Hope, Happiness and Pura Vida:

Pursuing a dream for the "pure life" in Costa Rica

Debbie Knight

DEDICATION

To my husband who participated on this journey with me. To my mom
who was my biggest fan. To my dad who went along for the ride
unwillingly but was always supportive when I needed him. To the rest of
my family, my friends and others who supported me along this journey.
Finally, to all the couples and families whose jobs lead you to live apart,
whether it is to serve in the military or to do what is best for your family, as
your sacrifice of time apart earns my deepest respect.

Table of Contents

ACKNOWLEDGMENTS

The author wishes to thank several people. I would like to thank my husband for his unending love and support. I would like to thank my parents for always being there. I would like to thank my friends who suffered through the early version of my book to give me good editing advice. I would also like to thank my editor, Paper Perfect Editing, for their editing work and creation of my book cover

PART 1
JUMPING INTO A BLACK HOLE

1 HAPPINESS IS

WE LIVE IN A WORLD where far too many people go through the motions of life to acquire material things and can never seem to buy enough to make them happy. I know, because I once lived the same way. There will always be someone with more than us, and this world of technology constantly invents new things, making it impossible to keep up with the ever-growing desire to be on top. Unfortunately, those expensive packages of new toys, regardless of how they are wrapped, will only bring short term satisfaction. I finally realized this and made a decision to change my situation.

When people hear my story, they are often excited to share their dreams, with a sparkle in their eyes. However, nine times out of ten there is always a "but" as to why they can't follow them. The spark drains from their eyes as they reveal the reasons for not pursuing their passion. As you read about my journey, you will see it is not easy to follow a dream. However, to be successful you must find a way around the obstacles laid before you.

My hope in writing this book is that more people will find the courage to follow their passions. Do what you are passionate about, and you will find happiness. You may not be able to go full throttle, but maybe you can follow your dream on a smaller scale. Life is short, so dare to pursue your dreams. After all, it is your choice, and happiness is a wonderful feeling.

My Dream: to build a Bed & Breakfast in Costa Rica, in pursuit of a happier life for my husband and me. During this journey, over the past five years, there are three important lessons I have learned. First, no matter how hard your life may become, never lose sight of your hopes and dreams for the future. Losing hope can lead to depression and self-pity. Thinking positively and always having hope for tomorrow are what helped me push through the bad days of my journey. Second, always remember to live in the current moment to enjoy happiness before the moment is lost. This was one of the hardest things to do. Often I wanted to wish away the time to being finished, as I think many of us do in our daily lives, in a rush to begin the next thing on our "to do" list. But if we constantly wish away the time, then our life will pass us by before we realize it. Last but not least, we must live an uncluttered life with a deep appreciation for the simple things, such as our health, family, friends, faith and nature. To be truly happy, that is all you need. It is the essence of Pura Vida. You will see evidence of these lessons throughout my story, along with my advice for others who wish to pursue their dreams, including the most valuable lesson of all.

What we do with our lives should bring us long term happiness, so we must be sure not to become sidetracked by the glitter and focus on what is truly important in living life. Somewhere in our culture we have confused our basic needs with a desire for material objects. If we can change our culture to return to an appreciation for a simpler lifestyle, then I believe we can have a world full of happier people benefiting each of us as individuals, as well as employers—happier, healthier, more productive employees.

The Pura Vida or the so-called pure life of Costa Rica is a great place to find it all. The people there are reported to be some of the happiest on earth. My husband and I felt the eternal optimism of Pura Vida on our first visit to Costa Rica in 2005, and little did we know how it would change the course of our lives forever.

As we left the country, the seed had been planted to build our own B&B (bed and breakfast) in Costa Rica. That seed grew on our return flight to the U.S., and hence began the journey of a dream for a happier life. We never imagined the roller-coaster ride that awaited us or the sacrifices to come.

17 years ago, when we were both students, we fell in love at a stoplight in Pensacola, FL. Our love for the ocean eventually led us to live in St Petersburg, FL. My husband, Chuck, worked as an architect, and I, Debbie, as an insurance underwriter. Chuck had worked his way up as the first employee of a firm in Atlanta to open the Tampa office and become a minority principal partner. We were DINKS (Double Income No Kids) with dogs. We owned a house on the water and two nice cars. Chuck's pride and joy was a 28-foot twin-engine catamaran that he used for offshore sport fishing on the weekends. Heads turned wherever we went in the boat. It was fully rigged out with equipment as good as any charter fishing boat guide would use. In exchange for all the trappings of success, we both worked long hours, especially Chuck. He was under heavy pressure in the economic boom of the early 2000's to complete projects by their due dates. Like many people with heavy work schedules, we had little time to eat properly or exercise. Over the years, combined with stress, this lifestyle affected our health.

From the outside it looked as if we were successful and happy. Despite appearances, that was far from the truth. Chuck started to bring his work pressure home and take it out on me. It was a strain on our marriage. One day Chuck declared in frustration he would rather have a heart attack than to go to work that next day. I still recalled the shock I felt at hearing those words. Although I knew he was unhappy at work, I had not realized the depth of his misery. It was a turning point. The moment he said those words I knew our lives needed to change—quickly. Chuck knew it as well, but it was hard for him to give up the money. He didn't know what to do either, since there were consequences to quitting his job.

I imagined there were a lot of people in the world who found themselves in the same shoes. It was a scary situation. Without a solution, we continued to march onward as "normal" with our "typical" lives. We had lots of stuff, and we did have happy moments. But overall neither of us was truly happy.

2 OUR PASSION

CHUCK'S 40TH BIRTHDAY in January 2005 required a special celebration. Since looking forward to retirement excited Chuck, I decided to celebrate his birthday while vacationing somewhere we might eventually retire. Finding the right place to retire might take some time, so I thought it would be good to get a head start looking while we were young.

After a friend in my bunko group suggested Costa Rica as the next hot spot for expatriates, I researched it and was blown away. It had so much to offer–adventure, rainforest and wildlife; I was sold. I gave Chuck his birthday vacation options, but I pushed Costa Rica. Being a smart husband, he quickly agreed with my recommendation.

Prior to our upcoming Costa Rican vacation, Chuck and I had a short list of true vacations during our 15 years of marriage. It was a headache when it came to taking the time away from our jobs. Vacations seemed like a waste of money. Little did we know, Costa Rica was about to change our vacation philosophy.

Our Costa Rican journey began upon arrival at the Juan Santamaría International Airport, close to San Jose, the capital of Costa Rica. Our travel agent had given us driving directions to guide us on our way to the Arenal area. Even so, there were not a lot of road signs, and we often wondered if our rental car was headed in the right direction.

A number of general comments about Costa Rica are in order here. When we say we are off to Costa Rica, people often tell us to enjoy the islands. I think they sometimes confuse Costa Rica with Puerto Rico. Although the Caribbean does border Costa Rica, it is not an island in the Caribbean. Costa Rica is in Central America. It is located south of Nicaragua and north of Panama. It stretches between the Caribbean on its east coast and the Pacific on its west coast. According to the U.S. Department of State website, Costa Rica's population is about 4.5 Million in

2010, and geographically, it is about the size of Vermont and New Hampshire combined. Spanish is the official language. However, in the touristy areas, there are usually plenty of Costa Ricans who speak English.

Back on the topic of our first trip, the drive throughout the countryside was beautiful. It was everything I had expected with a few exceptions. We were shocked to see a large number of pedestrians, even children, hitchhiking. This is a common occurrence, because so many Costa Ricans do not have their own transportation. The lack of streetlights can make it particularly hard to see pedestrians at night, and I believe is part of the reason some Costa Ricans have developed the bad habit of driving in the middle of the road, both day and night. We were also shocked to see so many Costa Ricans just park their vehicle in the road. I still don't know why this happens, but they don't seem to think twice about doing it, especially on a one lane road out in the countryside.

I was terrified when we arrived at a suspension bridge with gaping holes in it. Our tires had to be placed along the two pieces of metal that went over the holes in the bridge. There was a huge valley below the bridge, and I held my breath, hoping to cross as fast as possible. At this point I thought we were lost, because I could not imagine we were supposed to go across this bridge. Chuck thought it was totally cool. He wanted to stop on the metal strips and quickly changed his mind, when I freaked out. We would later find out from other tourists at the hot springs this was called the "Oh My God" bridge. The name says it all, because I certainly said a prayer before we crossed it. We heard not long after our trip that the bridge had been fixed. Of course, Chuck was disappointed at never having the chance to stop in the middle to take a photo.

We arrived in La Fortuna near Arenal at a cute little place called the Arenal Country Inn. It was very tropical and lush, with little bungalows. We felt like we were in paradise, walking around the tropical grounds of the inn.

During our stay in La Fortuna, we had our first lesson in dining out in Costa Rica. We enjoyed a great dinner, but it took us forever to receive our check. In fact, we realized that our waiter had actually left the restaurant after we were done eating. We saw him arrive back when a car dropped him off at the front door. Eventually, we learned you must ask for your check if you ever wish to receive it. It was something that was hard for us to become accustomed to when we went out to eat during that vacation, and it is something that we often have to remind ourselves about when dining out now in Costa Rica. However, Costa Ricans believe that bringing the check without your request is like asking you to leave, and they don't want to be rude. Therefore, if you don't ask for the check, then they will gladly let you sit at your table for hours to enjoy your meal, regardless of how crowded the restaurant may be.

For our first few days, our discoveries in Costa Rican food were incredible. We loved the taste of real butter. At breakfast, the butter was bright yellow and went great with all the fresh breads. The choices of jellies, made from fresh fruits, were outstanding. We found the bacon to be incredibly lean because the pigs were allowed to roam freely. The pizza was amazing as well, with all of the fresh toppings. I especially loved the sweet, juicy, Costa Rican pineapple on my pizza. We had a wonderful experience enjoying the many outstanding foods on our trip.

Although the highlight of the Arenal/La Fortuna area was to see the hot lava from the volcano, we learned it was difficult to see unless the night was very clear. Since we were there for a short time period, we did not witness the spectacle. However, we did enjoy several other activities the area had to offer.

The Tabacon hot springs was a lavish water park with various springs of different heat intensity. The springs were all warmed by heat generated from the Volcano Arenal. It was an amazing place to sit in the water and enjoy a tropical drink. It was very romantic, with all of the plants everywhere. Although at times we did have to ignore the crowd, we were usually able to find a secluded spot to ourselves. Sometimes, we found another tourist couple to chat with, where we learned several interesting tidbits on Costa Rica. Talking to other tourists got us excited about what awaited us for the rest of our Costa Rican vacation.

Our next big adventure was an ATV tour along the countryside. It turned into a private tour for Chuck and me, with the tour guides. It was a fun way to see the local people and venture off the beaten path. We rode down back-country roads to see beautiful scenery. When we passed some of the small Costa Rican houses, the little kids would wave at us. We got our first full glimpse of the Volcano Arenal during our ATV ride, as the sky cleared briefly. Chuck took a great picture of the volcano from his ATV. We drove by little streams and waterfalls, where kids and adults alike were playing in the water. We saw iguanas running along the roads. We saw cows standing in the roads. A memory I will never forget was a particular family, walking down the street. The man was carrying a huge pile of firewood, stacked up three feet high (or more) across his neck, with his wife carrying some, also holding her child's hand. It shocked us both to see the man with that much firewood. It had to be hard on his back. I also thought to myself that this man was probably happier carrying his firewood here with his family than we were in the U.S. doing less manual labor. Maybe he didn't have much, but it was enough for him to be happy. This is the real Costa Rica. It is how people live there. It was not for us to judge them, but it did make us feel bad driving by them that day. Chuck and I discussed later how we both would never forget what we saw.

Our ATV guide was amazing. He spoke such great English, I was surprised to find out he learned his English by watching TV! He called us "familia" the entire trip, which we found very endearing. He always beckoned, "Come, familia." Our ATV ride turned out to be a wonderful experience for us.

When we left the La Fortuna/Arenal area, we headed over to the Peace Lodge and the La Paz Waterfall Gardens. The Peace Lodge is where our travel agent fought to encourage us to stay, since it was one of her favorite places. It was a very tricky drive to get there. Our directions may have worked, had the signs been facing our side of the road, but we often learned they were only on the other side of the road for people coming from the opposite direction. Each time we thought we had gone too far, we learned to turn around, and sure enough, the directions would seem to make sense again. It was challenging, but oh, what a beautiful ride it was. It was our first true drive into the rainforest, and it was stunning. We fell in love immediately.

When we arrived at our room in the Peace Lodge, we were shocked. It was nicer than any hotel I had ever stayed in before. Keep in mind, I am not a ritzy kind of girl, so I don't like high class things. I prefer an "artsy-simple" style, and the Peace Lodge nailed it for me. We immediately settled into our room and then walked to the waterfall gardens adjoining the hotel. It was all breath-taking, which I mean literally. The hike took my breath away, along with the absolute beauty of it all. We were totally out of shape, and we hiked the falls rapidly, to finish in time for dinner. On the way back to our rooms, we discovered hotel guests could feed the hummingbirds, so we made a pit stop. It was an amazing experience to hold the feeders while the hummingbirds flew up and ate. They would buzz by my head like little helicopters. Chuck took some great photos. What an amazingly special place this was. We had an absolutely wonderful dinner on-site at the hotel that night. Dinner was followed by our fabulous use of the hot tub in our huge bathroom, as well as the hot tub on our balcony. We slept that night listening to the waterfalls below and awoke to watch hummingbirds, feeding on our balcony. A great breakfast topped off our spectacular first visit to the Peace Lodge. We could not believe how fabulous Costa Rica was so far, and our adventure was still to continue. We headed off to the beach to see all it had to offer, and I was thankful that we would not be crossing the "Oh My God" bridge on the way. We would certainly be back to the Peace Lodge another day.

We arrived in Jaco to find the weather more humid, as the other tourists at the hot springs had forewarned us. The sand was black, very beautiful with the blue water and tropical shoreline. The atmosphere was very different here. There was more of a big city vibe, with armed security guards patrolling areas, including our condo. It didn't bother us, but there was a noticeable difference in the town versus out in the country, where we had been previously.

We spent some time in Jaco exploring the city. In the restaurants, we learned that if musicians played at your table, that you better stop them beforehand, or they would want money afterwards, as they were not being paid by the restaurants. Also, we learned that there was some peddling going on in the restaurants in town. These were not things we were used to, but we quickly learned to deal with them in a big city. One of our favorite treats was enjoying drinks at Villa Caletas, while watching the sunset. It was a beautiful hotel outside of Jaco, with a cliff-side view overlooking the ocean. When I made our hotel reservations, I told our travel agent I wanted to be on the beach, and her opinion was that we really didn't. Standing at Villa Caletas, or from any of the mountain views, I quickly understood why she had given that advice. Being on the beach was certainly beautiful and convenient. However, the views we saw from the mountains were more spectacular than sitting on a flat beach. Plus, the altitude kept it cooler, with fewer bugs. As our travel agent suggested, we could appreciate the views from staying higher up all day and benefit from the cooler temperature, and it was a short drive to the beach, if we wanted to enjoy it for part of the day. Those were words of advice we would remember when we went to buy our property one day.

For adventure, we spent one day on a fishing charter from an area outside of Jaco, called Los Suenos. The place was an amazing community of houses, condos, a hotel, restaurants and a marina. We enjoyed looking around the area, and Chuck enjoyed catching his first sailfish on a fishing charter. Unfortunately, nobody else on the boat was as lucky. Little did we know during our visit, in the years to come, Los Suenos would grow tremendously and increase in popularity as a world class fishing destination.

We spent another day in Jaco, venturing outside of the area to go ziplining. A zipline is a cable stretched between two trees at different elevations. There are platforms created around the tree at each elevation, where you stand. With a helmet on and a glove used to brake, you sit in a harness connected by a pulley and cable, while gravity zips you from one platform, down to the next platform. The number and the length of the ziplines vary based upon the tour operator you select.

Chuck was adventurous, so he was excited about ziplining. I, however, did not share his sense of adventure. I am usually happy to have tried things once they are over, but I allowed my fears to overwhelm me, especially when I was doing something new. I did want to go ziplining, since that was one of the things you must do while in Costa Rica. Needless to say, I was nervous over the whole issue.

We had selected the Original Canopy Tour since their zipline provided two cables for safety, in case one of the cables broke. From a risk management perspective, this made me feel much safer. I was a nervous wreck the morning we left, and I was shaking like a leaf when we took off from the first platform. It was nice to have only Chuck and me with our two guides on the tour. We saw no wildlife while ziplining. If any had been in sight, they were long gone by the time I started to scream. I simply could not help myself. Ziplining definitely gave a new meaning to being a tree hugger, because there were certainly points when you had to hug the tree to stay on the crowded platform, high up in the air. Before I realized it, the whole thing was over. I was only starting to relax and enjoy it at the end, so I couldn't say it was a fun experience for me. Now that I had survived my first attempt, though, I felt it would allow me to be less fearful of the experience next time. Plus, I learned one lesson the hard way. It was important not to slow down too early. If you did, then you would have to pull yourself up backwards at the end of the cable to reach the platform, which could be difficult. Now, I was better prepared for my next attempt.

We meant to spend our final day in Jaco on a different tour. However, our tour operator did not pick us up. I broke down and cried hard that morning. I later realized I was not crying so much about the tour being screwed up but because we would be going back to the "reality" of our "normal" life soon. In Costa Rica, everything was peaceful and happy. I did not want to go back. My tears were very upsetting for Chuck. We always pulled each other up when the other one was down, so he got to work. We were going to do something productive and more wonderful than the tour we had planned, and boy, was he ever right about that one. It was the turning point of our trip and was about to change our future.

We decided to take a drive and venture further south down to Manuel Antonio. There was a national park there, which was the number one popular tourist attraction in Costa Rica. It also had beautiful cliff-side views of the water, where we could stop at any number of restaurants to enjoy lunch. It was very tropical from what he had read, and we loved tropical. We had a plan, and we were going for it. I stopped crying and got ready for our new adventure of the day.

The drive down south was yet again different than our previous drives through the countryside. Here, it was flat and relatively straight. We drove by a number of fields filled with palm trees, which we later learned were used for palm oil. It was an interesting drive, and it became more tropical as we arrived to the cliff-side views of Manual Antonio.

We walked through the park on our own. However, we later realized that we should have hired a guide outside. The guides had spotting scopes and already knew where a lot of the animals were located. The views from the park were beautiful. Unlike much of the rest of Costa Rica with black beaches, the beaches here were white sand.

After our visit to the park, we stopped for lunch at a restaurant with a great cliff-side view. We had an iguana run across the floor past our table.

It was exciting to see all the wildlife and such green lushness here. We talked at lunch about what a wonderful day this had turned into for us. If we had gone on our planned boat excursion that morning, then we would never have known what a great area we had missed. This trip had us excited to go further south on our next visit. I also felt happy and peaceful in Costa Rica. I really thought we should live there. It felt safe. People were out walking everywhere with their families. It wasn't as safe to walk around in the U.S. All of the people were nice in Costa Rica, and everyone seemed happy, even if they appeared to own very little. It felt like we were missing the whole point of life in the U.S. We were working to obtain more stuff we really didn't need. Plus, it was more stuff that seemed to wear and tear, creating even more stress to have it fixed. We didn't need all of our stuff. We needed to simplify. To be happy, we needed to return to the basics. I thought we needed Costa Rica. Maybe we could have a B&B and the simple life. Of course, Chuck said those were irrational thoughts of someone caught up in happy moments on vacation. Nobody actually followed through on them. Even though he agreed with me on all the other points, he thought I was crazy to actually consider moving to Costa Rica, having spent only a week in the country.

We packed up and headed back to the U.S. Our first trip in Costa Rica had exceeded all of our expectations. Even though Chuck said I had lost my mind in Manual Antonio about moving to Costa Rica, he bought a book at the airport on retiring there. I gave him a hard time on the plane, because I figured it was one of the few books he ever read in his entire life. The more he read the book that day the more excited he got about the potential to move there. He realized maybe I was not so crazy after all, but it would certainly require more research.

Why is Costa Rica so popular among expatriates? It is a peaceful democratic country that abolished its military long ago and used that money to invest into education. Because of this, it has a very high literacy rate with well-educated citizens. It offers a socialized healthcare system that provides quality care at affordable prices (around $75 a month for two people in our case). This health care system, combined with the unsurpassed beauty of the country, low cost of living, wonderful climate, open immigration policy, ability of foreigners to own property there with ease and the friendliness of its citizens has a lot to offer expatriates. It is important to remember though that Costa Rica is still a third world country. Expatriates who go there to live need to understand that things in third world countries do work differently, and they need to be prepared to live with that in their daily lives.

We arrived home to tons of office work that raised our stress levels to new heights. Was vacation worth all of this? Yes, it was. During this trip, we developed a sense of peace from being in Costa Rica on vacation. After all, on this trip, we had no cell phone service, and we had not watched much TV. We had disconnected. We realized that we needed the time to relax and enjoy ourselves, even if the work that piled up made the office more hectic afterwards.

Vacations are a necessity in today's fast-paced world, required to rejuvenate our body, mind and soul. With cell phones everywhere, it is hard for most people to really get away from their work as required for good mental health. Visiting family does not count as a vacation, with its own set of stresses. People really need to totally get away to relax. The whole concept of helping people rejuvenate on vacation fit in perfectly with what we wanted to do with our future. We wanted to have a B&B to help people enjoy themselves while they were on vacation, and Costa Rica was the perfect place to get away to relax and have fun. It was a good feeling to know we could meet people from all over the world, helping them to re-energize before they returned to their real lives. We didn't want to trade in our material possessions in the U.S. for more material possessions in Costa Rica, though the B&B needed to be nice to attract business. We knew Chuck's creative ideas would make our B&B special, and our place would enhance the experience we could share with others who come to visit us. We had found our passion!

When we weren't working, we spent time researching the Internet for everything we could find about Costa Rica. The more we learned, the more we liked the idea of buying property there. I still recall springing the idea on our friends one evening at one of our local hangouts, Woody's Waterfront restaurant in St Pete Beach, Florida. Chuck and I told them we had decided to move to Costa Rica and open up a B&B. Obviously, our friends were shocked. I was sure they thought we had probably been drinking too much that day. I knew they had their doubts that we would ever follow through with our grand ideas. Some of our friends were joking around that they would move with us and add on a casino and a house of prostitution (by the way, prostitution is legal in Costa Rica). They carried that joke on for years, but all jokes aside, we had not been drinking too much. We were serious about our intentions for moving and opening up the B&B.

While our friends didn't totally believe us, our family thought we had gone insane, especially my parents. I had to admit this was some outer space thinking for my family from Tennessee. My family was not worldly or well traveled. I couldn't recall when any of my family had ever been out of the country, and I had been only a handful of times. When I first met Chuck, I didn't know what alfredo sauce was, or a number of other basic food items most people knew. In our family, dinner revolved around southern home-cooked meals. I remember asking my grandma one day if she liked shrimp, and she asked me, "What kind of fish is shrimp?" It was a big ordeal for me to move away from Tennessee. Therefore, when we said we were moving to Costa Rica after our week long vacation there, they thought we had gone totally nuts. However, unlike our friends who didn't believe us, my family knew we did not say things without meaning them. They took us seriously, which only upset them more.

Many people, including my dad, didn't understand why we couldn't find a place to move to in the U.S. instead of going all the way to Costa Rica. That was an easy answer. I wasn't aware of any place in the U.S. that would give us a warm tropical climate with ocean and mountain views including toucans and monkeys, plus a lower cost of living. I obviously had not traveled around the world to testify that Costa Rica is the only country that offered all of this. However, I know Costa Rica has many species from both North and South America, because of the unique way the country was created. At one point in history, North and South America did not connect. Over time, a tectonic plate pushed upward to connect them. As a result of this connection, wildlife and plants from both continents were able to merge into Costa Rica, resulting in large biological diversity within the country. The nature and tropical climate there, along with the friendliness of the people, brings a sense of peace. We know we can obtain that sense of peace long term by living there. The ability to share that experience with others at our B&B one day is an added benefit of our Costa Rica plan.

3 TOUCAN REAL ESTATE

SINCE WE HAD LOVED the tropical rainforest, wildlife and beach area of Manual Antonio, Chuck learned via recommendations from people (mostly through www.welovecostarica.com) that we should look for property in the Dominical area of Costa Rica. It was further south than Manual Antonio and more affordably priced. We eventually made plans for our second trip to Costa Rica, determined to buy property.

The real estate market in Costa Rica is not like the real estate market in the U.S. Even though some websites state they have an MLS system, there is no official regulated MLS system of all the properties in Costa Rica. Each property owner is free to select their own realtor to use, so they can choose one or two or as many realtors as they like to sell their property. Therefore, appointments were required with various realtors to see what properties they each represented, which could be a very time consuming task. Chuck and I found calling multiple realtors uncomfortable, because it was so different than what we were used to in the U.S. Another thing we discovered was that most of the Internet property listings we called about were already sold. Properties were selling faster than realtors could keep the Internet postings updated, in the hot economic times of 2005.

Eventually, time for our second trip to Costa Rica arrived in September. This was our first time to drive through San Jose and over the mountains on the Pan-American Highway. Driving through San Jose was hectic. There were a number of roundabouts, lots of traffic and people walking everywhere. Motorcyclists did not seem to know what driving lanes were, and apparently, the police didn't mind this. Pedestrians wanted to challenge the cars to a duel, darting through traffic to cross the busy roads. My nerves were shot, but luckily, Chuck was not fazed by it all.

When we arrived in Dominical, it was more green and lush than we had ever imagined. After becoming lost in the back roads, we eventually found the right river crossing, which was required to reach the B&B we were seeking. As crazy as it seemed, we did actually have to cross a river to arrive there, and I did hold my breath while doing it. The owners were great, and it was wonderful to hear the story of how they had begun their B&B. He had actually lived in a tent when their B&B was under construction years ago, while she stayed in the U.S. to continue working, to earn more money. They had roughed it back in those early days, but they had made it into a successful business. They were happy in Costa Rica and were thankful they had made the leap to follow their journey. Their family had thought they had lost their mind when they said they were moving to Costa Rica, just like my family, but now their family loved it there. It made me feel much better to hear those words.

We had meetings scheduled with a number of different realtors during the upcoming days, and we were hopeful that we would find something to match our search criteria. We wanted our property to have spectacular views. To us, this meant we needed to be in the mountains, with views of the ocean. After our first trip to Costa Rica, we agreed that these views were better than the beach views. Plus, we had learned that in Costa Rica, there are some restrictions on beach ownership. All beaches were opened to the public for the first 50 meters from the high tide line, closed to development. Beyond this was a certain distance that could be leased for a time period, with approval of the local municipality, but not owned out right. We felt that the mountain views and the cooler temperatures at higher altitudes in the mountains, along with outright ownership with no limitations were a much better match for our needs. Therefore, we were not going to consider beachfront property. We wanted to be sure that our views to the ocean were not blocked or restricted in any way by neighboring properties, which meant it would be best if we were on top of the mountain. Although we had heard you could ask neighbors to trim trees, we were not too excited at the prospect of having an uncooperative neighbor. We did not want to see the rooftops of our neighbors either, so we wanted to have some space. We wanted sunset views too. Based upon our research, we needed to be sure that we had drinking water available to the property, since this was crucial in buying property in Costa Rica, and a lot already wired for electricity would be a plus. Most importantly, we needed to remain within our budget.

Going out with the realtors was an adventure. Property in Costa Rica was fairly spread out. Hence, it took a while to travel from one lot to the next. Some of the roads into certain areas scared me, so I ruled out some lots before we even reached them. In fact, road safety on the way to the property became a new item for my search criteria.

Typically, the realtors would ask if we had seen a particular lot, and if so, they would not show us the same one again. However, they would also have their own secret properties they would not want the other realtors to know about, since they wanted to sell the lot for the owner before the owner opened it up to other realtors. Remember that without an MLS system there is no splitting of commissions between realtors to list a property and sell a property. They sell it to keep all the commission, or they receive nothing. Apparently, only in rare cases do different realtors work together to split commissions. All of the realtors understood the position we were in. Because we were going to be their neighbors and part of their community, they believed we should buy what made us happy and not buy what they wanted us to buy. It was an uncomfortable situation for us, because we appreciated the time all the realtors spent with us. We felt like we were cheating on them regardless of what they said. This lack of MLS setup was one thing we did not like about Costa Rica.

By the time our trip was coming to an end, the pressure was mounting, since we still had not found the right place. Properties that we wanted to consider, despite not being perfect, were selling out from under us faster than we could make it to our next realtor appointment. We felt desperate to buy something.

One realtor felt that we should venture further south. It was where all the future development was going to occur, due to the new hospital being built, in preparation for an international airport. As soon as we got to the property and saw the views, we knew it was the one for us. It was practically perfect. We were on the top of the mountain, with a 360-degree view. We had Pacific Ocean and river views to the front, with mountain views to the back. We also had a view of the Osa Peninsula and Cano Island. We had a small waterfall at the edge of our property, which we could hear. There was a great road and water association in the neighborhood. The lot came with power. The drive up to the property was super easy, and the lot would be visible from the coastal highway. We had 4 acres, sufficient space to keep us from sitting too close to our neighboring properties. The only downsides were we had to share a driveway with one neighbor and we were a little further back from the ocean than we had wanted to be. Overall, it was as perfect as it was going to become. We were thrilled.

We made a stop at our attorney's office to take care of some business in San Jose before catching our return flight to the U.S. Since Costa Rica did not have street addresses, he had given us Costa Rican directions using landmarks. He referenced La Sabana Park, the KFC (Kentucky Fried Chicken) and said his office was located in the Embassy of Spain. Since the park was clearly marked on the map, we thought we could find his office.

Unfortunately, we missed a turn. Driving around lost in San Jose with little signage, heavy traffic honking at us and people walking everywhere was not much fun. We arrived hours late. We parked in unsecured street parking with luggage in the car, which made us nervous. A standard rule in Costa Rica is to never leave your luggage unguarded in your car. While violent crime is rare, petty theft happens frequently in a poor country like Costa Rica. However, we had no choice but to leave the car.

We saw the embassy and headed toward it. Someone was walking into the embassy gates, so I headed in behind them. We got through the first two gates and past the guards, until the guard at the third gate stopped us. As it turned out, our attorney was not located in the Embassy of Spain, but across the street from it. In hind-sight, that made more sense. When he saw our paperwork, the guard politely pointed us in the right direction. After I started taking Spanish lessons, I understood how easy it was to get words confused in translation. Obviously, our attorney had made the mistake, and it was a huge difference to mix up words like "in" and "across from."

Our attorney was fine with our delayed arrival. Costa Ricans are very laid back about time, and I believe that is part of why they are always happy. Just think how much less stressed we would all be if we didn't worry about how much time we had to do a task or how much time before we had to be somewhere else. We often hear of "Tico Time" in Costa Rica, because most Costa Ricans (commonly referred to as Ticos, since they often change the ending of their words to make them sound less harsh by adding the suffix "ico" to the end instead of "ito"), do not value time like Americans. Dealing with people in Tico Time can be very frustrating, however, especially if you really need something done quickly. Thankfully, things worked out all right with our attorney, and we returned to our car, still full of luggage.

We ended our second trip to Costa Rica having agreed to purchase the property. During the next few months, a corporation was set up for our purchase, purchase agreements were signed, escrow money deposited and a closing date set of December 5, 2005.

As the time for the closing drew closer, it was both exciting and scary. We were about to invest a huge amount of money in our future dream. I was all right with investing the money. What had my nerves shot was the fear of wiring over $250,000 to an attorney who we had only known for a few months and had only met once in person. He was highly recommended by a number of expatriates on-line, but these were not people we knew personally. We had done our due diligence as best as we could. Still, no matter how I tried to reassure myself, I was not going to rest easy until he showed up with our cashier's check at closing.

On our third trip to Costa Rica, I was a nervous wreck the night before our closing. Would the cashier's check be there the next day? I also couldn't believe we were really making the leap. We weren't jumping completely into the unknown on this deal, because we had researched it at great length, but fear was definitely kicking in. This was another big step into a big black hole to change our lives. It took a lot of courage to not fear the unknown, but courage yielded reward. Hopefully, our rewards were yet to come. We were giving up all we owned now to take a chance on a better life in the future.

When morning arrived, it was a relief to know we were close to having this chapter resolved. We went to the office of the seller's attorney for the closing. Upon arrival, I almost walked into an open water fountain in the lobby. The floor simply sloped downward into a pool of water, which blended invisibly against the glossy tile floor. Chuck later commented such a thing would never be allowed in the U.S. for liability reasons. We were told that in Costa Rica, such things were allowed because people were held to a standard of personal responsibility. Yes, people did fall in that fountain periodically. However, it was their fault for not watching where they were going. If they attempted to sue for that in Costa Rica, then they would not obtain anything out of it. Hence, people did not waste their time. Wouldn't it be nice if we had that concept in the U.S.?

Our attorney was not at the office when we arrived, which heightened my anxiety. As we sat in the receptionist area, he walked out of the elevator. I wanted to run over and hug him so badly, I could have screamed. It was like a huge weight was lifted off my shoulders. Everything was going to work out. We weren't going to be some couple on the news who got swindled out of their life savings.

Securing the check from the bank had apparently been difficult for him, due to the "know your client" paperwork required to prevent people from laundering large sums of money. Even so, he had pulled through for us. Once we were in the conference room for the closing, everything went very quickly.

Given it takes an amazing amount of paperwork to close on property in the U.S., and given Costa Rica is a paper intensive society where everything is about the process, we expected to sign lots of papers at closing. On the contrary, we signed only one piece of paper to close. The signed document was written in Spanish on the official numbered papers that the attorneys kept in their offices. These numbered pages started out blank and were to remain in their offices until they had items typed and signed on them to eventually be filed in the national registry. Our attorney translated the document from Spanish to English so that we could read it before we signed. Things went so fast that it was over before our seats were warmed up. We were officially property owners in Costa Rica! Before leaving the office, we asked our attorney to draft a will for us to sign on our next trip, so it was clear our investment would go to our family, now that we had assets to protect.

We drove south with plans to stay at the same B&B as last time.

Unfortunately, there was a major traffic jam. Truckers were sitting with chairs and coolers on the side of the road. As we sat on the two-lane highway with a ditch and mountain on one side and a drop off on the other side, we watched cars go up the wrong side of the road head to head. Eventually, one car would squeeze in between sitting cars to allow the other to pass. We could not find anyone who spoke English. We eventually saw a policeman pass, so we hoped he would be clearing the road ahead. However, after waiting for hours with darkness finally setting in and watching cars constantly passing us going up the wrong side of the road, we decided it must be the thing to do. We were starving by this time, and I really had to go to the bathroom. As I stated earlier, you always have to keep in mind that Costa Rica is a third world country which requires you to deal with the unusual at times. I finally told Chuck to go for it.

The next time a car passed, we followed it up the wrong side of the road. We went only a short distance before Ticos yelled for us to pull over. Many cars in front of us had already disappeared between all of the trucks. After a short time, a small utility truck pulled out ahead of us, and the Ticos motioned for us to follow. The policeman had left this group of truckers to decide whose turn it would be to go, even though they had no radios to communicate with the other side. Once we got further along, we saw a truck had overturned, blocking one lane and part of the other, enabling only smaller vehicles to pass. The utility truck in front of us cleared our path, pushing people coming up the wrong way over into the other lane or even into the ditch in some cases. There was little traffic past the wreck, making for a speedy drive on the rest of our trip.

We called the B&B owner to let her know we were arriving late and needed to stop first for food in town. We were happy to arrive at the Rum Bar, until we found out the kitchen was done for the night. However, once the owner heard our story and how much we loved their pizza during our last trip, he agreed to make a pizza for us. It didn't look like the kind of place to find good pizza. However, the ingredients were fresh and the combination on their Dominical pizza was wonderful.   My favorite ingredient was the great Costa Rican pineapple. After our second sampling of Rum Bar pizza, Chuck and I agreed it was definitely one of the best pizzas we had ever eaten. Thereafter, pizza at the Rum Bar became one of our favorite stops when traveling to Costa Rica.

When we arrived at our lot the next day, it was as beautiful as the day we first laid eyes on it, and we could not believe how lucky we were to have found it at the end of our last trip. During the past few months, we had discovered that our property was owned by a family the government had given it to as farm land. The land came with the stipulation that they were not allowed to sell it for a set number of years. The long time frame had expired just before our closing date.   Timing was everything, and this property was meant to be for us. Our timing on this trip was also good, and we were even able to see a few toucans during our visit. As a little girl, I would never have looked at a box of froot-loops and thought of someday owning property with toucans on it, yet here I was, with toucans in Costa Rica.

4 DREAM BREAKS

WE DECIDED TO BUILD a furnished garage we would use as a vacation home. Someday we would use it to live in and oversee the construction phase of our house and the B&B. At first, we weren't planning on construction to happen anytime soon. However, it was not long before Chuck became convinced that there was really no reason to wait. Since I already telecommuted for a global company, it didn't seem unreasonable to relocate my job to telework from Costa Rica. Chuck could do drafting work, which I hoped might take him back to the roots of architecture and what he loved about it. Teleworking seemed feasible for both of us. Moreover, the housing market in the U.S. was skyrocketing, so it appeared, at least on paper, that we should be able to sell our house to fund our dream in Costa Rica. If we were willing to make the jump, then it seemed we could sell and have money left over after construction. With income from the B&B, we shouldn't need to make much from our regular jobs, even though we could still have the other income. Chuck was so burnt out with his job that he began to see this path as a light at the end of the tunnel. I was worried about his health and the consequences if he stayed in his job, so I agreed we had to take the chance. After all, we couldn't change our lifestyle if we weren't willing to take chances. It would be a major commitment to take us to that end vision, but we were going to go for it. Our plan was to live in Costa Rica in 5 years.

A dilemma arose when Chuck's partners decided to offer the opportunity to run another office to his right hand man. Should he tell his partners now about our potential move to Costa Rica? We didn't even know yet when we were going for sure, since our 5-year plan might not work out on schedule. Chuck felt he had to in order to give a fair opportunity to the other person in his office. It was agreed that at the end of two years, the person in his office would become principal, and Chuck

21

would step down to become an employee, if we had not decided to move yet. Chuck certainly felt some relief from his work pressures, knowing that he could see a date to exit his job.

Based on a two year time frame for his job ending, Chuck picked a contractor who built on a construction cost basis with a flat fee per week for his services. He hoped to have the garage ready to move in by January 2008. Chuck designed the garage but had to pass the work off to a Costa Rican architect. His duties included translating the architectural notes to Spanish, coordinating the engineering drawings, obtaining the permits and completing the inspections.

Property maintenance is an important part of owning property in Costa Rica. There are squatter's rights. Therefore, if you don't take care of your property, then there is the possibility that others could earn a right to keep it. We paid the property maintenance people at the realtor's office where we had bought our property to fence our lot. This was completed in March 2006. To put in concrete posts with three lines of barbed wire fence cost us close to $3,000 for our four acres. We paid $50 a month to have the building site and boundaries chopped so that we could find our lot in the fast growing jungle. It is good to use a property management firm for maintenance instead of hiring someone directly, since there are legal employment issues if you hire someone individually. The property management company can handle it if you hire them instead.

In March 2006, we also completed a land survey of the building pad on our property. We wanted to obtain a better idea of the topography of the area, as our building pad was small. We were going to need every inch we had to lay out all of our buildings effectively. Since it cost more money to build on the slopes of a mountain-side, our plan was to keep our construction on the flat part of the mountain, using what was already cleared out for us. We needed to fit in a B&B, a separate house for us, a pool, a tiki hut and a garage with driveway and parking, all in this area. Chuck had a lot of hard work ahead. We later decided to have soil test done as well, to be sure we were on solid ground. A lot of people did not go to those extremes, but we wanted to be very safe with our construction.

As time progressed, we made a commitment to learn Spanish. Although we could travel on vacation just speaking English, we felt people should take the time to try to learn English if they decided to live in the U.S. It seemed only fair that we should learn to speak their official language if we wanted to live in Costa Rica. With our heavy work schedules, we did not have time to go to a language course in person, so we decided to buy some CDs to teach us the language. We bought the Pilmsleaur Language Program. I completed my 30 minute lessons late at night. Chuck, on the other hand, played the CD's in his car during his commute to work. He was making progress, which discouraged me over my lack of progress, until

I eventually gave up. To my surprise, I would attempt those CD's again two years later to realize that I learned more than I had thought. I had established a good foundation during my late night struggles. What I had not realized was I didn't need to be perfect to progress through each CD. I just needed to push myself to keep learning once I knew most of a CD, because with time, the rest would fall into place.

In April 2006, our architect told us he did not see the electrical lines that were supposed to be there, according to our purchase agreement. In June 2006, we contacted an electrical engineer to check into correcting the electrical issue and asked what size transformer we would require. The final decision was made that we needed the biggest transformer that could be put on a pole in Costa Rica. The downside of such a large transformer on a pole was that there were very few available in the country. There was a huge demand for them in China, so supply in Costa Rica was limited. After months of waiting, we received the initial contract for the electrical work. It was close to $12,000. Our transformer was $5,000 leaving a difference of $7,000, which we should recoup from the seller of our property. The electrical plan would later have to be tweaked, increasing the cost to $18,000.

Using the Costa Rican pony express, our attorney took care of what he had to do for our electrical engineer in order to proceed with the request to ICE, the Costa Rican Power and Telephone Company, to run the power. He gave limited power of attorney to our electrical engineer to complete the paperwork for us in Rio Claro. He sent the documents down to our engineer on the bus, which he said was like the pony express in the old days of the U.S. Buses ran from San Jose out daily, carrying packages like courier services to towns in the outlying areas. This was an efficient and cheap way of sending things that needed to be delivered. Chuck and I were amused by the analogy. Although things were different in Costa Rica, they had a way of making them work.

We would need the proceeds from the sale of our house in order to get started on the construction in Costa Rica. It was basically financing our dream. Since it seemed to be a hot U.S. real estate market, we thought we could handle selling it on our own. Unfortunately, the hot market had already started to fall, but we did not know yet. After trying on our own for four months, we finally gave in and signed up with the Simms Team in November of 2006. We went on the market and held out hope that things would go our way. Since we had faith the house would eventually sell, and we knew that we could not take our flashy boat to Costa Rica, we put it up for sale as well. It was difficult to think about letting go of all the things we owned, but in the long run, we knew that it had to be done to start us moving forward again.

It was not long before we had a buyer for the boat. It was a very sad day when they rode away in it. I knew it had to be heartbreaking for Chuck. I cried my eyes out watching it leave our dock that day. Regardless of how many times I had been seasick on that boat, I still loved all the happy memories we had, riding around Tampa/St Pete and even all the way down to the Florida Keys. But it was another material thing that we had to let go to reach our new dream in Costa Rica.

Like anyone who has a house for sale, we went through the highs that came, hoping that the next set of people would be the one to buy. We evaluated them from afar as we walked the neighborhood, wondering if they were the one. We went through the anticipation, waiting to hear what they thought. We got excited when we heard good feedback from our realtor. We went through the lows that followed when no offer arrived. And of course, we then thought afterwards they were not good enough for our house anyway.

We even had one deal we did not take seriously at first. The offer was to sell our house with a boat. Now remember we had sold our boat already, so it meant we had to buy a boat to meet the terms of the sale. In theory, Chuck could find a decent used boat and negotiate a better deal on it than the buyers who knew nothing about boats. Our realtor said we should acquire a small used bay boat with a good mechanical report. We agreed it all made sense. The family was coming back from Orlando after the weekend to do the paperwork, so we had the weekend to look for the specific boat. It was going to be a 100% cash deal on the house. As I was standing on a boat that weekend, our realtor called to say they changed their mind and decided to move to Orlando instead of St Petersburg, so it was good we hadn't bought anything yet. It was a huge disappointment, since we had allowed ourselves to become excited at the potential we would be moving on with our dream in Costa Rica. It was a rollercoaster ride of emotions for us, waiting for the right buyer to arrive, but we knew that lucky person was out there somewhere.

While we waited for things to move forward with our five-year plan, one of our favorite things to do was to dream. Sitting on our dock was our meditation moment where we could unwind from a day of work and strategize on our future. All of the basics for our dream came to life among many a night, while Chuck and I kicked around ideas on our dock or sat in our kitchen talking about our future life in Costa Rica. These "dream breaks" allowed us to survive through many tough work-days.

We named the B&B Ocaso Cerro. It meant Sunset Mountain in Spanish, which we felt was appropriate for the mountain and sunset views that we would have to offer. Chuck planned out the design of our house and the B&B. Curved walls were involved, as he always had to have curves. The B&B overall design from above looked like a butterfly, which seemed appropriate for Costa Rica, where butterflies were prevalent. We came up with paint colors to coordinate with the Spanish names of our four B&B bedrooms. Ocaso would be orange for sunsets. Cerro would be green for the mountains. Rio would be blue for the river although we would later change the name to Cano because of the great view it offered of Cano Island. Lastly, Vista Mar would be the master suite painted yellow for its all-encompassing views, promoting joy and happiness. Chuck designed and redesigned the tiki hut, with swings taking inspiration from a place we had stayed in Mexico on vacation. The swimming pool had an infinity edge and a spa. It too was designed with everything we had always wanted in a pool. We came up with names for the drinks we would serve at the tiki bar. We tried to plan out all aspects, even down to the minor details. For example, we decided where a towel bar would hang so that it would not block the beauty of a room and designed special niches, in which to place some of our paintings.

We began to shop for items like bathrobes, when we found things on sale. Over time, these things added up to quite a collection of items for the B&B. We stuffed these items in any empty spot we could find, like under the beds and in closets. Eventually, we lost track of everything we had bought. Talking about our dream got us through a lot of hard and difficult times, as Chuck continued to work at his job. We always felt like we were working toward a goal, and he could see the light at the end of the tunnel, which helped him survive through the day. I held out hope he would be able to push on with his job until we made our dreams come true, but I constantly worried about his health and the toll stress from his job was taking on him.

Design was important to us, so we felt like it was important to have a good logo design for our place. We kept a notepad on our tables and countertops and worked really hard at trying to come up with good ideas. In the end, we decided we needed professional help. A friend in the advertising business referred us to Bev at www.theinnovations.net. We gave her an idea for what we wanted. We told her about ourselves, about Costa Rica and about what we envisioned for our place there. She took those ideas and then within a short time set up a meeting to show us her designs. I still recalled sitting at a Starbucks one Saturday morning excited about what she was going to show us. Sure enough, as we sat there, we were amazed. She had one logo design that nailed what we wanted. The funny thing was that she had numbered her logo designs on the back as she had thought of the ideas. The one we loved was one of the first few she had done. We were thrilled. Over a short time period, the logo was tweaked. From that she took it a step forward to design our business cards. Unlike most business cards, which were typically one-sided, she made our business cards a glossy two-sided card, taking full advantage to advertise the benefits of Ocaso Cerro. She embossed a portion of the imprint of the sun as a backdrop, giving it an artsy feel to go along with the artistic character of our place, as well as fit in with the sunset translation of our name. It was amazing that she captured our spirit so well, having known us for such a short time. She was very talented. She also added the Experience Nature theme to our business card, which apparently was something we had consistently stated we loved about Costa Rica. She went further and suggested we use the experience theme when we developed our website, to provide some consistency. Chuck would later design the website with the experience nature, experience adventure and experience relaxation tabs on our webpage. We stuck with the experience nature theme for our t-shirts, as we felt that was the true heart of Costa Rica. We were very fortunate to have found Bev to help us with our logo and all the added benefits of her experience.

It was important to have a good mentor. Chuck and I were very lucky to develop a relationship with Ginette, a B&B owner who we stayed with in Escazu, during our trips down to Costa Rica. She loved the passion that Chuck and I expressed about our place and thought that we would do well as B&B owners. She thought this because we loved the idea of the people we were going to make happy on vacation, rather than seeing it as a job. During our stays at her B&B, we had great little chats, during which she gave us advice on being a B&B owner. Those little nuggets of gold were a lot of help to us. Her place, Casa Laurin (www.casalaurin.com), was often booked full, because people liked the service and personality she offered. We were truly lucky to learn from her experiences.

Progress continued throughout 2007. The final electric line was powered and checked by our electrical engineer. It felt like our first small victory. At the end of September 2007 we got a quote for $14,500, which included building a concrete panel at the road to contain the electrical feeders for the house, digging a trench to run the wires underground up the hill to our building pad and the cost of the wires. We had selected copper wire, since we were going underground, so it was very expensive and the majority of the cost of the garage. In December 2007, we received an email from our electrical engineer that ICE connected our service.

The expiration of Chuck's two-year notice to quit his job came at the end of 2007. He officially stepped down as principal of his office. It was a huge relief for him. He went to the doctor shortly thereafter for a checkup, to find his high blood pressure had dropped by over 20 points. What an amazing difference stress makes in a person's health. In his case, it was very visible too. It was like night and day in his personality. He became a much happier, healthier person.

Over the next few years, Chuck backed away from working at his old office. He knew that the situation would never work as it should with him in the office. A lot of clients and employees had a difficult time making the transition away from him as the principal. He knew remaining around the office was not good, as it undermined the authority of the new principal, regardless of how hard he tried not to do so. Plus, he knew that his old office didn't have the work to support paying him in the poor economy. No doubt, we needed the money for our Costa Rican dream, but that was no comparison to other employees in the office who needed money to pay day to day bills and put food on the table. Others, such as the new principal or his old partners, never truly understood Chuck's reasoning for backing away.

Chuck eventually helped another friend start up a new architecture business. He had even required in working for the new company that they were not allowed to take any work away from his old office. Of course, that was tricky, to be sure. It really limited the market that his friend could reach, but he honored Chuck's request. Personally, I would have preferred Chuck went to a fishing store to work in sales instead. However, Chuck always thought that he would make more money and help his friend out doing the architecture work, despite being burnt out on it. It was his choice to make, and I was proud of the guidelines he set to protect the people from his old office and help out his friend. If the economy had not crashed hard, things would obviously have worked out better for both his old office and the new company as well. However, that was out of everyone's control.

5 DIRTY TEETH, DIRTY POLICE AND DIRTY THIEVES

AS WE WAITED FOR THE HOUSE to sell, we continued with vacation to de-stress. Some vacations were in familiar places like Costa Rica and the Florida Keys. Some vacations were in new places we found once we discovered our love for cruises. Our Costa Rican vacations, detailed below, were always an adventure.

OUR FOURTH VISIT TO COSTA RICA

In October 2006, we started our vacation with a bang, beginning with a few days stay at the Peace Lodge. The hotel had gained popularity since our first stay. The Travel Channel featured it on Trista and Ryan's Honeymoon Hotspots as one of their international destinations. The increased popularity allowed the hotel to grow, adding some new exhibits, such as one for frogs. After seeing this exhibit, I certainly had a much bigger interest in frogs than I ever had before. Yes, the Costa Rican tree frog is a real frog you can see there, and even hold. Keep in mind, it is nocturnal, so you'll have to sign up for a night tour to see it. We left the Peace Lodge after a short stay and headed south towards Dominical.

As we were driving back into town, a soccer ball came rolling out into the street. Chuck slammed on his brakes. He stopped the car in the middle of the road and ran over to retrieve it. It was the flattest soccer ball that we had ever seen. The kids in the local schoolyard were yelling like crazy for him to throw it back over the fence. Once they got the ball, they started kicking it around happily again. At first, it broke our hearts to think that they had to play with such a flat soccer ball. However, it also made us smile to think they were still all grateful for that flat soccer ball. To them, that flat ball was all they needed. Isn't that really the way things should be? Shouldn't we be grateful for what we have instead of being unhappy with what we don't have? These kids really seemed to understand how to be happy more than we did. It also made us think about how many toys most kids in the U.S. own and how unhappy most of them would be with a flat soccer ball.

We didn't have kids. If we did, I thought it would be great to raise them in Costa Rica. Many people thought the opposite and often told to us, "Oh, well, you can move to Costa Rica because you don't have kids." However, I thought that raising kids there would teach them to appreciate the basic things in life. In fact, I admired people who moved with their children to foreign countries. I thought it taught them to become well-rounded individuals with a true appreciation for the basics of life. It was a simple soccer ball we saw that morning, but it was a moment that stuck with both of us. We would be happy, as long as we remember to be grateful for what we have, just like the kids playing soccer that morning.

As a side note, when it comes to children, I don't like that many people constantly judge us as selfish for not already having kids in our lives, as if it were an obligation since birth, expected of everyone, instead of a responsible decision to be made. I know a number of people who would love to have kids but physically can't. It is painful to see people judge them. Also, I see many kids who are not well cared for by their parents. I guess those kids survive the best they can with what life deals them, but I don't think it is fair for some to have parents that give them a disadvantage in life. I admire others who are good parents. Maybe we will be someday, but I don't really see children in the cards for us. When it comes to having children, I believe happiness is up to the individual, some are happier with them and some without them. It is a decision that we each must make, as both roads lead to different experiences. It is not for any of us to judge the choices of others.

Now, returning to our drive, our vehicle was not in the best condition. In fact, we ended up naming it "The Worbbler." We also realized the new rental car company we used had not given us the 4x4 we paid for, requiring us to do some walking to reach our property. When we reached the top of the hill, the view was as beautiful as we had remembered it. We were happy to see it had been fenced and was being well maintained too. We stayed at our place for a long time, listening, watching and dreaming about the future. It was peaceful being in Costa Rica. The rest of the world did not exist to us when we were there.

That night, we had a wonderful dinner with neighbors Chuck met on-line. We loved the community feel of the neighborhood already. We had not gone far from our neighbor's house when we discovered a landslide had blocked the road. We returned to ask them for alternate directions. Our neighbor said he could tell us how to go, but his wife rolled her eyes at me. She said we could spend the night in one of the cabinas (i.e. cabin) they were building. They were still under construction, but they were completed enough that we could sleep in one. I was immediately in favor of spending the night. I had no intention of becoming lost in the jungle in this downpour, and I particularly did not want to cross a creek, which was part of her husband's alternate directions.

Chuck was not happy. He really wanted to brush his teeth, but those are the breaks in Costa Rica. You had to go with the flow. It got worse as the night wore on, because the power went out in the cabina. Whenever it went out, two things happened. The ceiling fan quit, making it really hot, and worse, the light strip flashed on right in our eyes. Apparently, they had a safety light set up in the cabina, for power failures. The power would go off for only about one or two minutes, which was just long enough to wake us, but not enough time to reach the power strip. After coming on a number of times, it stayed on long enough for me to unplug it. However, the light did not turn off. We eventually realized it had a battery backup, so Chuck pulled out the bulbs. Finally, we got some sleep, although it was hot with the power out and no ceiling fan.

By morning, we thanked our neighbors for their hospitality. They said the road would probably be cleared out soon, if not already. We headed out, and sure enough, the road was almost cleared. Some Ticos had come along and were almost done clearing it with their shovels. Yes, there was no machinery here. We waited only a short time before heading back to our hotel to clean up for the day. It had not been a great night of sleep, but it was always an adventure in Costa Rica, which kept it exciting. We never knew what experience the day would bring us, and that was part of the fun. In the future, I might need to carry around a few toothbrushes.

One day, Chuck hiked alone, down to the waterfall at our property line. We had a stick shift vehicle, which I could not drive if something happened to him, so I was very nervous. He had no fear at all. Thankfully he came back all right. Upon his return, he admitted it was not the smartest thing he had ever done. It was not scary going down, but it was very creepy coming back up. On the way down, he did not see all of the big spider holes he left in the hillside, but on the way back up, he had to look at them. As he went deeper into the rainforest, the canopy grew thicker, making some areas black as night. Once he went down a certain distance, he grabbed a stick to help climb back up, using it to poke into the holes as he went. He promised he would never go back into the jungle without a machete again.

We spent a lot of time driving around the area to obtain our bearings. During our time in Dominical, we killed many a crab with "The Worbbler" while driving down the coastal highway. They lived in the mountains and travelled back and forth to the ocean. Around sunset, it was amazing to see hundreds of crabs on the road, trying to cross, as we and many other motorists were driving. We simply tried to stay off of the highway around sunset, to avoid the crabs.

We spent one morning as tourists visiting Hacienda Baru, where we took a hike through the jungle. We learned about some of the plants and trees. We had the opportunity to see sloths, toucans and monkeys, and we also heard some wild pigs.

We had decided to see what it would be like to drive the road between Dominical and Quepos. This stretch of road has since been paved, but at that time, it was not. Although the distance was short, it required a lot of patience to transverse all of the potholes in the dirt road. We were in "The Worbbler," which did nothing to improve the situation. It sounded like our car was going to fall apart at any moment.

After about an hour, we came to a halt. A young Tico spoke to us in Spanish. We called the hotel and asked them to translate, and they said the gate was out. It was going to be hours before it was fixed, so we needed to turn around to take the other highway. Chuck and I both stared at each other in horror. First of all, we figured they meant the bridge was out. Secondly, we did not want to drive all the way around on the other road. It was going to cost us a ton of time and would make us miss out on our great night we had planned in Manual Antonio. We sat there for another five minutes thinking. Finally, Chuck decided the other drivers must know something we didn't know, because they were not turning around. He thought we should wait it out. Waiting turned out to be a good idea. After about an hour, they had the bridge fixed. The bridge was nothing more than a big metal panel that spanned the river. They had brought in a piece of heavy equipment from nearby and used it to relocate the metal panel to the proper position. The bridge was now passable again, and traffic was flowing. The young Tico smiled at us happily as we drove by across the bridge.

We were happy to arrive in Quepos and see pavement again. I wanted to jump out of the car to kiss the pavement, and I thought Chuck would have liked to as well, although he would never admit it. We arrived in Manual Antonio and settled in for a nice night there.

The drive back to San Jose from Manual Antonio was fairly uneventful, with the exception of being stopped by the police. In Costa Rica, you have to wear your seatbelt. I always wore my seatbelt in the U.S., but it was very uncomfortable to wear a seatbelt in Costa Rica, especially on bumpy dirt roads. The seatbelts in "The Worbbler" were definitely uncomfortable, even on the paved highway, so neither Chuck nor I were wearing our seatbelts that day. There is an area outside of Jaco where the police are known to wait to pull people over for violations, such as no seatbelts. At that time, we were not yet aware of that area. However, we were guilty and got stopped.

The police though did not want to give us the ticket; instead, they wanted us to pay money on the spot. Chuck knew what they wanted, and he wanted the ticket. Since they spoke Spanish and we did not, the police did not think we understood. They kept trying to tell us to just pay them instead of taking a ticket that we would have to pay at the bank. To us, it was not a big deal, because we were already on our way to the bank to acquire our ATM cards. They were right in the fact that we did not have our seatbelts on, so we deserved the ticket. After a lot of sign language and discussion the police finally understood we were not going to pay them bribe money. We were shocked when they told us to put on our seatbelts and to keep driving. Apparently, they really did not want to do the work of writing up the ticket for two tourists. Perhaps they did not want us to take the ticket to the bank, with their name on it, and get them in trouble for requesting money on the spot. In any event, we counted ourselves as lucky and felt good that we had not given them the money to corrupt them. Hopefully, more tourists will stick to asking for the ticket, so they will turn into honest policemen.

As usual, we were somewhat depressed by our inevitable return to the U.S. and to work. However, it was the real world, and what we had to do to make our dream come true.

TIME FOR ANOTHER COSTA RICAN VACATION

March 2008 turned out to be a hectic month. We were losing faith in selling the house anytime soon, as the real estate market was sliding downhill. The right person didn't seem to be coming along for us. Chuck really missed not having a boat. It was a shame to be living on the water without a boat, when he loved to fish so much. Plus, there were a lot of great used boats for sale at reasonable prices. We finally decided to buy a small fishing boat he could have for now, and later we could take it with us to Costa Rica, to fish in the rivers there. He was excited and immediately turned up a great deal within his budget. He was still getting it all accessorized before our next Costa Rican vacation, when we heard the sad news that my grandmother died. We jumped on a plane to see my family in Tennessee.

I felt drained when we returned home from traveling and from working so much to keep my desk caught up between traveling. However, Chuck and I pressed onward. We hoped our planned vacation in Costa Rica would give us the sense of peace that we needed to rekindle our spirits. We quickly unpacked and soon repacked to take off out of the country.

We headed off for our next Costa Rican adventure. Unfortunately, Chuck was already starting to feel sick upon arrival in Costa Rica, and the airline lost my luggage. Even though our trip was not going well yet, we were starting it out with a stay at the Peace Lodge, so I was convinced things would improve once we arrived at the hotel.

We made the drive to the hotel with one interesting new discovery. During our drive, we came upon a construction zone. One lane of the road was shut down for paving. We were stopped for a minute, until we were given a stick with a piece of red cloth on the end. We assumed this was the method they had developed to allow people to take turns on the road, and we would drive until we reached another construction worker, to whom we would hand the stick. We drove for a while without spotting a construction worker and wondered how far we had to drive. We saw a guy at a restaurant on the side of the road, so with limited Spanish, we waved the flag and decided to ask him. He started laughing and pointed back to where we came from. Obviously we had passed it up. We drove back fast to see where we had gone wrong. By the time we got back, Chuck had figured it out. He thought that we were expected to go past the limited amount of road-work we had seen and stop to wait for the next car to approach us. At that time, we would hand it off to the next car, to take in the opposite direction. Sure enough, we arrived back at the construction site to find a worker to whom we could hand the flag. We were making hand gestures, and he was laughing. Apparently we were not the first foreigners to run off with their home-made flag. He was grateful, and we continued on our journey to the Peace Lodge with another lesson learned.

Upon check-in at the hotel, it was good to find out that a package had arrived from our new attorney. It was our first Costa Rican cell phone. Like many things in Costa Rica at the time, the phone system was a monopoly, controlled by the government (ICE). In order to acquire a cell phone in Costa Rica, you had to have a corporation. There were limited phone numbers released by the government at certain times, so a waiting list was required. Therefore, it was very exciting to finally have our first Costa Rican cell phone. The rates in Costa Rica for a phone were very cheap, usually around $7 a month at the time. Now, the government monopoly for cell phones and internet has been opened up allowing for advancement within the country as more providers enter the marketplace.

We went to the hotel gift shop, hoping I could buy a few things for the night, like a toothbrush and hairbrush. I figured some underwear would be asking too much. It turned out even a toothbrush was asking too much. Chuck was disappointed that we had not divided the luggage when we packed to half my stuff and half his per suitcase, in case we lost a piece. It was another lesson learned which we now do when traveling together. Nevertheless, we had a wonderful night at the hotel, and my luggage arrived early the next morning.

We checked out the aviary exhibit, where a blue macaw landed on my shoulders. At first, Chuck was trying to take a photo of him on my shoulder, but I freaked when Chuck started to panic, as the bird reached for my ear. He had a grip on my shoulder and would not let go. I kept trying to pull my head away from him, but Chuck told me to stay calm as he walked over. Apparently, the red strap on my sunglasses, which went behind my ear, fascinated the macaw. Chuck got him off of me, and I packed my sunglasses away. The blue macaw still followed me around the aviary the entire time we were there, so I felt like he was going to swoop down on me at any moment.

Once again, we had a nice short stay at the Peace Lodge to begin our trip. This was followed by an uneventful drive down to Dominical, where we grabbed pizza at the Rum Bar, which had become our traditional first dinner down south. We happily talked about how we couldn't wait to see our property the next morning.

It was exciting to finally have power to our property, but the power pole standing there with an enormous box for the meter stuck out like a sore thumb along the small country road. Chuck peeked in a manhole cover to look at the expensive copper wires we had installed. However, it was empty, and he became furious! We rushed back down the driveway to the power pole where we could clearly see that the copper wire had been cut. It was heartbreaking to have our power lines stolen after our long wait to acquire power. In hindsight, we should have known better. At that time period, copper was even being stolen in the U.S., with one theft causing a huge blackout in Miami. Of course, in a third world country, to leave the copper lines with the lot unattended was simply asking someone to take it. It was another lesson we learned the hard way.

Our stay in Dominical was short lived, since we were venturing further south into the Osa Peninsula. Our destination was the Lookout Inn in Carate. We had heard about potholes the size of cars, but we didn't see anything that big during our drive. We crossed a few rivers I would certainly be fearful of in the rainy season.

Fortunately, we had a separate cabin away from the main inn, as there were two snakes (one a boa) in the bathroom of the main inn. Our cabin was built up off the ground with slats in the floor that did not totally meet. The walls were built only waist height, to allow a view of nature. The bathroom had no door. The bed had a white mosquito net surrounding it. We heard the pounding waves of the ocean and watched the macaws.

Like many hotels in the Osa Peninsula, the Inn was all-inclusive, given its remote location with limited restaurants surrounding it. The food was very good. Most dinners ended with wonderful desserts. Many included bananas and chocolate in tortillas or crepes, and although I was not a big banana person, you couldn't go wrong with bananas in Costa Rica. One interesting tidbit of information we found out was the monkeys could smell the different types of bananas. The inn kept the high quality bananas locked away, but the smell still lured the monkeys in to try to eat them, even though they had set bunches of less desirable bananas around outside for the monkeys to eat.

This area of the Osa was off of the power grid, so they were very conservative with energy usage. It made it interesting to return to our room at night. I did not realize we needed to bring a flashlight, but fortunately, I carried a small one in my purse with me. After eating dinner each night, we used the light to find our way between the inn and our cabin, since it was pitch black otherwise. Another reason for the lack of lights was you did not want to attract the many bugs into your room, given its open walls. I learned this the hard way when trying to take my prescriptions and brush my teeth the first night. By having the light on for only a short time period to find my prescriptions and take them, I ended up with bugs flying around everywhere in our room. It was very gross to then try to brush my teeth with them flying around. Moreover, when I was done, I had to leave my toothbrush out in the open. I grabbed some toilet paper to at least wrap up the bristles to keep them bug free.

Going to bed that night, I was a little upset by the openness of the room. Before our arrival, I had dreamt the monkeys would come into our room and steal my underwear. Now, I was thinking more about snakes crawling up the bed-posts into bed with us, or bugs crawling up through the slats in the floor and into our bed. Chuck was tired from being sick, so he went to sleep right away. It took me a while to relax and fall asleep. I awoke in the middle of the night to go to the bathroom. However, it totally freaked me out to walk across the floor in my bare feet, thinking about what things might have crawled up through the slats in the dark while I was sleeping.

We awoke in the mornings to macaws sitting in the trees right outside our cabin, chewing on nuts. They were everywhere. This allowed for some great macaw photos during our stay.

We eventually found out there was a photography tour that was going to end at the inn, which was the reason for the snakes being held in the bathroom of the Inn. The boa had been caught in the hen house, so the joke was that the boa was not hungry for a few days since it had already eaten a chicken. Even so, I did not want to be close to the thing. We would be gone before the photography tour arrived for their photo shoot. I was satisfied knowing the boa would not be let loose until after we left.

We saw a number of great sunsets during our stay at the Lookout Inn. I did not see the famous green flash that happens after the sun hits the horizon, but Chuck witnessed it one night, along with a few of the other guests.

We ventured down to the end of the road and saw the landing strip for the small airplanes that passed the inn. We couldn't believe it. The bumpy landing strip was hard to tell apart from the dirt road that we drove in on, which made for an interesting photo. The airport was a guy sitting under a tree next to his truck. It was the funniest thing to see, but it worked sufficiently down in this area.

When I booked our trip, I had hoped to go to Corcovado National Park which has been called the "most biologically intense place on Earth" by National Geographic. Even though the road ended past the airport landing strip, down from where we stayed, the park entrance was not at the end of the road. Due the long hike to reach the park entrance and avoid the hot weather conditions, we saw hikers with their flashlights pass our cabin, starting at 3:00am. They had to carry their own supplies and time the tides right, as the hike to the park entrance was past the end of the road, down along the beach. It was basically an all-day hike by the time they hiked into and out of the park, along with spending any time in the park itself. They were handsomely rewarded for their abilities. We heard there were pumas along the hiking trails during our stay. Since most people who went to these extremes to see the animals had a deep appreciation and respected them, the animals apparently remained in place, undisturbed, while the hikers continued down their trail. I was sure that would scare me, but it was an opportunity I would love to see someday. Even if we had been great hikers, it was not meant to be on this trip, as Chuck was too sick to go anywhere. I still planned to visit there someday, but I was guessing it would be on a boat ride, using another park entrance. This was closer to our B&B, making it possible to do without hiking the beach.

Since our original discovery of the stolen wires, we had been given a lot of time to contemplate things. We had planned to build an expensive garage to live in during the construction phase. Now that this had happened, we were going to be short on money and realized we didn't need an expensive garage. If the garage were there, where would the workers' quarters go during construction? There was not really room for both. It didn't make sense to build a garage that was nice on the inside, to then rip it out and replace it later on, simplifying it into a normal garage. We decided the best thing to do was to kill the entire garage idea. Instead, we would have the workers' quarters built where the garage was planned, and we would use temporary power during construction the next time. We would rent a place to live during construction. Maybe, it was really all meant to work out this way for a reason.

Overall, the trip had not been what we had planned when we arrived in Costa Rica. However, we still made the best of our vacation. We headed back to the U.S. and back to work. Our future Costa Rican plans had changed slightly, but we were still ready to go forward. At least, we would be if our house sold.

6 FOLLOW THE SIGNS

FINALLY, AT THE END of August 2008, we closed the deal to sell our house in the U.S. It was both sad and exciting. I was sad, because it was difficult to leave behind the house where both of our dogs were buried. Chewy had lived with us for 15 years, and Shoes had lived with us for 17 years. We had them for almost as long as Chuck and I had been married, so they had been a big part of our lives.

I would miss the house, because we had put our hearts into renovating it. We had a lot of good times in it with our friends. Many of them had thought we were insane when we moved from our big fancy new house in Tampa to this dumpy house on the water. We had even paid more for it, but we had seen the potential in it. Once we were done fixing it up, they had all grown to love it, just like we had. It had been an important move for us, as waterfront prices, although expensive, had not yet skyrocketed. Now, a lot of our friends wanted to live on the water and realized what a smart move we had made earlier. That move was one of the big reasons we were going to be able to afford to finance our dream in Costa Rica. I felt like we were passing the house on to a buyer who would love it and appreciate it as much as we did, which was important to us both.

Our realtor helped us find a place to rent. Chuck and I selected a condo, thinking it might be our last chance to live close to the beach in the U.S. We also picked a place that did not allow dogs. We figured it would stop our temptation from getting another dog in the U.S., since we wanted to wait and adopt one of the many homeless dogs in Costa Rica.

For a long time, Chuck did nothing but pack. Packing was allocated into two different groups. There was the packing of things that would be put into storage for later shipment to Costa Rica, and there was the packing of temporary things that would go to the condo with us. He was very good at keeping the boxes labeled, with a list of what was in them. I tried to help when I could, but I was swamped at my job. I was a pack rat, so my contribution was making a commitment to throw things away. I actually got pretty good at it, as far as I was concerned. However, I was sure Chuck would disagree.

A short time prior to our moving day, Chuck's next step was to rent a Pod. This is a small storage unit that gets delivered to the driveway of your house and later taken away for storage in a large warehouse, where you pay a monthly fee. By the time Chuck filled it with all of our items for future shipment to Costa Rica, every square inch was used.

On the day prior to closing on our house, I was teleworking from my office while Chuck finished packing the last few items. He was running around the house like crazy that morning. Chuck rarely made mistakes, but that morning he made a big one. He decided to raise the boatlift so that it wouldn't be sitting in the water for the new owner. However, he got distracted in the house. I heard a horrible screeching noise followed by Chuck running out of the house to the dock. I knew immediately he had forgotten to stop the lift before the boat lift reached the top. He was devastated. How were we ever going to get the lift fixed? We couldn't close that next day with a broken lift. I had no faith he could get it done, but Chuck started to make emergency calls. Luck was on our side, and he found a company that was willing to come out to see us. Believe it or not, they said this sort of thing happened quite frequently. It made him feel better to hear. They got everything fixed, back to working order that day. To me, it was a sign we were meant to be out of the house and on our way to Costa Rica.

Chuck did most of the work loading the U-haul, and it was stressful for him, doing this while waiting to see if the lift could be fixed in one day. By bedtime, he was exhausted. Surprisingly, neither of us was sad. We were actually ready to move on. Other than leaving the dogs buried here, I had no problems with leaving. The fact was, we were excited about our future, and we knew deep down that our new place in Costa Rica would one day be much better than our place here. Our future was bright, and we were ready to go there, even though we knew the road ahead was going to be a hard one. We didn't know then how hard it was going to be.

At first, our condo was an unorganized disaster. After not much time at all, Chuck had paintings on the wall, with plug in art lights to brighten our pieces. It looked like a really nice place to live while waiting for our plans to proceed in Costa Rica.

Next on our agenda was the boat. Without a dock, we needed a tow vehicle for our boat. Our plan was to sell Chuck's car and buy a 4x4 vehicle that we would use to tow the boat in Florida. Later, we would ship it for driving in Costa Rica. Initially, we had always read on-line to buy our vehicles in Costa Rica; however, that advice had changed over the years.

Now, it was recommended to bring a vehicle from the U.S., where you knew its history, to avoid flood-damaged cars left over from some of the major hurricanes. The problem was we absolutely had to have a 4x4, and they were hard to find in Florida. Eventually, we got lucky to find an Xterra. It would work out to be a nice vehicle for us, as the parts were readily available in Costa Rica, which was important to think about when picking a vehicle to take there.

In September of 2008, Chuck returned to Costa Rica to look for a contractor, since the original contractor we had selected still did not have the time to begin our project. Chuck stayed at the cabinas in our neighborhood and made appointments to meet with potential contractors, who had been recommended to us.

By chance, a neighbor recommended her boss, an expatriate from the U.S., living close to our neighborhood. Chuck met with him, saw some of his work and loved it. He charged on a cost of construction basis plus a percentage for himself. Chuck's concern was that he was older and did not look in the best health to hold up to a project like ours, which might take a few years to build.

The other two contractors Chuck met had provided fixed-cost bids. They were both Costa Rican contractors from outside of our neighborhood, with great reputations. Our hearts had sunk, because their fixed-costs bids were over our budget. At this point, our options were limited. Apparently, since our trip in 2005, material costs had risen dramatically. The worldwide demand for items such as steel had driven up the cost astronomically. This hit us hard as we already had sold our house in the U.S. for less than anticipated in the falling real estate market. It was a double edge sword. We had less money to spend and would need more to build. We had given up everything to get to this point. We considered our odds and decided in the long run it was best to take our chance to continue. Some things would simply have to go, and we would not be able to finish our house right away. It was the reality of the situation, but rewards in life rarely come without some risk. It was scary, but we were hoped for the best things would work out.

Chuck had a meeting with a contractor recommended by our architect. Chuck was very upset when he found out during his meeting the entire cost of the pool had been left out of the bid. This upset our architect as well, since the pool was clearly on the drawings as part of the bid, and this bid was already the highest one we had received. That led to some heated discussions in Spanish, which Chuck obviously did not understand.

The other construction firm was out of San Jose. Chuck had set up a meeting with them while he was staying in Escazu. Their bid seemed to be fairly well in line, also for a fixed price. They were very professional, and Chuck really liked the guy he spoke with. His biggest concern with them was they were located a distance away, so it might be difficult to have any problems resolved after construction was completed.

Chuck returned home from his trip to think things over. After a short time, he was convinced we should go with the cost of construction plus a percentage, using the local contractor. First of all, he really liked the contractor. Secondly, he liked the fact that we would be paying the true cost of things, without having to worry what kind of curve balls might be thrown at us when it came to picking out the detailed items, like tile and granite. Third, with the economy going down the toilet, he felt that material costs might drop, and the cost basis would eventually allow us to make our money go further. Fourth, we would have a local contractor who could communicate with us in English. Finally, he loved the quality of all the workmanship and woodwork that he saw on the houses this contractor had built.

My fears were that I didn't want to create trouble in the neighborhood by using our neighbor's boss. Hopefully, nothing bad would happen, but sometimes things could become out of control in a small community, if relationships turned sour. I also had not met the guy, but I was worried about his health, just based on what Chuck had said to me.

One day, the realtor who sold us our Costa Rica lot emailed to apologize for not recommending the local contractor before now. This seemed to seal the deal for us as a sign it was meant to be. We had to take our chances with someone, so we agreed to proceed with him.

In the middle of October, Chuck signed the agreement with our contractor in Costa Rica and set up a meeting to introduce him to our architect, since the two had never worked together previously. This turned out to be a very intense meeting. After two hours of what Chuck felt like was a lecture by our architect to our contractor of what he expected of contractors on his jobs, the meeting came to an end. Since it was all done in Spanish, Chuck caught only a word here and there. Chuck didn't know if this was a lecture our architect gave to all of the new contractors he worked with for the first time, or if this had something to do with us not selecting the contractor he had recommended. In any event, Chuck tried to smooth things over with both of them and was hopeful they would work well together in the future. He later apologized to our contractor, who was all right with the meeting. He said he built things the right way. Therefore, our architect would have no reason to complain, and he would find that out soon enough.

After having some time to review the job, our contractor suggested a few changes to improve our project. First of all, we needed to build a water storage tank for our property. While our association had a great water system, it still had outages when the pressure from the water upstream would break the lines, causing outages that might last for days or even weeks. Secondly, we needed to install a second electric meter at the road. This would allow us to track the power separately for the B&B and the house, for expense purposes. Also, it would make the bill cheaper, given rates increase above set wattage limits. We agreed with both recommendations.

In early November 2008, our architect obtained the permit for our buildings. Our contractor started to work right away. He began by cleaning up the site. He got the driveway in better working order, so it could handle the delivery of materials easily. After the driveway was ready, he got the workers' quarters built.

Having workers' quarters built on-site was a typical situation in Costa Rica, since many of the workers depended upon the public bus system for transportation. Usually, our workers stayed on-site during the week and went home on the weekends, as some had to travel hours on the bus. However, a few of our workers with unique expertise, like our plumber and wood worker, were from Nicaragua, so they traveled home only a limited number of times during the year. It must have been very difficult on their families to have them away for such a long time. Looking back, our crew was always very happy. Construction was a way of life for them. Being away from home for long periods of time was part of what they knew as reality.

In November, we celebrated the sale of our house by taking a Panama Canal cruise we had signed up for months earlier. After learning we were over budget to build in Costa Rica and that our friends had to cancel the cruise, Chuck and I seriously thought about canceling. However, we were not people to pass up opportunities, and we felt this was a once in a lifetime experience. Plus, as I already expressed earlier, we felt vacation was a necessity that we owed to ourselves, so we decided to go on the cruise by ourselves.

When talking about this cruise to one of my friends, she was laughing at me, because I was so on top of planning out our vacation, I had this cruise planned out along with our vacation plans for 2009. It bothered me that she did not plan in advance and would lose vacation for 2008. She would complain about losing vacation time every year and was burnt out on her job, yet she didn't take the time to plan for her vacation to re-energize herself. I told her to laugh all she wanted, but I was not going to lose my vacation days.

In addition to seeing the Panama Canal and many other stops, this cruise included a stop in Costa Rica, which gave us a chance to paddle down one of the many rivers in Costa Rica. Overall, we had spent a lot of money on the cruise, but we felt it was worth it in the long run. We were re-energized, ready to start back to work and ready to see the progress at our property.

By late December we had officially broken ground on our project. The dry season had started, and we were in good shape to make progress. Our contractor was positive that things were going to go smoothly. By early January, the footings were dug for our house, and the lowest level of the B&B had been dug out. The crew moved on to laying block in January, and by the end of February, much progress could be seen. By early March, the panels for the floors were being laid, and the building really began to take shape. Chuck had wanted some unique columns for our house and for the tiki hut we would build. Our contractor found some wood to use for the columns, called Mano de Tigre. They were incredibly unique, and Chuck fell in love with them immediately.

As worried as Chuck had been about our architect and contractor getting along, given their first meeting together was intense, everything actually worked out to be fine. As promised, our contractor built things properly, and, as promised, our architect stayed on top of him. Our architect visited the job site to run concrete tests and other inspections, to be sure things were done right. All the concrete tests came back fine. He found a few minor things that were wrong, and our contractor admittedly said the crew screwed up. In a short time, our contractor gained the respect of our architect. They were able to work together well, and we had no significant problems.

Our contractor kept us current of what was happening in Costa Rica by sending us periodic email updates and photos. We would wait impatiently for the photos to arrive, usually on Thursday or Friday. Initially, we got them every week or so, but eventually, things started to spread out more and more.

There was even one period of time where he did not return our phone calls or our emails. With no updates arriving and no return calls, I knew there was a problem. His last word to Chuck, before dropping all communication with us, was that he was going to San Jose to take care of some things. I speculated that he had checked into the hospital there. At first, Chuck thought I was over exaggerating, but then he tended to agree with me. I finally resorted to calling our neighbor, who worked for him. I felt bad to put her in the middle, but I wanted to know if our contractor was all right. She was put on the spot, but finally admitted he had not been feeling well. I didn't ask if he was in the hospital, because I already knew the answer. She said she would be sure he got the message to call us. Sure enough, it was not long before he called and admitted he had checked himself into the hospital in San Jose. It worried us not only because we really liked him as a person but because our project was just beginning construction. We were thankful that he was at least getting medical help, but it was stressful to wonder if things at the job site were being taken care of while he was away.

7 A TASTE OF COSTA RICA

FINALLY, MARCH 2009 had arrived. This time we were not just off to Costa Rica for vacation. We were off to see our dreams come to life. We arrived in San Jose and spent days there doing some shopping. We paid our driver, Eduardo, by the hour. He not only drove, but also translated for us in stores, when necessary. He was amused by some of our purchases. For example, the cheap clay light fixtures we loved versus the big massive American style light fixtures, which he preferred. He added his two cents when he could and took us where we wanted to go. In addition to shopping, we made a stop at the bank.

When you enter the larger banks in Costa Rica, there are numbers at the front for two types of service, one for regular teller service and one for customer service. The waiting area has chairs, where you sit until the individual teller windows or customer service desks show your number above them, so you know which window to go to for service. It is a very efficient process.

Since nobody spoke English on our prior trips, we were a little nervous about being alone on our third trip to the bank. Our attorney was with us to set up our account on our first trip, but on our second trip we were left alone, with our limited amount of Spanish, which created some difficulty. On this trip, once again, our teller spoke no English. Nevertheless, we figured things out, with no problems this time. We were initially annoyed that our driver didn't come in with us to translate, like he had done on our shopping stops. I supposed it was human nature to be lazy and take the easy way out by relying upon him, but he had forced us to learn to communicate. It was a good feeling to have accomplished the task on our own.

Overall, shopping was both fun and exhausting. It was a lot of work to go shopping in Costa Rica, as the stores we needed were usually very far apart. Also, most stores were typically specialty stores, so it required many stops to find what we wanted. We hit the jackpot in a few stores, like Constru Plaza. We checked out many different lighting stores, but in the end, nothing was as Costa Rican as the simple clay fixtures. Chuck would be able to design the perfect ones for us. The one thing we never found was good pre-colored stucco. The ones they showed us were paint with sand thrown in it, as far as I was concerned. By the time our shopping days ended in San Jose, we were pretty happy with our choices and tired of shopping. We realized it was much easier to buy things in the U.S. than to find them in Costa Rica, regardless of what people said on-line about having no need to bring things to Costa Rica. I was sure you probably could eventually find most everything you needed there with enough time, but time was a luxury we lacked.

During our stay in San Jose, we decided to take advantage of being close to the ARCR (Association of Residents of Costa Rica) offices, by paying for their help to obtain our driver's licenses. The ARCR can be a very useful resource in keeping expatriates informed on matters affecting them, especially for those just becoming established in the country. We hired the ARCR to walk us through the driver license process.

I was not sure why the driver's license facility needed to be protected like a fortress, but it was very tightly secured. Once we parked at the facility, we had to walk off-site for a blood and medical test. The blood test was needed to confirm our blood type, to place on our driver's license, to make it faster to provide medical help should we ever be hurt. After the blood test, we went through an eye exam and a quick medical review with a doctor to complete our paperwork. Once back at the driver's license facility we went through several more lines to pay our fees, show our existing U.S. driver's licenses, take photos and do other paperwork, before obtaining our Costa Rican driver's licenses.

The worst part for me was being fingerprinted at the police station. The fingerprint lady did not click with me. I tried to cooperate, but my hands apparently did not relax enough for her. She was not happy that I was a foreigner obtaining a driver's license in Costa Rica, who was unable to speak Spanish. I tried to apologize for my hands not doing what she wanted, and I tried to tell her I was going to learn Spanish. My attempts to talk to her did not help my situation or improve her mood.

I looked at Chuck for help, and he rolled his eyes at me to stop creating trouble. There was nothing I could do. The lady was brutal. She yelled at me. She yelled at the lady who was helping Chuck to tell him to yell at me. Finally, she yelled directly at Chuck to tell him to yell at me. It wasn't only me who she had trouble with, either. She had to ask another policeman to fingerprint one or two people while we had been waiting, who she couldn't convince to cooperate. Anyway, after messing up two cards on me already, we were doing well to almost finish the third card, when she put my right thumbprint in the left thumbprint slot. I watched her do it too, knowing it was wrong. What was I supposed to say? She went completely nuts at that point.

A really nice policeman came over and took my fingerprints next. He did it with one try! She stood there the whole time, talking furiously in Spanish, giving me looks that could kill. The policeman told me I should learn to speak Spanish, and I promised I would. It was humiliating to stand there, with the long line that had now formed behind us. He ignored the lady, and when he was done, he told her I did well. My fingerprints were incredibly sloppy on the card, but that was fine with me. I was so happy to wash my hands and exit that room.

What would we tell the driver's license people to use as our address? Given there is no daily home mail delivery system in Costa Rica, we had no idea what our address would be. All we really knew was that it was off the Costanera Highway, which was similar to telling someone we lived off Interstate 275. Obviously, they would not have a clue where we lived if this is all we said. We were discussing this in the waiting line, and a number of the Costa Rican's had a good laugh over it. Costa Ricans are very nice. They started trying to help us figure out what to do by asking questions to see what our address should be or telling us to use our hotel address. Fortunately, our ARCR rep was able to use their association address, for now. He said we could change it once we figured out what our Costa Rican address was supposed to be. Obviously, this was another good reason to have someone walk us through the process the first time.

Another interesting part of the driver's license process was when we had to put our fingerprint on a machine that recorded it for future voting purposes. As foreigners, we are not allowed to vote, but fingerprinting is part of the standard process we had to follow. I thought it was an interesting way to obtain fingerprints of most people living in Costa Rica. After all of that, we were off with our new driver's licenses. Mine was great, but Chuck realized later, his name was misspelled. Oh well, guess we would have to fix our address and his name at renewal one day. The good news was that it took only half a day to accomplish our mission, instead of the full day we had planned. This worked out great, as it allowed us to have the afternoon to grab a taxi to Constru Plaza, to look around some more.

After we left Constru Plaza, we walked back along the road, stopping at the various places to shop to acquire more ideas where to find things for our house. This experience made me sympathize with the Ticos, because walking was not fun. There must be an art to learning to walk along the road with no sidewalks. I had not mastered it, but I was sure many of the Ticos had. I seemed to step in tons of holes, mud puddles, dog poop and about everything else you would want to miss. I was embarrassed to see my messy tennis shoes and the muddy tracks I left in a little soda we entered to grab some lunch.

To clarify, sodas are a combination family-run restaurant and convenience store. You can find these all over Costa Rica, as many Ticos have them connected right to their houses. I felt like the people were giving me the eye for making their floor dirty. I wanted to crawl under the table. After all, this was Costa Rica, where they are very picky about having clean floors!

As we walked back along the road, the trucks and cars seemed to be so close that the mirrors felt like they would clip my ear at times. I personally did not enjoy the walk, and I suppose we were lucky it was not raining on us. I often see Costa Ricans out in the rain with no protection. I think about how miserable it must be to walk in wet shoes or to arrive somewhere with your clothes and hair totally wet. Many times, they are carrying lots of groceries and other items that you know are also soaked. I had a new appreciation for Ticos who walked on the side of the road after our little trek that afternoon. I also had a new appreciation for our car and realized how spoiled we were to have our own transportation.

Chuck had taken the regional commuter prop plane down to our property previously, but this trip would be my first time. Because I am prone to motion sickness easily, I was not looking forward to it the next day. It was a short 45-minute flight on the prop plane from the international airport outside of San Jose to Palmar, a city about 15 minutes south of our property. We were each limited to a 25 lb piece of checked luggage and one carry on, which included my purse. It was the first time I had ever stood on a scale to be weighed with my carryon bag, making check-in rather interesting. They also tagged my purse for carry-on, like you would tag any piece of luggage, which is fine, except the sticky stuff didn't really want to come off later. We learned it was best not to look at the scale, since it was highly likely you would weigh more on your return flight than when you left, which could be depressing. Breathing in the plane fumes as we waited for our plane was probably not very healthy, but the wait was interesting. We've never seen so many people mopping floors. At one count, I think we had seen at least 5 different people with mops in this small area of about 800 sq ft. We noticed the bathroom was mopped at least 4 times, yet not one person had been in there to use it. We never saw them clean the mops, but we did see them use the mops often. Based upon our observation in the airport, along with a number of other things we saw on this trip, we came to the conclusion that clean floors must be very important in Costa Rica. This was certainly something I would have to remember once we moved to Costa Rica, because I was not great at mopping.

Although I had been fearful of the flight, it turned out to be amazing, just as Chuck had promised. The views down the coastline were gorgeous. We had an excellent view of the "Whale's Tail," a land formation off the coast that resembled a whales tail at low tide, and Chuck shot some great photos. I had worried for no good reason. As usual, I had pushed past my fears, and it had been worth it.

Upon arrival, the airport terminal was an open-air structure with a roof and one small office, where they gave out the tickets for departing passengers. Of course, the scale sat outside the office, for weighing departing passengers with their luggage. There were no rental car companies here, but we had pre-arranged for a car to be delivered from a nearby city. Once we got our car and arrived at our property, the first thing we were asked was if we had felt the earthquake. Apparently, we had been in the car during the earthquake, so we did not feel it. Chuck was very disappointed, since neither of us had ever felt an earthquake. The construction crew stopped for lunch to watch TV, and they informed us that it was a 6.7 quake that had occurred off of the coast of Golfito, about 1.5 hours south of us.

After all of the planning we had put into building in Costa Rica, it was very exciting to finally arrive at our place, to see the construction site in person for the first time. Even though we had received photos almost weekly since construction began in January, it was amazingly different to physically be there. It seemed like we had been dreaming the whole time, but this trip made the reality of the situation kick in for us.

After touring around the job site for a while, in a stunned daze at the reality of what we had created, we sat down to talk to our contractor about details. It was not too long before one of the neighbors came running up, shouting there was a wildfire nearby. She needed some of our crew to go help fight the fire, which was close to a neighbor's house, and of course, she would pay for them.

Now two things seemed odd about this to me. First of all, there were wildfires in the rainforest where it should be wet and raining. Unfortunately, we learned this was an unusually dry year for our area with scarce rainfall, so wildfires had been rampant. According to some of our neighbors, who had been living in Costa Rica for a while, this year had been unlike any other they had seen. The dryness was obvious to us on our drive in, as typically we saw all lush greenness instead of the dry brownness. Plus, there was the occasional smoke along the roadside, which we assumed was caused by someone throwing out their lit cigarette, creating the fires, as was the case in a number of wildfires in Florida a few years ago. Secondly, she said she would pay for the guys to help fight the fire, and our contractor asked us if we wanted to charge her. We said we did not as we were shocked by the thought of it. Things we would take for granted in the U.S. like helping to fight fires was something there that they seemed to think was perfectly normal to pay someone for to obtain their services. This was certainly a way of thinking that we will have to adjust to in the future.

We stayed at the job site for a while longer, talking to our contractor, working out details on what we needed to accomplish during our trip, then laying out a timeline in order to finish things. For example, we needed to come up with the right mix for the concrete aggregate and the color we wanted for the floors before we left. The crew had worked on samples, but we didn't like them. It was going to take some time to bring things in line with what we wanted before we departed for the U.S. Before we knew it, time had flown by quickly. We decided to grab some food to eat and drive up the hill to see if we could help out with the wildfires. We had no shovels or anything, so we didn't think there was much we could do. However, Chuck thought we should offer to help.

While we ate our chips in the car, we talked about what we had seen at the job site. From a positive perspective, the buildings and the work that had been done were excellent. We had known there would be some problems. After all, nobody could expect to build and have everything perfect. We had simply hoped to find no major problems. I had lots of fears running through my head for the last 3 months, but the worst one was that they had built the buildings on the wrong spot. Since Chuck is an architect, he could truly appreciate how much progress had been quickly made and how well built things had been done. In fact, he commented that construction was going better than we could even expect it to go had we been building in the U.S. From the negative side, the reality was that all hope of having enough money was lost. It was obvious, seeing the buildings only half finished, knowing how much money we had spent. There was no way we could finish, and it hit us pretty hard. We had known from the start that we were over budget; however, given the drop in construction material prices and the higher exchange rate of the dollar, we had held out hope we were close to possibly having a miracle, to squeak out enough to finish.

It was an unsettling feeling to lose that last little bit of hope, but it was reality. We realized we needed to face up to the fact and adjust accordingly. We unhappily accepted we would not be able to finish our house and decided to replace finishing it with completing the tiki hut instead. Hence, our new goal was to be hopeful that we would have enough money to finish the B&B, the pool and the tiki hut. After all, we could live in the B&B and finish our house someday in the future. It was not what our plan had been when we first envisioned it years ago, but if you obtain everything you want, then you don't appreciate it as much as when you have to work harder to achieve it.

Chuck was able to follow the smoke up to the wildfires. It was amazingly hot. Our crew was down the hill, in the thick of it cutting in a firebreak. How were they breathing? I remember being nervous about how close to the edge Chuck was standing, when I felt the earth move. Only a few of the crew seemed to notice. It was minor, but I count it as my first earthquake. It was a very strange feeling. It was odd that Chuck did not notice, but he was lost, staring into the wildfire. Eventually, the crew finished the firebreak, to cut off the fire from our neighbor's property, and we all left for the evening. We had started this Costa Rican adventure with a bang already, with earthquakes, wildfires and seeing our place under construction in person for the first time. I hoped that things would become a little bit calmer, as we hadn't even checked into our room yet.

Over the next few days, we enjoyed ourselves spending time at the job site, looking around. It actually turned out to be a good thing, because Chuck realized in conversations with the crew that they were trying to build from the pretty pictures he had shared with our contractor. Our foreman had a notebook full of them. Chuck had to point out that he drew those pretty pictures for me to have an idea of the overall concept, which he then shared with our contractor; however, they should be building from the real drawings. Chuck had not put all of the real details in the pretty pictures for me. Now the missing roof beam they were asking Chuck about made sense! They knew it should have been there. Nevertheless, they really liked the pretty pictures and wanted Chuck to keep sending those too. Going forward, though, Chuck knew to be more careful about what he shared. We were very lucky to have a great crew and an excellent foreman.

Our contractor got a big kick out of the fact that we liked seeing the site in its grey stage, since most of his clients usually did not care too much about things at this point. I still had a hard time visualizing it, even with my pretty pictures, but I loved being there. On the other hand, Chuck could understand the bigger picture, and he liked to see the fine details of how they had built things. He was intrigued by how they had come up with methods to do some things. They had developed their own hand tools, to bend all of the rebar (i.e. reinforced steel bars) on site. In fact, we had a dedicated rebar guy, whose only job was to bend the rebar. I must admit, the rebar guy was my favorite, because I thought I could learn how to do it. I wanted to have him teach me how to bend all the rebar, but Chuck wouldn't let me. He said we were paying the guy to work, and he did not want to spend the money for me to learn how to do it. Plus, he didn't think I realized how much strength it took to bend rebar by hand, even using their tools. Man, did we have a lot of rebar on-site! Our "rebarman" was fast too. It was impressive during that visit to see how much rebar work was involved, but it is even more mindboggling to look back now at the sequential construction photos that Chuck kept of the progress from start to finish at the amount and size of rebar that went into our project.

We continued buying things for our property. We decided to make a trip to Golfito. This is one of the few duty free ports in the country, where every person is allowed to spend a limited amount of money on items at a specific place, free of duty charges (i.e. taxes). It can add up to a lot of savings, especially if you need to buy big items, like appliances.

Since we had two kitchens to fill with appliances, we wanted to get started on spending our money, as we needed to spread out our purchases. For example, at that time, I could only spend $500 every six months and buy one refrigerator every two years. This might not be the actual rule for a refrigerator but things like this were tracked by the government's computer system, all using your passport number, to keep up with specifically what you purchased and when. We were not sure what to expect, so our neighbors sent their daughter to help guide us along the way.

We began the 1.5-hour drive to Golfito early in the day. We had only gotten to the main highway, before our young guide wanted to stop at the store to pick up something. Chuck stopped, and she jumped out. We could see her from the car. However, I was nervous. How would we know what she was really buying? Was she buying something she should not be? We were DINKS and not used to this. We both started to feel pressured about being responsible for her. She was very mature for an eight year old, so that got us even more worried. She returned to the car with a pack of gum. The panic mode we had gone into was for nothing, but I was determined not to let her out of our sight from that point forward. She sat in the backseat and played on her computer quietly for most of the ride. When I asked how she was doing, she told me she got car sick sometimes. Chuck and I looked at each other again, about to panic. When I told her maybe she should sit up front and not play on the computer, she insisted she was fine in the back. This was certainly not going to be an easy day, like I had hoped it would be. The kid was stressing me out. I was glad we were not parents.

The ride to Golfito was beautiful, though we had to dodge many potholes along the way. Our guide helped us acquire our tickets, which we had to obtain and hold for the next day, to actually pick up our purchases. There were lots of great appliances. All the big-name brands were there, like GE and Whirlpool, along with some brands that we did not recognize. In addition to appliances, there were tons of other items, from clothes to cosmetics. It seemed like this place had it all. We were very fortunate to run into a salesman who spoke excellent English and explained the entire purchase process to us. We spent the morning deciding what we wanted to purchase, then headed off for lunch. We would return the next day to pick up our items.

We stopped at a popular place called Banana Bay, recommended by local expatriates, for a hamburger called the bilge burger. While we were waiting for our food, we were admiring all of the beautiful boats docked there. One particular yacht was amazing. Some of the crew came to sit at the bar. Our little guide was very mature and very outgoing. She was fascinated by this particular yacht. Who wouldn't be? It was a huge 100+- foot yacht with magnificent white sails and beautiful wooden decks. It was not long before she had worked her way to the bathroom and by the crew for a few discussions. Before we knew it, she had managed to talk her way into obtaining permission to tour the yacht. I was a nervous wreck. They had varnished all of the railings, and I knew she would be touching everything. Chuck was all for it, because he could tag along. I stayed back and waited for our food. I warned them to please be sure she didn't touch the newly wet wood! They had a wonderful tour, and as I expected, she touched the wood. I was sure the crew knew it would happen too, but she was very hard to resist. The burgers arrived, and they were great, just as recommended. We headed back to our neighborhood, having had a great day and a little more adventure than we had planned. It seemed like that was always how things went for us in Costa Rica.

The next day, we returned to Golfito with our tickets, to pick up our purchases. It didn't look like we had bought very much, so we tacked on a few more items. Our salesman held our hand through the whole process (more specific details on the process to come in a later story) from start to finish. Overall, it was painless for us, other than requiring some patience. The funniest part of the whole ordeal was seeing the two guys who carried our purchased items back to our SUV shake their heads, laughing like crazy at the small size of it. Maybe we were a bit overzealous. After a lot of work trying to put things in, taking them out, changing them around and moving all the car seats up as far as they would go to the front, they eventually fit everything in the SUV. When they got close, the sweat was pouring off of their faces. The one really tall guy was pushing and yelling, "Bueno! Bueno! Bueno!" They had such huge smiles on their faces for having accomplished their goal. I could hear them going home to their wives that night, telling them about how much stuff they had fit into this one small SUV at work today. It reminded me of seeing a car with all these clowns exiting it. You wouldn't imagine they could all fit in there, but they did somehow. Well, we were happy to see the items in the SUV and glad that we did not have to resort to Chuck's backup plan, to un-box items.

We got into the SUV, and we both busted out laughing immediately. The front seat on my side was pushed so far forward that my knees were bumping the dash. This was not going to be a fun ride, on a bumpy road where we had to swerve to dodge potholes. Although Chuck's seat was not as far forward, it was up pretty far, which meant he was bumping his knees every time he tried to shift gears. It was a brutally long few hour drive back to the neighborhood. My knees were red by the time we arrived. Now, when I see empty boxes lying around the parking lot in Golfito, I know someone else bought too much stuff on their shopping spree, and I remember our overstuffed SUV-ride, with the one tall guy yelling, "Bueno! Bueno! Bueno!" in triumph, which brings a smile to my face.

One day, Chuck decided to take me to a tilapia farm. He had once visited it while on an ATV ride with one of our neighbors. Back then, the family's excitement over soon getting electricity installed at their place had made an impression on Chuck, and he was now interested to see if they had gotten it. I had never been to a tilapia farm, so I wasn't sure what to expect. It turned out to be a cute restaurant with fishponds behind it, and Chuck was happy to see that they had electricity. We watched the cook use a cast net to catch our fish in the pond. If we had not been rushed, we could have caught our own fish with a hand line. Chuck ordered his whole. I ordered mine filleted. There were no choices for side dishes. The fish arrived with rice, yucca, salad, and patacones (i.e. fried plantains). The food was amazing. For those non-fish lovers, chicken is now an option, but please don't go all the way there without at least giving their tilapia a taste. After we ate, Chuck took me for a walk to a beautiful waterfall, where a rock was stuck at the edge of the cliff. If we had brought our bathing suits, we could have gone swimming. These were the unique experiences that Costa Rica had to offer, where you remembered not only the food, but the entire dining experience. This was now a place we would certainly look forward to on every visit. It was also a place where we would plan to send our future B&B patrons for a wonderful, truly Costa Rican experience. As a side note, this family ran restaurant is named Tilapias El Pavon. If you plan to go here, be sure you are at the right place before you stop as there is now another tilapia farm located on the same road.

We were shocked on our most recent trip to find that our closest neighbors, who had just finished their house since our last visit, had listed their house on the market. Apparently, they thought they would be happy, but they later decided maybe Costa Rica was not for them, once the building experience was done. It made me question if Chuck and I were doing the right thing. There were many a day recently, as reality was setting in more, where we were asking ourselves if we were totally crazy. We had to maintain a sense of humor by laughing about it and saying it was going to work out somehow, without really knowing how. Even if it didn't work out, we could always say we tried. We would never regret jumping over the edge to take the chance.

The last day of our March trip started with us meeting a neighbor at our property, to show them our construction site and finish discussing a deal to buy their recreational utility vehicle, called a Teryx. We were a little frightened when they said they thought they had been ambitious on their house, but we were really ambitious with our place. This certainly added to our fears that we were in way over our heads, when it came to being over budget. We ended up with a verbal agreement and a handshake to seal the deal and buy their Teryx. Isn't it interesting that in the modern day world, people can still conduct business with only a handshake and no contract?

The morning of our departure, we were so focused on finalizing everything at the construction site and closing the deal on the Teryx, we locked the keys in the car, along with my purse. We were not flying out in two hours, unless we could get into the car. Chuck and our construction foreman tried using a wire to pick the lock. Obviously, neither of them was experienced at the job. As time went by with no luck, Chuck told me to walk to a neighbor's house to ask for help. It was my first adventure hiking in our neighborhood, and I can attest that the mountains were steeper than I thought.

By the time I got back with the neighbor, Chuck had found an experienced construction worker on our site who took two seconds with the wire to pick the car lock. I was very thankful for the lock picking expertise. However, I was also scared at the reality of how unsafe it was to leave anything in a car in any country, given they were that easy to break into. Thankfully, we made it to the airport in time to catch our flight.

8 BAD NEWS

SO MUCH HAD PROGRESSED on our trip in March 2009 that we realized I needed to ask to relocate my current teleworking job from Florida to Costa Rica. Being able to telework was a big part of us being able to live there, as far as I was concerned. I liked my job, and I preferred a security blanket with a fixed income. On the other hand, Chuck was more entrepreneurial and willing to go with faith that the B&B would support us. After we realized we were short on money to finish the construction, it had since become a priority for me to relocate my job. It had been very stressful, waiting to tell the people that I worked with what we were planning, and to see if I would be able to relocate my job. Until then we had faith that things would somehow work out. It was time to see if that was really going to happen.

Now I must point out that this was not going to be a total surprise. My boss and his boss knew we were building a house, just not a B&B too. They also knew I had issues with obtaining a DSL or cable modem Internet connection at our Costa Rican house, and they felt that renting space at my own expense was an adequate alternate proposal until I could obtain Internet to our house. Therefore, this was a request that they knew might someday occur. We had all joked about me teleworking from Costa Rica for years. It was finally going to be a formal request, actually coming to fruition.

At the end of March, I told my boss we were building the house and the B&B. I asked to relocate my telework office from Florida to Costa Rica, effective January 2010. He was surprised to hear about the B&B, but very supportive of my request. Even though I didn't know all the specifics about how things would work, I was convinced that I could do my job from there, and I would figure out the specifics if given the go-ahead. I hoped I would have an answer soon.

Unfortunately, the timing of my request was bad. That week, my employer announced we were laying off 10% of our staff worldwide, as a result of the poor economy. Plus, we had recently come under new ownership. Although the prior owner had been very open to teleworking, the new owner, despite being a global player, was still making the adjustment to embrace teleworking. In my opinion, the main point was that I could do my job bearing any extra costs that this might raise, and that should present a lot of freedom to me and to my employer. As such, it was a win/win for my employer, our clients and me to relocate, or at least to give me the opportunity to prove I could make it work. I tried to remain hopeful.

While I waited for a response about relocating my job, things continued to progress in Costa Rica. We continued to drain our bank account, wiring money to Costa Rica at a fast pace for the construction. Chuck kept trying to do architecture work in the U.S. to make some money to help out, but the economy remained poor. He also spent his time concentrating on things for Costa Rica, like learning how to design the website. Even though we had no photos to use, he laid out the website and used dummy photos, with an idea in mind of what needed to go there. He also started to practice with breakfast ideas for the B&B. It was fun to test out new ideas. Unfortunately, a lot of Chuck's ideas would involve the use of puff pastry, which we would later find out was not an available commodity in our Costa Rican neighborhood.

One day we received bad news from Costa Rica. The police had arrested one of our neighbors. We were shocked. They were wanted for tax evasion in the U.S. As far as we knew, they didn't have much money, so it didn't make any sense to us. Our contractor called to explain the situation as a mix up. He was working to straighten things out for them, but he didn't think they had a lot of the paperwork they would need, regarding their prior business in the U.S., in order to fix things. They were in a Costa Rican jail, while friends were left to watch after their place, and their daughter was taken back to the U.S. It was very sad news. They fought extradition. After almost a year in a Costa Rican jail, they ended up back in the U.S.

It was surprising to many people in our area that the U.S. government would come down to our small little Costa Rican neighborhood to pick up people who did not owe that much in back taxes. We heard that our neighbor had put his name on a list of people who were against paying U.S. taxes. Maybe this got them red flagged as a target. All we knew was they served time in a Costa Rican jail, then ended up in the U.S. jail system, where they eventually worked a deal to be released. We would go back to Costa Rica without them ever being there again, which was sad, since most of our memories of our property thus far had involved seeing them. Good people made mistakes, and they would pay the penalty for it.

A few months passed with no news about teleworking from Costa Rica. On June 1st, I emailed my boss. Although I was prepared for bad news, it was altogether another thing to hear it announced formally. He was sorry to tell me that HR had turned me down. It had not gone any further up the ladder. Even though I was devastated inside, I took it well over the phone. I asked if HR would work with me as an independent contractor at a reduced salary and benefits; however, they were totally inflexible. I didn't like it, but I had to accept it. The reality was harsh. I had hoped that things would work out somehow, but they didn't. It was like a cold slap in the face. Chuck and I would have to find a way to deal with the news.

I would be better prepared in the future, when I asked to relocate again at a better time. I knew that someday, I would ask again. For now, I had to let it go and find a new solution. But in a company where we offer solutions to our clients, it hurt to have no flexibility from my employer to make my situation work as an employee. Looking back now, it might have worked to my benefit to not go to Costa Rica right then. However, at that time period, it was devastating news, and it has been a hard road to think about all the things I missed out on in Costa Rica. My morale did not stay down for long, since I simply can't go without doing a good job at something, by my very nature. It was a difficult time period for me to accept the rejection and have all of my hopes squashed without any chance to prove I could do my job from Costa Rica if only given the opportunity.

Now that I was turned down to telework in Costa Rica, we needed a plan. What were we going to do? Chuck was still not making any money in the U.S. doing architecture work. He would be more productive in Costa Rica. Construction would soon be down to the finishing details, and he would need to be there to make decisions. We simply had no choice but to live apart. I also thought it might be a good idea for me to move back to Tennessee. It would be a good chance for me to become close to my family again and have their support while Chuck was gone, instead of living in a Florida condo alone. After all, I was not a big fan of condo living. In one way, it was exciting to think about being close to my family again. In another way, I couldn't imagine living with them, where my mom would constantly try to tell me what to wear, and my dad would be smoking four packs of cigarettes a day. Moreover, I would have to live without Chuck, which was heartbreaking in itself, and I would have to miss out on all of the details of the B&B that we had said we would do together, which was also heartbreaking. It was not what we had planned, but life often threw us curve balls. We had to go with the flow.

I went through a stage of depression over the harsh reality. Finally, I bucked up and realized it was going to come. I had to do it, and I would. Chuck and I had dated for two years apart. I could stick it out for two years in Tennessee. It would not be easy, but I could do it. After all, we could all do things that we didn't think we could. It might not be as bad as I was imagining it to be either. Certainly, turning 40 years old and having our 20th wedding anniversary, both while living apart and at home with my parents, were not things I would have imagined would be in my future. We certainly were going backward before we went forward to reach our dream. Nevertheless, we would get through it somehow. It was our new plan, and we had to get through it.

9 BITTER SWEET

THE END OF JUNE 2009 rolled around, and it was time for our next trip to Costa Rica. We were off on another adventure. For this trip, we had decided to mix up our mode of transportation yet again. Our plan was to ask our driver, Eduardo, to pick us up at the airport and drop us off at our property. Once we arrived at our property, we would pick up the Teryx to use as our mode of transportation around the neighborhood. We would then test out a local shuttle service on the way back to San Jose, so that we might recommend it one day to people staying at our B&B.

Eduardo was waiting for us at the airport. He had a large van, which was perfect for transporting our luggage and the custom light fixtures we had pre-arranged to pick up after departing the airport. We were thrilled to see all of our lights at the lighting store. It was our first time to see Chuck's designs in person, and they had turned out awesome.

Eduardo drove slowly along the bumpy roads, to protect the fragile light fixtures in the van. Although I was grateful, it made for a long drive. However, we had fun in the van, talking along the way. He liked to talk, and so did we. We were starving and stopped at our favorite place, the Rum Bar, for pizza. By the time we arrived at the cabinas, it was pouring down rain, so we got soaked unloading.

Our friends in charge of the cabinas gave us the key to the Teryx we had purchased on our last trip. We had an appointment to walk up to retrieve it the next morning from the seller's garage. For now, we were exhausted and ready for bed.

We woke up the next morning, glad that it was not raining. We had a long walk ahead of us to pick up our Teryx. I was out of shape, so it was an exhausting walk for me. It was not difficult to walk along the main road, which was flat. However, the walk up our driveway to see our property before picking up the Teryx was a killer. I made it, but Chuck was relentless, nagging me along the way. I was embarrassed at being out of breath. I had to let Chuck walk ahead, while I stopped to rest before going onto the job site, where all the workers could see me. I hoped that I could become healthier once we got to Costa Rica. I was going to make it a goal to learn to walk these hills without becoming out of breath. It was bitter sweet to see how beautifully things were turning out and to know I was not yet in Costa Rica to stay. We quickly looked at our lot and the progress that was made before heading further up the road.

I was very thankful to see the caretaker when we arrived. We left with the Teryx, and as normal for me with anything newly adventuresome, I was terrified riding in it. I felt like it was going to turn over at any moment. I wore my helmet and held on for my life. Chuck trying to do donuts did not help relieve my stress at all. Eventually, by the end of our vacation, I would learn to relax just a little.

In the Teryx, we headed back down to our property to take a closer look at the construction. Most of the exterior walls for both the B&B and our house were completed. With all the walls up, the form of the whole house and the B&B were visual to me now. Construction of the pool was underway, and it looked amazing. So much had progressed since our last visit, yet there was still a long way to go to reach the finish line.

We spent most of our trip at the job site. We noticed some potential problems, which were bound to happen on any job. A beam had been added by our Costa Rican architect at our front patio, hiding the top of our curved front door. We had to decide if we were going to now use a square front door. Obviously, it was the easy answer. Nevertheless, after sleeping on it over night, I couldn't live with a square front door when we had curves all over the place. The decision was made to nip out the beam slightly, to finish off the curve enough to show our curved front door. It actually worked out to be a good compromise. We also had to make a few other changes, like moving some electrical boxes around. It was easier to do all of that now, rather than later. In fact, we double-checked any electrical boxes that we were unsure about against Chuck's drawings.

The outside of both the house and the B&B had a wave pattern in it. Chuck wanted to be sure the pattern was conveyed properly for the crew to follow when they added the stucco. Our foreman decided that they would use a PVC pipe to let Chuck bend it to form the curve he wanted. It was actually a great idea and worked out well. One day, several of the crew, along with our foreman, held the pipe against the house according to Chuck's instructions, while he marked the line with a pencil. They went around both buildings. When they were done, our foreman had a crew member go back with a hand grinder and grind the curve into the concrete, so the pen mark would not disappear. He asked Chuck to correct any areas that were not curved out enough, to match what he wanted. It was actually pretty funny to watch the crew as we went around the buildings with the PVC pipe. Our foreman liked the idea, but most of our crew thought he was nuts with no idea where he was going with this curved line. Our foreman had seen the pretty pictures Chuck had drawn, so that helped him see the overall design.

We found our green plastic chairs that we had bought on a previous trip and sat on the upper patio of our house. We spent a lot of time sitting there and enjoying our place. I couldn't explain it, but once again, a feeling of peace came over both of us. It sucked knowing that I would not be able to move with Chuck, yet sitting on that patio made it feel like it was going to be all right. It was all going to be worth it one day. There was this sense that it was where we belonged, and our journey was going to get us both there one day. We were both going to reach a new stage of happiness that would require us to cross a rough road, but it would be a road that was worth traveling, no matter how hard it was to walk. I felt rejuvenated by the time our trip ended. It was once again the motivation that I needed to go back to the U.S., to take care of business and keep moving forward toward our goal.

Although we thought the Teryx would work to take us around the neighborhood during our stay, it did not turn out to be the best vehicle to have during the rainy season. For the first few nights, it started to rain every night at dinnertime. The first night, we ate our leftover Rum Bar pizza, but the second night, all we had to eat was a few potato chips. I did not react well to lack of food, so I was nagging Chuck to stop at the rental car place the next day. Our contractor overhead our conversation and was nice enough to loan us his old pickup truck. However, it would mean that to get the loaner, I had to drive the Teryx back from his office on the main highway to our cabina. Our contractor seemed worried about me driving it, which simply made me more determined. I had never driven the Teryx before, so Chuck had me drive a test run once through the neighborhood. I wasn't too crazy about driving on the main road. However, I was less crazy about not having anything to eat for dinner again.

I made Chuck follow me home, so I at least didn't have to worry about someone running up too close behind me. I got out on the highway with no problems and was going a decent speed. It turned out to not be as scary as I had envisioned. The further I drove, the more I relaxed. I watched behind me and drove close to the white line, in case people were passing me. Before too long though, Chuck was honking his horn at me and passing me up. It scared me to death. A thousand thoughts ran through my head. Was I leaking fuel? Was the engine about to blow? What else could be wrong? He pulled over on the side of the road and waived me over. Something had to be wrong. He came back and asked me where I was going. What? I was going to our house, of course. What was wrong?

Since he thought I might keep driving all the way to Panama, he wanted to tell me I passed the road to our house a long time ago. I couldn't believe it. I mean, I had never driven a car in our neighborhood before, but I thought I would recognize our own road. Apparently, I had been so distracted watching the road in front of me and watching him behind me that I had passed it right up. Chuck said I sure must have been having a lot of fun to keep right on going. We turned around and headed back to our road. This time Chuck took the lead but drove slow enough that I could stay with him. It turned out to be a fun little driving adventure for me, and the loaned truck turned out to be a lifesaver, since it rained close to dinnertime every night.

Before we knew it, the time had arrived to depart to San Jose. The ride on the shuttle was not what we had expected. It was more like someone's personal van than a van that was part of a professional fleet of vehicles. The van was not in the best condition, either. Once we arrived in San Jose, the driver took us through back roads, into parts of town that would be best for a tourist not to venture down. We were exhausted by the time we arrived at the B&B in Escazu.

The next day, Chuck had set up an appointment for us to meet at the ARCR offices to move forward with our residency paperwork. We hoped that we had all of our paperwork in order, as it had been a difficult task to complete to that point. I hated to think that we would have to start over now. Plus, we were trying to beat a deadline for a new law that was going to kick in soon. The new law would increase the amount of money we would be required to have, under the residency laws as Rentistas.

I'll back up for a minute and briefly mention the residency categories in Costa Rica. The two main categories are Pensionados for individuals who have a permanent pension source or retirement fund (i.e. social security) and Rentistas for individuals who do not have a permanent pension source. The amount of money required per month for Pensionados is much lower, but the other requirements, such as length of time required to be spent in Costa Rica, are currently the same. After a set time period in one of these two categories, an individual can apply for permanent residency. This deletes the monetary requirement and allows an individual to work as an employee. As a Rentista or Pensionado, you can own a company, though you cannot work as an employee. There are several other less used categories like Representante and Inversionista with their own requirements, but I won't go into those. Due to constant changes in the residency laws, it is best to check for the most up to date information to better understand the requirements for all of the categories as this is a hot topic that continues to evolve with time. The ARCR website is a good source for a quick summary of this information. By the way, although a lot of people are permanent tourists (i.e. exit the country every 3 months for only a few days before returning), this is not a legal residency category. In fact, immigration used to turn their head to this practice; however, expatriates can't always count on it anymore. They have now started to crack down harder on permanent tourists by randomly limiting entry into the country for shorter time periods than 3 months.

As mentioned above, some residency categories restrict a person from working in Costa Rica. The government does this to protect the jobs of Costa Ricans by allowing foreigners to own companies but not to work as employees to take their jobs away. There are ways to obtain permission to work, when you are not taking a job away from a Costa Rican, including teleworking for a foreign company or getting a work visa for a certain job (i.e. English teachers). Eventually, foreigners can obtain permanent residency with no work restrictions. It is an honorable concept. Although I'm not sure it was heavily enforced in the past, immigration has started to increase enforcement with stiff consequences for those who are caught violating the law.

Now, back to explaining the process Chuck had followed to get us up to the point of our meeting at the ARCR. When we had been at the ARCR offices in March to obtain our driver's licenses, they had given us a sample bank letter that we would need from our bank to apply for residency. They had also given us a list of some additional information that would be required, like police letters of good conduct, birth certificates and a marriage certificate. I believe that covers all the items we had to collect. The tricky part was not obtaining these items themselves, but what had to happen to them afterwards.

Basically, everything had to be notarized, to show the official signature on the documents were authentic. For example, the county clerk's signature on a birth certificate had to be authenticated by the Secretary of the State as being the county clerk's signature. The Secretary of State's signature then had to be authenticated by the State Department in Washington as being the official signature of the Secretary of State. Finally, the appropriate Costa Rican consul for the document must then authenticate the State Department in Washington's signature. Now, if this did not sound complicated enough, it was important to remember that we were dealing with a number of states, such as Florida for our current residence, Massachusetts for Chuck's birthplace and Tennessee for my birthplace and our marriage license. Therefore, we had a number of Secretaries of States to deal with, as well as various Costa Rican Consuls. Because the Consul at the Costa Rican Embassy in Washington DC could authenticate documents from any state, they sometimes got backlogged from requests.

Chuck was working against time, trying to obtain all the documents collected and sent off to the next stage before our June 2009 Costa Rican trip. We were fearful documents would become lost, so he used FedEx to track what we sent, along with sending return FedEx envelopes for them to use. Luckily, we never lost any of our paperwork. Although, a few times, there were issues with the prepaid FedEx envelopes not working as we had planned. Eventually, we got it all worked out. Moreover, there were issues with how each state or consul got paid. They all seemed to work differently, which also complicated matters. In one case, Chuck had to prepay their bank account and send in the receipt, since they didn't accept either cash or checks. He had faced many challenges to obtain all of those pieces of paper full of stamps. They were worth gold to us at that point.

We were very happy when we arrived at the ARCR and met with our attorney, to find out that we had only one item, our bank letter, which was required to be redone. Given I had to live in the U.S. to earn money, I had also worried for months that we would run into problems meeting the 4 month a year minimum stay required at that time in Costa Rica to keep residency once we received it. However, our attorney said that Chuck was the primary person applying and that I was only a dependent. Everything was tied to him in regards to the 4-month requirement. It was another huge relief. We felt like a ton of weight had been lifted off our shoulders. Not only was our paperwork mostly in order, now this fear we had was gone. We completed the application for residency, along with a few other items that he required. We paid half of our fees for his services, with the other half due upon completion. The full residency process could take up to two years to complete. Once we got a file number, Chuck was good to use the letter he received to stay in the country. Until that time, he had to leave every 3 months as a tourist. We were hopeful we would receive a file number before too much time passed. We were relieved and now starving for lunch.

We walked over a few blocks to a nice hotel that we had heard about called the Hotel Grano De Oro. We enjoyed a nice lunch at the restaurant, walked around a little bit, then headed back to the B&B. What a wonderful way to end our trip in San Jose.

10 NO GOOD OPTIONS

AT THE END OF JULY, we finalized our plan for Chuck to live in Costa Rica and for me to live in Tennessee. I emailed my boss and his boss to thank them for being open minded in considering my relocation to Costa Rica. I told them I was disappointed at not going sooner, but I still knew that I would live there one day. I realized the timing was not good to push things. One day, that opportunity would come to light, and I would be better prepared to act at the right moment. In the meantime, I wanted to relocate to Tennessee, effective in October. This request was quickly approved.

August was a very busy month. In Costa Rica, the crew began work on our bamboo ceilings. Our contractor finally agreed to start on our wooden bathtub. He found the wood we would use and had it kiln-dried. He was still not happy about the idea, but he agreed to build it, excluding the warranty.

Because it took longer to clear and get registered, the Xterra had to be shipped earlier than the container and Chuck's fishing boat. On August 17th, Chuck delivered our Xterra to the port in Tampa, for shipment to Costa Rica. It was a strange feeling to leave it there and hope it would show up in Costa Rica the next time we saw it. We were now a one-vehicle family for a while, which would be another adjustment.

Finally, August ended with the realization that we were more over budget than we had ever expected. As things now stood, Chuck would be going to Costa Rica with no windows and doors in the house, because we simply did not have the money. I looked over our money situation while Chuck was in Pensacola visiting his family, and I was devastated. It seemed like things always got worse for us. I cried my eyes out that weekend. Eventually, I made the decision to borrow money from my 401K, without discussing it with Chuck. I had always heard not to borrow from your

401K. However, I had lost a lot of money from the economic crash already, and the value was still decreasing by more than I was putting in each paycheck. Taking all the factors into consideration, it seemed like a good option at the time; especially given we had no other options.

Chuck arrived back to the news of our poor financial situation and didn't have any answers. He was very upset to hear I had taken a loan against my 401K without discussing it with him. However, he calmed down when he realized it was our only choice.

11 SHIPPING AND SHOPPING

LUCKILY, WE LIVED NEXT TO one of the cheapest U.S. ports for shipments to Costa Rica. Chuck set up a meeting with the shipper we wanted to use. He was located in Costa Rica, but he also had an office at the port in Tampa. On a trip to the U.S., he was nice enough to stop by our condo to talk about our shipping needs. I had been worried about getting things to our property. However, he made it all sound so easy. In fact, our plan was to send as few items as possible, which he explained as a common mistake. We were paying the same price for the container, regardless of what we shipped, so we should fill it full. A full container at 39 ½ feet, minus room for the Pod items we had in storage (now full at 20 feet), would leave us a lot of room to fill with other things.

After our latest shopping experience in San Jose, where we realized how difficult it was to find things, we agreed that it made a lot of sense to use the extra space for a minimal cost difference. He also gave us a lot of other good ideas of things to bring, like mountain bikes for our guests. He had lived in Costa Rica for a long time, so he had some helpful ideas for activities at the B&B too.

We needed to tell them when we wanted the items in Costa Rica, and they would then give us a date to drop them off. His guys could wrap and pack things for us. However, if we wanted to save money, Chuck could help pack things. Chuck could deliver things to the port if he wanted, or they would pick them up. Chuck was interested in doing our own packing and taking our stuff to the port himself, since we were always about saving money.

He explained their normal shipping routine. They ship a container from Port Manatee in Tampa most Mondays. It arrives at the port in Limon, Costa Rica on a Thursday. They use specially marked containers to divert attention away from the true contents, so there is less chance of theft from their containers at the port. Also, they do not allow their containers to be opened at the port, which also reduces theft losses. The container is then trucked to Alejuela, outside of San Jose. Once there, they use a list of its contents, provided by the owner of the container, to take the container through customs. This can take up to 7 days. No chemicals are allowed, so cars and boats have to be drained of oil and gas. At the warehouse, everything is inspected, and the container is unloaded onto 24-foot straight trucks for transportation to its destination. If the property is hard to reach and requires a 4x4, like our property, they may not be able to drive there with the big trucks. In such cases, they (or rather the owner of the goods as we later discovered) will find local guys to shuttle the items onto their little pickup trucks to finish the delivery, including unloading.

When it came to how items were packed, he explained that they did stack things in the container and on the trucks. However, as long as they were packed well in the boxes, they had experienced limited breakage. They had limited theft for the reasons outlined above. We could purchase door-to-door insurance, including theft and breakage, for about 2½ percent of the declared value. He had not ever had his quoted price change dramatically. He had been in the business long enough (something like 30 years) to know the system and had never had a problem with his numbers.

We were very impressed with his knowledge, and after talking with him, very comfortable with the shipping process. We were also very excited to start shopping! Using his architecture software, Chuck immediately drew up the container and laid out all of our items, so as we bought things, he could pack it all in there. Now that we had talked to the shipper, we planned to stuff our container full!

We went on a wild buying spree. We looked for all kinds of items that we might need in Costa Rica. Our Costa Rican architect had already told us to bring ceiling fans. We needed 20+ of those. Chuck was able to call a place to find a good bulk rate on the fans. We had them delivered to the condo and stacked them in a corner. Chuck said the driver must have thought we lived in the penthouse of the condo complex, given so many fans. The bulk rate would only provide delivery to the front door, so Chuck had to carry them all upstairs. Our architect had also told us to be sure to bring faucets. We ended up finding those on Overstock.com, along with some beautiful vessel sinks. We went wild with those. We bought the motion-activated camera that the shipper had mentioned to us. We got a telescope and spotting scope as well. We bought two TVs. We bought retractable door screens for both the B&B and our house. Chuck had those delivered from Seattle, Washington. It was a big delivery that we again stacked up in the condo. We added cable railings to the pile. We then hit the pawnshops, looking for items that we might use and found some really great deals on mountain bikes. I continued to buy items for the kitchen, including many glasses –my fetish. We then moved to the great outdoors. Chuck bought 450+ feet of rope lights for the tiki bar. We bought a combination smoker/grill named the Big Green Egg, which we were dying to buy after tasting some food a friend had cooked on one. We moved on to pool loungers and lots of outdoor patio furniture.

Chuck arranged and rearranged our condo to make room for the growing piles of items we were acquiring. Things were becoming really packed up on Chuck's computer drawing of the container, but we really wanted to fit in a living room set for the B&B. I had seen a great deal on one that I loved. However, our condo was stuffed, with no room to breathe. Chuck figured we could make room for it on the container, and we had a friend offer to store it at his place. Therefore, we bought the living room set for the B&B and had it delivered there. I remembered waiting at our friend's place the afternoon it was delivered. We talked the delivery guys into leaving the furniture wrapped up with all the packing blankets around it. After all, there was no need to unpack it for us to repack it. The condo was busting at the seams by the time we were done shopping. Thankfully, we had rented a decent sized condo unit without knowing in advance how handy all the extra room would be for our planned move.

In mid September, we were U-hauling it. A friend helped Chuck load up the U-haul the first day. We then went to the friend's house that stored our living room set to pick it up. It had been so long since we bought it, we couldn't remember exactly what we had purchased. It turned out to be a sofa, a loveseat, a chair and an ottoman. We barely had space to fit it all in the U-haul. We stored the U-haul at a friend's condo nearby our place that night, because our condo rules prevented it from staying on-site at our property. I worried all night about someone stealing it with all of our new belongings, which were worth a lot of money. I was very happy the next morning to look across the water at our friend's place and see it was still there.

Chuck took the U-haul, with the boat in tow, to the port. Our pod had been delivered directly to the port that morning to be unloaded for our container as well. Chuck returned by lunchtime with everything resolved. It seemed that part of our plan had all gone smoothly, outside of the first day, when the U-haul people gave us the wrong key to unlock the back of the U-haul. Chuck was exhausted from moving so much stuff out of our unit, which looked massive, now that all the piles were missing. The reality of our relocation was drawing closer. Like it or not, we would be living apart soon.

12 FAREWELL FLORIDA

SAYING GOODBYE TO FRIENDS and our favorite places in town was hard. However, we knew that we would see our friends again and return to Tampa/St Pete to visit another day. We looked at it more as a happy time than as a sad time. We wanted to work in as much as we possibly could in the short time we had before the move, so we made out a "to do" list of our last places to visit, like Waltz, Carmalitas, Habana Café and Fetishes. We went to parties and dinners at friends' houses for the last time. We enjoyed a final outing, listening to Tony D play guitar at Caddy's on the beach, then walked back to watch a beautiful sunset on our last night in the condo.

We had accomplished a lot during our life in Florida. We had moved there knowing virtually nobody, yet we were leaving with a lot of friends. Chuck helped his firm build a successful architecture business from scratch and sold his stock back to them, to continue on without him. I had switched jobs several times and was now happy with my current role. We would be leaving without our dogs, which had been with us during most of our marriage. We had built one house and remodeled another. We had many boating and fishing adventures along the way. Florida had been good to us. We loved it, without a doubt. We were taking away many happy memories.

It would be nice in the future, not have to worry about hurricanes and for Chuck to be less stressed about work. We hoped to reach a point someday soon where we would be less stressed about money, and we would reach the happier, simpler lifestyle that we dreamed about together in Costa Rica.

Since I had decided to move in with my parents and forego the expense of renting my own place in Tennessee, I really didn't need to move a lot of furniture, outside of my work desk. We decided to ship a few boxes of clothes and take only what would fit into my car. Everything else would have to go. We slowly spent the next month and half disposing of all of our remaining furniture.

By the time moving day came around, at the end of October, we had very few items left in the condo. It was a happy day for us, though. Just like moving out of our house in St Petersburg, we were ready to move forward. A friend came over and helped us pack up the car. It was stuffed to the hilt that day. There was not room for a pen to fit into it anywhere. We happily turned in our keys and headed out to grab some wings for dinner. We met a friend at the restaurant and then headed over to his house to spend the night. Our friend still couldn't believe we had actually followed through on our plan, just like we had said at Woody's Waterfront restaurant all those years ago, but it was happening.

We went to bed exhausted and got up early the next morning. Our friend was up already, making breakfast. Chuck and I were still half asleep. Breakfast was wonderful and got us off to a good start for our early morning drive to Tennessee. It was Halloween, and we arrived at my parents' house before nightfall. We were tired, but ready for the challenge ahead of us.

Over the next few days, we unpacked the car and I settled into my new space. Mom had actually done a great job cleaning out the two bedrooms I would be using. The hardest part of everything was getting used to living in the house with my dad's cigarette smoke. After not living in it for so long, the smell was over-powering again. It hurt my eyes and made it very difficult to breathe. At times, thinking about staying here almost brought me to tears, but I had to do it. There was no turning back. My parents were trying to be great, and it was a habit my dad couldn't kick. The worst part was I knew Chuck would be leaving soon. He was my best friend, and I didn't know how I was going to be apart from him. We did everything together for the past 19 years, including going to the grocery store. Going to work was the only thing we had done on our own, outside of the occasional bunko or fishing trip. During the past few years, Chuck had been working at home, so we were basically together 24/7. What was it going to be like without him around? I had to be strong, and I had to deal with it. After all, I had no choice.

There were a number of positives to living in Tennessee. I was not a condo person, so I had to admit it was nice to be back living in a house with some space. To look outside of a window and see a yard again was wonderful. To not hear someone banging around in the unit above me was wonderful too. I had been away from my parents for almost 20 years, so returning home was a golden opportunity to become close to them again. I had many people with deceased parents tell me I was getting an opportunity I should cherish. We were also saving money by having me stay with them.

I still hoped it was a short-term situation, until Chuck and I could be together again. I knew he would be leaving soon. It broke my heart to think about it as each day passed, and his departure grew closer.

PART 2
A DAILY ROLLERCOASTER RIDE

13 A NEW BEGINNING

I COULD'T SLEEP. It was the last time for a while that we would be snuggled in the same bed. What was it going to be like to sleep without him? Not only was I going to miss him, I was going to be scared staying in the house at night by myself, while my parents were at work. The long road ahead of us living apart was about to begin the next morning.

We dropped Chuck off at the airport terminal, dressed in an orange Tony D short sleeve t-shirt, with a big smile on his face. It was only 30 degrees outside, but he didn't mind. After all, he was going to Costa Rica. He promised to call when he arrived, but I didn't hear from him all day.

I woke up a few times during the night. Was Chuck sleeping OK? What did he eat? Was it raining in Costa Rica? It was strange not to be able to talk to him, despite all of today's technology.

Fortunately, Chuck had an email waiting for me the next morning. Our Costa Rican cell phone was not working. He hadn't eaten anything since he left Tennessee at 6:00am, other than a bag of chips. He was emailing me from a hotel, where he was eating breakfast. The howler monkeys woke him up this morning. There were squirrel monkeys everywhere and some hummingbirds too. He was grateful for no biting bugs, given we had only a few windows in our house, instead of all of them installed as planned.

A short time later, I received calls from friends in Tampa. Chuck had apparently emailed two of our couple friends to call me, in case I had not checked my email to see he had written. How sweet of him. I was worried about him, and he was concerned I would be worried.

Chuck called several days later. Our house was simply not far enough along for him to stay there. He had been taking cold showers, since the electrician forgot to hook up the hot water tank. Grinding the concrete floors was a very messy process, so there was no way he could stay while they finished them. Plus, the windows and doors were being installed. On top of all that, there were bats in the roof, which were noisy while he tried to sleep, and he still had no grill to create a makeshift kitchen. He had a change of plans and was upgrading his accommodations to house sit for a neighbor. The neighbors needed a house sitter during their vacation, so it made sense for him to move over to their place until things progressed further on our house. He was postponing delivery of our shipping container for another week. Things were going well, and I didn't need to worry about him.

Later that afternoon, I was shocked when Chuck called again. He finally had our Costa Rican cell phone working, and he wanted to finish telling me his big news from the prior night. He had finally experienced his first earthquake. It woke him up from sleep, shaking the walls and the bed. Our workers had not mentioned it at first. However, after Chuck asked them, they noted it was "muy pequeno" (i.e. very small). The earthquake turned out to be a 4.7, located offshore from the "Whale's Tail" in Uvita, some 20 kilometers away.

Chuck relocated into his new temporary living quarters and settled into the neighborhood. He called me one night, excited there was a neighbor who had the NFL package at his house. I had felt bad for him that Sunday, yet he had actually watched the football games all day. I realized it really was a small world. Even in the rainforest, guys got together to watch football on Sunday.

Eventually, Chuck posted photos on Facebook from his first days in Costa Rica. I had to laugh. They included a picture of his first machete. Months earlier, while lying in bed talking about Costa Rica, I had asked him to make a picture of the first machete he bought, and he had laughed at me. However, he remembered to take the photo! He had photos of our place, some monkeys and the neighbor's house, where he was house sitting. Everything looked awesome. His comments on the photos and what everyone else wrote on his page made me smile. It was nice going to bed knowing Chuck was happy in Costa Rica. How different his life had become from working in architecture.

My 40th birthday arrived. On top of the fact I was becoming older when I looked in the mirror, I was still adjusting to letting go of our material possessions, giving up our Florida outdoor lifestyle, living in a separate country from Chuck and living back home with my parents in Tennessee. It was not exactly the picture of where I thought my life would be at 40 years old, but I knew our future was headed in the right direction. Chuck and I always had to take a step backward before we could move forward again. It had worked for us in the past. It seemed we were taking a pretty big step back this time, so I hoped it only meant our step forward would be a giant leap. Chuck was not with me to celebrate my birthday, but it was nice to celebrate with my family. Mom even threw a surprise party for me, with some old high school friends showing up.

Chuck went to work on our job site. Despite concerns from our contractor that the crew would not react well to him working on-site, the crew received him very well. They were not used to seeing a lot of foreigners (i.e. gringos) work, so they were intrigued at first. After some time, they developed a huge respect for Chuck's hard work ethic and skills. They would encourage him with a thumb up or a smile. They would move scaffolding for him or do some prep work for him. Just as our crew respected him, so did our subcontractors. Knowing that the owner was on-site had made a difference, and seeing him work on-site also had our subcontractors showing up to complete their jobs.

One night, Chuck asked me what I had been eating while I was living in Tennessee. He was the chef, so one of my big hurdles was figuring out what I was going to cook with him away. He had a good laugh when I told him my dad commented my chicken soup was better than the can. Obviously, that was not a big compliment. Chuck responded that my dad's taste buds weren't sharp, because of his bad smoking habit. He was so sweet to defend me, but honestly, my chicken soup was not very good. He had no idea how much I missed his cooking, or even more, how much I missed our time together in the kitchen.

Chuck worked on painting the inside of our house and the B&B. He posted photos as things progressed. It was exciting to finally see color on the walls and rain chains (alternatives to traditional downspouts) in some of the photos. I had always loved rain chains, since the first time I ever saw one in Costa Rica, and I knew one day we would have a house with them. It was exciting to see it become a reality.

The contents from our shipping container finally arrived on November 17th. Since cell service at that time was not working in our area, Chuck waited at the Dome restaurant in Uvita for the planned phone call from the delivery driver. He saw two large trucks drive by that looked suspiciously out of place. After waiting a while longer without an incoming call, he knew they had passed without calling, so he raced south to find them.

It was important to always have a backup plan in Costa Rica! Thinking ahead, our contractor had placed one of our crew at the store in Coronado to flag down any big trucks, just in case they happened to pass by Chuck without calling. Chuck was not aware of this and arrived very happy to see the two suspicious trucks from earlier, sitting there with one of our crew.

Given the steepness ahead and the weight of items in the trucks, they could not drive very far beyond the store. They unloaded items onto a few smaller trucks to shuttle up to our place. Eventually, a friend of our contractor arrived with another truck to help, but he was delayed when he ran out of gas. Yes, there were never dull moments in Costa Rica. They used all three vehicles to shuttle items slowly, from the road below, all the way up to our house. Since progress was slow, our contractor called the hardware store to bring a bigger truck. Once that truck arrived, Chuck stopped carrying items and went up to our house to mark off the numbered boxes from our packing list to be sure we had everything. It was chaos, as boxes arrived faster than he could mark the numbers off the list. Plus, some of the boxes had been wrapped in brown paper, hiding the number, so he had a hard time finding them.

As chaotic as things were, it was inevitable there would be damage. While Chuck was busy verifying the boxes, the guys tried to move the large center section of our entertainment center with the TV still sitting in it. It was damaged when the TV shifted inside. Our dining room chairs had not been wrapped well by the shipper, and Chuck could see damage to those. All things considered, it appeared we had received most of the items, but he would have to sort through it all later to be certain, as well as to assess further damage. It had been a long day, and he was exhausted.

Although it had been a few weeks, I could not wait to visit Chuck in Costa Rica. Getting there turned out to be a bit of a challenge, though. The airport security guard was not happy to see the kitchen faucet in my luggage. After a major scene was created, where the security guards disagreed over my faucet being a deadly weapon, the supervisor decided I had to check it. It was the nicest kitchen faucet she had ever seen, so she knew I didn't want to have it scratched. Nevertheless, it was technically a metal pipe, which was not allowed.

My previously checked luggage was no longer up front, so the airline attendant threw the faucet into a blue bin down the luggage chute. He promised me he would put it in my luggage with my towels wrapped back around it for protection. I walked away with no identification placed with the faucet in the blue bin wondering if I would ever see it in Costa Rica. However, when I opened my luggage upon arrival, I happily found it there, neatly wrapped as promised.

Chuck was waving as I exited the airport. Traveling on the new highway to the coast was great. We stopped for our favorite pizza and arrived at Chuck's temporary house sitting accommodations. While I waited in the car, Chuck had to run into the house to open the gate, because the remote batteries had died. It scared me to think he did this by himself, because I knew he would leave the car running while he was gone to open the gate. Once we were inside, I was shocked at all the piles of clothes he had everywhere. They were in suitcases, on nightstands and on the washing machine. It was hard to live without a permanent home. I hoped he would be in our own place soon. For now, I couldn't think about that. It had been a long day, and I was exhausted. I was with Chuck, and I was happy. It was good to be in Costa Rica.

I awoke early the next day. It was weird to be in a strange place, but also exciting. It was beautiful to look out from bed, over the mountains and ocean as the sun was rising. I walked around outside, amazed at the views, and tried to imagine how wonderful it would be to awake in this beautiful setting every morning. It seemed odd to think Chuck lived here now. It made me anxious to see the views and the progress at our place.

It was an amazing feeling to be at our property. The view was spectacular, and I once again knew this was all going to be worth it someday. Yet, it was overwhelming to see all that still had to be done. It was hard to imagine that Chuck arrived here the first day with nothing except his suitcase. I was very proud of him for the guts he had to do it.

Chuck had a small piece of black felt at both door entrances to wipe our feet on before entering the house. He was trying to protect the polished concrete floors, which were my favorite new detail of the house. They were absolutely beautiful. It made me smile that he was trying so hard to protect them, but it was an impossible task.

The house downstairs was hardly passable, with all of our items piled up from the container. The enormity of the task it had been to take everything we shipped up the driveway into our house hit me. I wasn't that upset any longer about the damage to the dining room table and chairs. I knew we wouldn't be unwrapping anything on this trip to check for damage. There simply was no room to un-box anything. I was certain we would find more broken items when we did eventually un-box everything. However, the reality that we received most of our items was something to be thankful for at the moment.

We left to do our errands. Our first stop was the hardware store. Chuck had already become familiar with the guys who worked there. They mixed some sample paints for us to test on the house later. Our second stop was the grocery store, which was an adventure for me.

There was a lot to discover at the grocery store. There were International brands and Costa Rican brands. Some brands were easy to recognize. For example, if you saw Tony the Tiger on a box of cereal, you knew it was Frosted Flakes. The Costa Rican brands were cheaper but hard for us to read, since they were labeled in Spanish. For instance, a stick of butter could look like cheese. Some items were found in different places than would be expected in the U.S. For example, the milk was not refrigerated. It was in a box, sitting on a shelf in the store. Also, a lot of items were packaged differently than found in the U.S., like liquid soap and ketchup, which were in collapsible containers instead of bottles. The meats were all sitting behind the meat counter, at which you ask to have them packaged for you, as nothing was prepackaged. The fruits usually had lots to select from and often required having them weighed before going to the checkout counter.

Basically, everything was in the store, including wines and beers. They offered most of what you could find in the U.S. It just took time to find things and figure out what some things were. The aisles were smaller, and most people were not buying a ton of stuff like us Americans, so it felt crowded to me. At times, we didn't have a clue what we were looking for or at. I felt like we were often in other people's way, but maybe it was just me being paranoid. It was a different experience to shop there, but it all worked out. This particular grocery store had it all, though there were also specialty stores for meats, breads and fruits, if you wanted to make a number of stops.

I felt completely stressed after only a few days in Costa Rica. I awoke several times, lying in bed with tears in my eyes. How were we possibly going to make this work on the little amount of money we had left? I kept telling myself it would be all right, but it seemed we were on an impossible mission. I also felt disjointed from Chuck now. It felt like we were already drifting apart. How would our relationship ever make it through construction, when we had so much more time yet to go living separately?

At times during the night, I thought I needed to go to the bathroom to throw up. In fact, I did go to the bathroom at one point and almost totally freaked myself out. I used a flashlight to keep the dog from barking at the overhead bathroom lights. I came very close to screaming, when I realized what I saw was only a reflection of my knees, caused by the flashlight staring back at me in the glass shower doors. I was overly paranoid, because the open nature of the house had already yielded indoor encounters with a snake, a frog and a bat. Otherwise, I would not have been on edge as much when I thought I saw something moving in the shower. It made me laugh to think the flashlight had scared me so badly. How stupid would I have felt had I screamed, only to have Chuck come running into the bathroom to find nothing in the shower and me sitting on the toilet? It was funny. I couldn't help but tell Chuck about my near emergency the next morning. He called it the "knee monster" and teased me about it the rest of my trip.

Morning eventually arrived. At our contractor's office, it was surreal when upon our arrival he wanted to talk about building kitchen cabinets for our house. We didn't have enough money to finish the B&B, so we could forget working on our kitchen. We needed to talk about laying off the crew. Eventually, we got the message across. We wanted to keep a few crew to live on-site and help Chuck continue what he could to move forward. It was a traumatic experience for us to not only let most of the crew go, but also to see our dream come to a standstill.

Our contractor called our foreman on the radio to come over to his office. On the highway, we drove past our foreman, who happily waved at us. He had no idea what news awaited him. It made us more depressed to think about how disappointed he would be. The crew certainly would not want to work for free, so we had no choice, given we were out of money.

At the job site, Chuck and I painted that afternoon without talking much. We were both going over the whole situation in our heads and still letting it all sink in. After being given notice, the crew was obviously sad, and I felt like they were blaming me. I arrived in town, and the first day they saw me practically everyone was laid off. Chuck seemed even more depressed. He was blaming himself. It was awkward cleaning up at the end of the day, while the crew was moping around. Hopefully, they knew we would keep them all, if we had the money.

Our contractor had decided on the two members of our crew that we would keep. They both had special skill sets that would be hard to replace, and neither would have a place to live if we had not kept them. Plus, we wanted guys who were willing to live on site, so Chuck would not be alone. It all made sense at the time. However, after thinking about it all day, I thought he had made a mistake. We were keeping legal workers in Costa Rica, but they were both from Nicaragua. It bothered me that neither was Costa Rican. As we thought more about it through the day, it began to bother Chuck too. We wondered if the crew was upset about it. Hopefully, our contractor explained how he determined whom to keep. If we kept three guys, which would include the Costa Rican guy Chuck liked, then we would feel a lot better about the situation. It seemed like a long shot, but we wanted to look at our budget again, to see if it was possible to keep a third guy.

We spent two days going to Golfito to pick up appliances with different sets of friends. Our friends thought dodging the many potholes in the road was like skiing moguls. They would grade them on a scale, depending upon if you could drive over them straddling them, if you could dodge them while staying on your side of the road or if you had to cross the center line to totally avoid them. It was very funny. On the way home, Chuck and I graded the potholes according to the new scale. It made the drive home go by faster. We felt bad, though, showing up at our place having spent money on lots of new appliances, when our workers had been told they would be laid off, because we had no money.

We celebrated our first Costa Rican Thanksgiving. The food at our friend's house was fabulous. It was a true American feast, including turkey, stuffing and potatoes. We were in Costa Rica, yet we were eating the same Thanksgiving foods as many people in the U.S. In fact, our neighbor bought some of her food at a place in Costa Rica similar to a Sam's Club, where the food was made in the U.S. and packaged for sale in Costa Rica. It truly was a small world.

Finally, the day had arrived. I didn't sleep much, because I was worried about the trip. It was going to be hectic, since we had to pick up our boat and car in San Jose, then wanted to make it back in time before the crew left their last day of work. It would look really bad for us to bring yet more stuff to our place with them being let go, but we wanted to say goodbye before they left. We hoped we would make it back in time, even though we knew it would be a challenge.

After the 6:00am check-in call, where a number of the neighbors call in on the radio to be sure everyone is all right every morning and share any neighborhood news for the day, we began the drive to San Jose. After we reached the other side of Jaco, there was a problem with the rental car. Chuck thought the power steering was slipping. We went a little further up the road before he pulled over to be sure there were no branches under any of the wheels. There was nothing that we could see. It looked like we were in for an unexpected detour. We decided to drive the rental as far as we could go. We headed out on the road once again. By now, I was praying for a miracle. We had not gone very far when the car problem seemed to clear itself. My prayers were answered. We both were very grateful.

We arrived at our attorney's office in Escazu. Once there, we finished the registration for the car tags in order to pick it up from the shipper and completed a few other items that the attorney needed for our escrow account. We left having crossed another major hurdle.

It was wonderful to see our Xterra when we arrived at the shipper's warehouse. I had expected it to be dirty, but they had it spotless. Because it was year-end, the 2010 vehicle inspection was required, but the guy who spoke English and would be taking us to the inspection site was not in the office yet. One of the other guys decided to take us, even though he only spoke Spanish. He did not have a driver's license though, so Chuck had to drive. We stopped at the gas station on the way, in order to avoid filling up while pulling the boat later. However, the car would not restart at the gas station. Chuck remained calm and thought to check the battery. They had disconnected it when shipping on board the boat to avoid running the battery down. Luckily, with a quick fix, we headed for the inspection site. It felt like yet another small miracle. After a long drive, we arrived at the facility, where we simply needed to pay for the new sticker. There was no need to retest for 2010 when the 2009 test was recently completed.

Back at the shipper's warehouse, we hitched the boat up to the Xterra and drove to the interstate with ease. We rarely held others up in traffic, since Chuck drove a decent speed. There were times we even passed other people. Once we reached Jaco, I felt victorious, even though we still had a few hours to go to reach home. What a day!

Although we were close to home, it was late. We felt bad that we had missed the crew's last day at the job site. In fact, we passed our foreman on the highway on his way home. We hoped it would not be the last time we saw our foreman or many of our crew.

Our good luck for that day continued. We made it to the house with no problems. Our next big challenge was to take the boat up the driveway. Thankfully, Chuck successfully completed the drive around the tight turns with minimal light in the sky. We were highly relieved at our success and headed out for dinner to celebrate.

We arrived at the restaurant before our friends. It was a new Italian place in Ojochal called Mamma e Papa. I had previewed the menu and wanted the lasagna. The restaurant apparently made it a day ahead and ran out often. Since I was leaving town soon, I got first dibs on the last remaining piece, and it was excellent. We deserved a good ending to our memorable day.

Sometimes, good luck did happen in Costa Rica, and we had a lot of it that day. For months, I had worried about driving the car and boat to our house from San Jose. I had many nightmares involving the boat going over a cliff instead of safely up our driveway. I was very relieved at what we had accomplished that day. However, I still knew it was a sad day for most of our workers, who were now gone, and it weighed heavily on me. I still hoped one day we would have the money to finish construction. I didn't know how, but I felt confident it would happen eventually. For now, I was thankful for our good fortunes of that day and ready for some well deserved sleep.

While we were painting on one of the last days of my trip, a neighbor came by with our potential future guard dog. His name was Jefe, which means "the boss." Chuck had wanted us to meet before he agreed to adopt him. He was big with a huge head. He was not my type of dog, as I liked medium-sized dogs, but Chuck reminded me he was a guard dog. He was an unusual, very pretty gray color. As we were showing the neighbors around our place, Jefe tagged along with his tongue hanging out. He was not overly anxious for attention. He was more curious to see what he could find. Well, he found the wet lid of a red paint can and decided to lick it. His owners laughed about it, but I hoped we didn't kill the dog before we even took possession of him.

While showing the neighbors around our place, we realized the bamboo ceilings outside of the B&B sunset deck were done. We couldn't believe it. The crew had kicked butt to finish it that week, despite notice of the layoff. They were amazing.

By the end of the tour, we agreed to adopt Jefe. He seemed like he was big and muscular enough to scare people off as a guard dog, yet he seemed nice enough that guests would be all right with him once they met him. The neighbors agreed to drop him off in a few days. Finally, we would be dog owners again.

After cleaning up, we headed out for dinner at Citrus. We called it fine dining, Costa Rican style. Chuck and I tried the Costa Rican nachos. This was a first for us, and a surprise selection from me, the picky eater. It blew us both away. They were nachos in a limey juice with black beans (not any but the special Costa Rican kind), cheese and tomatoes, with lots of cilantro and very toasty nachos. We had excellent entrees, but nothing topped the Costa Rican nachos. Dessert was amazing, and the wine, once again, was good. Overall, everything was great for a wonderful last night out in town. I liked this place before, but I really loved it now. We both did.

I tried my best not to cry when Chuck dropped me off at the airport. I had no desire to live in a house under construction, and I was not sure he was looking forward to living in the chaos at our house either, even though I knew he was happy to be in Costa Rica. However, I missed him a lot, which made it hard to leave.

All morning, I sat in the airport and struggled to hold back tears. While waiting for my flight, I realized it was hard to travel alone. Almost everyone in a foreign country was traveling with other people, and almost everyone was having fun. Being alone while everyone else was so happy simply made me sadder.

By later in the afternoon, I started to focus on our February cruise. It was the next time I would see Chuck. I tried to think about how much fun it would be, since I would see him and lots of our friends. All those thoughts kept me from crying at the airport, but no matter how hard I tried, I could not shake the sadness I felt.

14 UNFORESEEN CHALLENGES

I LOVED IT WHEN I SAW things that reminded me to never give up on my dreams. Sometimes when my hope for the completion of our Costa Rican dream started to fade, it was great to watch TV shows such as "The Biggest Loser," which renewed my spirit. I was amazed at the determination many participants had to accomplish their goals. With this show, the dream was losing weight for a healthier happier life, but for me, it was getting to Costa Rica for a healthier happier life someday. This show proved you really didn't know where life would take you, but it was a journey you created when you believed in yourself and when you took advantage of the opportunities given to you. It didn't come easy, but with hard work, participants crafted their future into what they dreamed them to be. Some participants certainly had more obstacles to overcome than others on the show, but every day, they took the opportunity to change the direction of their lives and move them toward a course that would make them happy. If only everyone periodically re-evaluated their own life to work toward a goal that continuously strives to help them and those around them to be happy, the world would be a much better place for us all. Chuck and I had chosen a path to a healthier and happier life, but we weren't certain how winding that path would be in order to reach our destination. Therefore, it was important to remain hopeful and determined to accomplish our goals, just like those participants on the show.

In preparation for departing his house sitting duties, Chuck worked on getting things organized for his return to our house. His first priority was requesting Internet service set up, in order for us to continue to communicate after his move. He set up a makeshift kitchen with microwave and mini refrigerator in the master bathroom, along with the grill outside for cooking. Unfortunately, without a kitchen sink, dishes had to be washed in the pedestal sink or shower. He was not looking forward to that part. He slowly got things set up in the house and completed normal activities that we all take for granted, like getting his first hair cut in Costa Rica. It cost him $4.50 including the tip.

Chuck proceeded to paint the interior and exterior of the B&B throughout the month of December. He learned that something as simple as the paint machine matching up the paint was not so simple in Costa Rica. It was a constant struggle to buy matching paint. He did his best to make things work out, but it was a frustrating and costly process.

Since our contractor couldn't find large enough quantities of door hardware, Chuck asked me to order it on-line and ship it on a boat to Costa Rica. I called our shipper for details of the shipping process. The next boat was scheduled for Jan 11th, and it would cost us about $180. Due to stocking issues with the hardware, Chuck got some temporary hinges to hang a few outside doors at our house. This allowed him to turn on the lights without attracting bugs into the house at night, which made a huge difference in his living conditions.

In mid December, I awoke not feeling well. I immediately knew there was a problem, and it was a big one. It was over two years ago that I had felt a lump. That experience turned out to be a miserable week for me, ending at my doctor's office, being yelled at for not going to the emergency room. I was told the next time this happened, I would need surgery. Given I had not selected new doctors since moving back to Tennessee, how was I possibly going to find a doctor who would not only see me right away as a new patient, but commit to doing surgery on me that week? I was in a total stage of panic. It was hard without Chuck nearby for support, but I had to find a way to get through this without him. Fortunately, I calmed down and found a doctor with a cancellation that morning who would see me, after listening to my prior history. She was wonderful and set me up for surgery the next morning. I couldn't believe how lucky I was.

Not long after my return from the hospital, I was shocked when Chuck called on Skype. He was thrilled. The Internet people had arrived at our house at 4:00 pm on the last Friday before most Costa Ricans started their two week Christmas holiday. It certainly was exciting for him to have Internet service, so we could communicate again. Plus, he could stay connected to the rest of the world. The Internet was such a lifeline for him.

Chuck sent me an email to say the dog, Jefe, showed up while he was away from the house. The photos were really cute. Unfortunately, Jefe ran back to his prior owner's house already, so Chuck had to retrieve him. He felt bad about tying him up afterwards, but he had to in order to keep him from running off again. Jefe cried a little bit when Chuck first went to bed, and he barked once when he smelled monkeys close to the house. Overall, though, he did not make much noise. Jefe didn't seem to eat very much at first either. However, that changed after Chuck mixed some wet food with his dry food. Chuck also got him some foam on which to sleep, but he seemed to want to chew it up instead. Other than being worried about the dog liking his new home, Chuck sounded happy in Costa Rica.

A few days before Christmas, Chuck was having a really bad day. He was upset with everything, but mostly over Jefe. I just listened. He felt horrible about having him tied up all the time. The prior owner came by when Jefe was tied up in the shade and Chuck was painting on the B&B, where it was sunny. She took him for a run back to his prior house. Chuck felt like the run back to his old house was teaching Jefe bad habits, when Chuck was trying to make him forget about his old house. He very badly wanted to set Jefe free without having him run back to his old house. He was still upset about Jefe chewing up his bed. He also began to think there was a chance Jefe would run through our door screens. He was completely overwhelmed by the dog not being settled into his new home yet.

I tried to comfort him by saying I agreed that if Jefe ran home five times or whatever he thought then his old house was too close, and we would have to send him back. Our retractable door screens were a potential problem as they were nearly invisible, but Jefe could learn to notice them in time. Plus, I reminded him it wasn't easy with a young dog. Our last two dogs (Chewy and Shoes) were a pain when we first got them. They peed every two seconds when they were really young, and they chewed on the walls and cabinets in the house as they got older. They even dug out of the fence during one phase of their lives, requiring us to pour a cement footing around the whole fence line. Eventually, we worked through all of it, and they grew up to be calm wonderful dogs. It took time to get through all those phases. I knew it was now harder on Chuck, being by himself without help from me. I so wished I could give him a big hug to make it all better.

Despite my comments about the dog, Chuck was still upset with everything else, like doing dishes in the shower, the muddy job site, people not showing up to work on our place, the continuous painting and repainting. He was sick of the bats in the roof and told me they had even moved over into one of the other roofs now. He was totally upset and overwhelmed at all we needed to do at our place. Plus, one of the things that had upset him the most was that our security guard might not make it back in time for him to go to the Christmas party the next night, where he had planned to take Jefe, so he could play with the other neighborhood dogs. It sounded to me that we had come full circle, and once again, we were back to the dog, which was the real reason Chuck was so upset.

I told mom about my phone call with Chuck. She was sure that Jefe would learn to come back once he knew where he slept and ate. Mom was willing to take out a second mortgage on the house in Tennessee, so we could finish construction which would help to resolve a lot of the other issues that had Chuck upset. However, Chuck and I were not willing to go down that road. We couldn't afford to pay it back. Plus, we already agreed we were not going to borrow more money. Hopefully, something would work out. However, I didn't go to bed that night as happy as I would have liked. I really hated trying to sleep when I knew Chuck was so unhappy.

Chuck didn't sleep at all that night, thinking about Jefe being tied up. It bothered him, and he felt Jefe was restless as well. He got up early and let Jefe loose. He fed him breakfast and waited. Of course, Jefe ran off. Chuck decided to take him back at that point. He loaded up the Teryx with his stuff. However, before he could leave, Jefe's prior owners arrived. They saw Jefe down at the road and decided to drop by. Chuck explained he couldn't keep him tied up, and they should take him back where he would be happier. They explained that they had kept Jefe tied up at their place, because he jumped the fence and roamed around. That was a surprise to Chuck. They thought Chuck should let him loose and not worry about it. Jefe would come back to sleep and eat because he knew now where his new home was. They thought Jefe would be happier with Chuck than being just one of their twelve dogs. Chuck decided to keep him and see what happened with him untied.

Life was now good and in order for Chuck, given the dog situation seemed improved. He really wanted the dog to stay. Jefe ran off again to his prior owner's property, and Chuck chased him down. The turning point came when Chuck yelled for Jefe to come back, and Jefe stayed at the fence wagging his tail, while the other eleven dogs ran back to their house. Jefe jumped in the Teryx like he was ready to go back to his new home, now that he had been on his big adventure. Chuck was thrilled they had finally bonded.

One day, Jefe was so excited that he jumped into a neighbor's car to go for a ride. Chuck decided to take him for a ride in the Teryx instead. Jefe loved it, and that started a new routine with the two of them. Chuck also took Jefe over to another neighbor's house for dinner, to play with their dogs. It was the start of a love affair between Jefe and one of their dogs. Gradually, Jefe settled into a new routine of life with Chuck, and their bond grew stronger.

It was hard being separated during the Christmas holidays. Fortunately, Chuck was able to attend the Christmas party at our neighbor's house. He took Jefe, and everyone there loved him. It was nice that Chuck was invited to attend many Christmas celebrations in our Costa Rican neighborhood. I was very thankful he had others to keep him company during the holidays. Although I missed him, I loved being home with my family to celebrate Christmas. Christmas dinner was incredibly good at my parent's house. We had a long list of food for our small group. I remember seeing the following: honey baked ham, fried chicken, chicken casserole, dressing, fried sweet potatoes, sweet potato casserole, green beans, mac-n-cheese, rolls, cornbread, fried corn, potato salad, fruit salad, Chinese chicken salad, coleslaw, pinto beans, fried apples, fudge pie, coconut pie, brownies and butter finger cake. There would be yet another Christmas dinner with even more food the next day, to share with other family members. Eating too much was certainly a downside of living in Tennessee.

A few days after Christmas, disaster struck. Chuck was very upset. Our copper power lines to both the B&B and our house had been stolen during the night. This was the second time we had our lines stolen. Although our place was unguarded the first time, this time someone had been bold enough to come very close to our house to cut the lines while both he and the security guard were there, along with Jefe. There had been a bad storm raging outside that night, so they had heard nothing. Chuck wanted to forget having the crew return from Christmas vacation and was thinking of giving up the whole project to return to the U.S. himself. Also, there was a leak in the roof of our house, which let the heavy rains create a flood inside. He was more upset than I had heard him in years. He was sitting in the dark. He had no food, since it was all ruined from the lack of power. The money problem we faced was weighing on him. What were we going to do without power? How would we stop people from taking the copper lines again, if we could ever afford to replace them? He was overwhelmed.

I tried to calm him down. It was a setback. I was not sure why it happened. Obviously, I thought we learned our lesson the first time, but I guess we didn't. Now we knew we had to do more. We would get through it, but he had to have power. This sort of thing was part of living in Costa Rica, and we would have to learn to deal with it. Our contractor told Chuck we could file a police report, but it probably would not do any good. Chuck didn't want to, because it would ruin his San Vito trip with the neighborhood guys, planned for the next day. He certainly deserved to go. However, I would feel better if he was there, protecting our place.

The setback was depressing. However, we didn't need to make any rash decisions. We still had to finish the bamboo ceilings, to get rid of the bats. That was an absolute must. We agreed we could not keep three guys working for us. One of them would have to go, as we had stretched to work the third guy's salary into the budget already.

My stomach was in knots, thinking about the whole situation. I hoped there was a lesson learned here somehow and Chuck could come through this OK. I wished I could give him a hug. On the positive side, Chuck was not physically hurt. I knew he needed a break from our place, but I was not sure how he could leave things to go on a previously planned trip with the neighborhood guys. I would want to stay at our place to install the temporary power and call the police to file the report, on the chance we might have our copper lines back. However, it was his choice to make his own decision. Hopefully nothing new went wrong while he was away. I didn't think he could take another setback so quickly. I knew I couldn't.

I did not sleep much that night. I was still upset that someone would be so bold to come that close to our house to cut the lines with Chuck, Jefe and the guard there. Secondly, the realization was setting in that Chuck would not have Internet access, yet again. The Internet was our lifeline, and cutting us off from communicating bothered me more than the financial loss of the lines. Plus, I felt sorry for Chuck, living without power and going backward on all of his progress, when we had been making such headway moving forward. Finally, I was not sure how we could stop this from happening to us for the third time.

I had a very hard time concentrating at work that day. I kept thinking about the stolen copper lines. No matter how hard I tried not to be angry about the theft, my mind kept going back to it. Did they take them to sell to put food on the table for their family? Was there some way to justify what they did? Chuck and I didn't deserve to have something stolen from us. Maybe we should have done more to protect the lines, but whoever stole them was wrong. I felt like somehow there should be a way to track the thieves down and stop who was buying the copper from them. I told myself it was over. I needed to not dwell on the situation, because it was out of my control, but I couldn't stop my mind. I wished I could cry and make it all better. I really wished Chuck was close by. A hug would have made it all better. I missed him a lot that day. This was emotionally exhausting. It was such a roller coaster ride to be up, going good with everything, then down with a problem. I guessed that was life. It was a ride. Some of it was fun, and some of it was not so fun. Chuck and I could certainly say that our Costa Rican adventure was not a boring ride.

I called some friends after work. I hoped it would make me feel better to talk to other people. It cheered me up some. It reminded me that everyone has their own problems. We had a lot of friends pulling for us to succeed. If nothing else, I knew we should do well once we opened, because we would have many people marketing for us. In the whole scheme of things, we had come a long way, so we had to stay focused to succeed.

One of our friends was so much like me, it was scary. Like me, she liked to plan things out. We talked about how we wanted to set goals for 2010 as part of our strategy for the New Year. However, it was hard to set goals when sometimes we felt like we did not have a clue where our lives were going. We tried to plan, but some things were out of our control. We were not comfortable with that at all. Like me, she had not been feeling well. I had lots of tests done during that past year, and so had she. Without a doubt, the pain I had felt was very real. I had kept Chuck awake many a night in Florida, to the point where he wanted to take me to the emergency room at times, but I had refused. I had continued to hope the tests would reveal something. They showed minor issues, but there was never a lightning bolt moment to explain things. After arriving in Tennessee, my final conclusion was that my body was physically reacting to stress in my life. All of those years I had worried about Chuck's health on his job, and it had been part of why we decided we needed to start our Costa Rican adventure. Yet, the stress from our Costa Rican adventure was taking its toll on my health. I noticed that I started to feel better a short period of time after things had settled down in my life in Tennessee. Now that things had gotten very stressful again, both at work and in Costa Rica, my symptoms were starting to act up again. I couldn't change the copper lines being stolen or the fact that Chuck was probably not watching the stuff in our house that night. However, I was obsessed with it all that day and would worry about it all that night. It was out of my control, and it was draining me physically. I really wanted to let it go, but something in me wouldn't. Controlling my stress was a weakness I needed to learn to overcome in order to survive our Costa Rican adventure. I hoped I would figure out how to control it soon.

Just as I suspected, it was difficult to sleep. I constantly wondered if someone was stealing stuff from our house in Costa Rica. I slept for 15 or 30 minutes at a time and awoke to wonder if something had been taken while I was just asleep. It was a restless night, and I was glad to get to work the next day.

It was a relief when Chuck called to say he had a great time on his trip to San Vito with the guys. It was nice to get away, to take his mind off of our place and problems for a while. He was upset to come back and find there was still no temporary power at our place, due to a misunderstanding with our contractor. He at least had water pressure to take a shower. He was convinced we could secure the copper wire better, and we had learned our lesson this time. I hoped he was right. Anyway, Jefe did well at our friend's house while Chuck was gone. He was very excited to see Chuck and jumped in the Teryx, ready to go home with him. It made Chuck's day to see Jefe happy.

After dinner, I did some research on the Internet in regards to the theft of copper wires. It was strange when you didn't realize how prevalent something was until it peaked your interest. I learned it was a problem in lots of developed countries, as well as third world countries. I was actually shocked at how frequent copper theft had become. It was big money and big risk. Many of the articles I found on-line included stories of people dying from the electricity in attempts to cut the power. This proved we definitely had to do more to protect our copper lines.

I awoke the next morning, crying uncontrollably. I couldn't stop myself.

I was starting to forget what it was like to have Chuck snuggled up in bed with me. I felt the weight of everything from the last few months heavy on my shoulders. I had to find a solution that would work to bring us together. It had only been a few months of living apart, yet we could potentially be looking at years of living in separate countries. It was too hard to fathom. I had to pull myself together and not think about the overall concept. I would have to learn to take it one day at a time.

Chuck finally got temporary power. He was still in a bad mood. I kept telling him to think positive thoughts for the New Year. However, he was living in the moment, doing dishes in the shower floor, living with the mini fridge and taking cold showers. I knew it was harder for him to look ahead, but I felt that at the right moment, things would work out for us. I certainly couldn't explain to him why. However, most of the time, I felt our dreams were meant to come true. Despite the doubts that crept into my thoughts, there was mostly a light that told me things were supposed to work out for us if we only continued to push forward without giving up.

After contemplating our financial situation more, I decided I would consider taking up my parents' offer on the home equity loan. As much as I had been against going into debt again, especially on my parent's house, it actually made sense to do it. Mom was really pushing it, because she hated to see me and Chuck stressed out. If we got the money to finish our place, then we were less likely to have problems with thieves, since there would be guest traffic on the premises. Plus, the B&B income would help pay the loan back. Hopefully, Chuck would also have better living conditions as a side benefit. Having a plan again that I thought would actually work gave me new optimism. I hadn't mentioned any of this to Chuck yet. Even though he was depressed that night when we spoke, I didn't feel like I could tell him until I checked into things more, to be sure we could obtain the money.

Looking back on 2009, we had started the year under construction in Costa Rica. If we had not run out of money, then our contractor would have delivered on his promise to finish construction in 12 months. We had not finished, but we had accomplished so much. We had to hope that in 2010, it would somehow all work out to completion.

New Year's Eve arrived, but it didn't feel like it. It was strange to ring in 2010 without kissing Chuck at midnight. I missed him. I wanted to call him, but he planned to be in bed long before midnight. He was on his Costa Rican timetable now, and staying up until midnight was not going to happen. We had survived living apart until the New Year, which was a major accomplishment. What challenges and what joy would the New Year hold for us?

15 OVERCOMING FEARS

THE NEW YEAR STARTED OFF with an email from Chuck, telling me to look at his Facebook photos of the flight of a toucan. It was amazing to see a toucan, with his large beak, in flight. It reminded me of a story we heard once from a neighbor. His friend commented toucans could only fly downhill because of their big beaks. Chuck laughed and said if that were true, then toucans would all be sitting on the beach, unable to fly back uphill. Our neighbor commented that was exactly the reason he told his friend that his theory did not make any sense.

Chuck felt a little better now about where we stood with our money situation. Our Costa Rican architect had answered him back about the new luxury tax form. We had an extension, since we were still under construction. Also, it turned out we had more money in our escrow account with our attorney in San Jose, since we had already paid for some expenses that we had not realized. All of this was excellent news, so we would be able to keep a few workers, as planned.

One night we chatted for a while on-line. There was a party going on up the street at one of the neighbor's houses. Chuck wondered if they knew a party was going on at their house, since he thought they were out of town. He was worried and was going to have to leave the dog outside to guard the house. I agreed it was a good idea. He hated to punish the dog, because he didn't deserve it. How funny? I told him it was not punishing the dog, because he was an outside guard dog. It was obvious by his punishment comment that Chuck was keeping him inside all the time. I suppose the dog helped comfort Chuck's loneliness, but we needed a guard dog. I wondered if we were going to have to get a second dog to guard the house, since it seemed Chuck was turning the first one into an inside house dog.

We talked about our New Year resolutions. He did not make any. I told him mine was to find out why those roosters were tied standing on top of a log for a few hours a day at a house on the end of our road. He thought that would be an easy resolution to keep, but I told him so far everyone was stumped. He thought mine should be to live in Costa Rica. I told him that was a good one. I didn't tell him, but I didn't think I could honor that one this year.

It was a brutal winter so far, with temperatures outside down to 6 degrees at times. No wonder my feet were always freezing in Tennessee. It was difficult to be here in this cold weather and know Chuck was living a warm life in Costa Rica. However, I felt a little better when mom cooked my favorite foods, like fried pork chops. They were amazing. They were so good that I ate three one night and really wished I had stopped at two. I was feeling sick from eating too much at dinner. Why was it hard to resist too much of a good thing?

I received a lot of nice well wishes from our co-cruisers in response to the email I sent to tell everyone about all the bad luck we had in December. Everyone said they would keep us in their prayers and would help cheer us up on the February cruise. I was really looking forward to it. I knew we shouldn't be spending the money in one way. In another way, life was about memories, and this cruise would create a lot of great ones for us. Plus, it would give us both a break – me from the cold weather and Chuck from daily construction life – and allow us some well-deserved time together.

I decided to call an old friend, and the funny thing was she had needed someone to talk to as well. We always got philosophical about life when we talked. We had a friend going through a divorce, and we discussed why it always seemed that one person usually didn't want to let go of the relationship, despite being unhappy with it. Maybe it was the fear of the unknown versus the security of the unhappiness that seized people to stay. I certainly thought many people stayed in their jobs for that reason. I didn't look forward to fear, but sometimes we needed to challenge our fears and venture outside of our comfort zone to find happiness. Chuck and I would not be building our place in Costa Rica otherwise. My fear still gripped me at times, and I thought Chuck had the same emotions. However, when we rationalized our situation and sat at our place, the fear disappeared. When I got scared, this was the vision that I put in my head and my heart, so I knew we were doing the right thing, despite the many setbacks, including the copper power line being stolen twice and living separated for now.

Our new copper power lines were finally installed. They were incredibly heavy. Chuck guessed probably in total about 600 pounds. They ran the lines and foamed them in the pipe to make it impossible to pull the wires out, if someone tried to steal them again. They installed one new metal panel on one of the boxes. The other box had to remain open until the power company came to install the meter, which would hopefully be soon. Chuck was looking forward to his first hot shower in 10 days, as the water heater had not worked with the temporary power. The best thing of all was having hot water to do the dishes with again. It was hard to take grease off the dishes in the shower with cold water. Yuck! At times, I was glad I was not there roughing it with him, even though I really missed him a lot. I still recalled one day long ago when he had commented he would live in a tent to get to Costa Rica. I was never under that illusion, but I didn't think living in our house during the construction was as easy as he thought it was going to be either. Eventually, our crew concreted over the trench that contained the power lines all the way up the driveway, and the power company did their job so the meter could be closed. I lost a lot of sleep many nights, worrying about the exposed wires. I just hoped that we had learned our lesson and protected the lines properly this time.

As Chuck and I were talking one day, two toucans flew up and landed in a tree outside of the office window where he was sitting. I couldn't imagine what it would be like to sit in Costa Rica someday and for it to be normal to have that happen. Chuck was still getting used to it. He described to me over the phone how amazing the toucans were.

In a small community, it was important for people to volunteer their time to keep the neighborhood well organized. At the annual association meeting for our neighborhood road and water, Chuck volunteered to be V.P. of operations. The association now had enough money to hire a full time Costa Rican worker. Chuck and the new worker trained together, so they both learned the job. The worker took care of the daily work, and Chuck supervised him as needed. However, the job turned out to be more than Chuck expected, given he already had his hands full building our place.

One day, I got an email titled "The Boat" from Chuck, and I knew right away it meant trouble. Someone had stolen both batteries out of the boat, and worst of all, they had cut the wires, which meant he would also have to rewire it. He was ready to sell the boat. As frustrating as it was, the odd thing was it didn't upset me that much. I was expecting something like this. I had been telling Chuck since the theft of the copper wire that he needed to keep the dog outside to guard our place. Chuck and the crew were all obviously working hard during the day and sleeping like rocks at night. Without a guard dog at night, people could do what they wanted around our place with no problems. I knew something else was going to happen, although I was shocked it was so soon. I was thankful it was only the boat batteries. Selling the boat was no solution, because next time it would be the car or the Teryx or something in the B&B. We did not have theft coverage on any of these, so it was a scary thought. Obviously the answer was to leave the guard dog outside or maybe get a second dog. We had to put in some security lights, and we had to eventually put in a gate at the entrance. A combination of factors would eventually spread the word that people couldn't take things from us easily. Chuck promised he would leave the dog outside but pointed out that the dog had to sleep too.

The poor economic conditions around the world had led to theft being more prevalent everywhere, not just in Costa Rica. Before we started to build, I remembered seeing how some people lived in neighborhoods behind huge walls with barbed wire on top and telling Chuck that I would never want to feel like I was in a prison, living in fear. Even after having stuff taken, it did not make me want to resort to that scenario. Although I was not sure I would ever feel everything at our place was completely safe, we had to learn to live with it as part of being in Costa Rica. My opinion was still after we got open with guest traffic around that we would be less vulnerable, so the theft would stop.

After Chuck told me about the batteries being stolen, things got really hectic at work. However, in the middle of the day, I went into girly mode, and for some reason, I started thinking about changing my hairstyle. I had no idea why I thought of this, other than the fact I needed something to think about, to take my mind off of all the stress. Mom was funny. She thought I should talk to Chuck before I cut my hair, but she didn't have a problem with me borrowing money on a home equity loan without talking to him. I thought most guys would want the opposite. I wondered which one of us was right.

That night, I watched an International House Hunters episode on a couple moving to another country to start a B&B. They bought an existing house in France, but it needed a huge amount of renovation. They selected the house that needed the most work but had the most potential when they were done. Thinking about our situation made my stomach knot up, because like them, we were investing a lot of money in another country on the hopes we could make a successful business. Also, like them, we all had dreams of living a freer lifestyle. It made me smile at the end, because even though they had made little progress in the first year of their journey to renovate, they said it was the best decision they had ever made.

When Chuck went outside in the mornings, he found Jefe looking very sweet, sleeping on his tattered piece of foam bed. I was relieved, as I had worried he might keep Chuck up all night crying, or worse yet, break the door screens trying to get inside. So far, he was doing very well outside at night. During the day, he wandered off at times and spent part of that time at a neighbor's house, playing with their doberman. Chuck took him out every day in the Teryx for a ride or to let him chase it. The workers had a pile of dirt left that they were using to mix with the concrete, and Jefe loved the dirt. He had been digging and lying in it under the shaded tree a lot. It was now one of his favorite spots.

Late one afternoon, I received a call from the mortgage guy. Everything looked fine on the home equity loan. It was just pending final approval. I was thrilled. I might have to bring Chuck into the loop on this before I left on the cruise, but my stomach still knotted thinking about how he would react.

I couldn't sleep one night. My migraine was raging, and my mind was racing about Costa Rica. Where would we place a gate and wall for our property? What would it cost? Would it keep Jefe in our yard? Where would we put a sign for our place? What would it look like? What was Chuck going to do with the Teryx when he was gone on the cruise? How would he protect it (i.e. take out the battery or let the air out of the tires)? What would he do with his computer when he was gone on the cruise? Was there anything else he needed to hide while he was away? Did he have an updated balance sheet from our contractor? Was he going to sleep in on the cruise or be up every day by 6:00am like he was used to in Costa Rica? My mind was going through lots of questions and scenarios. I hated when I did this, but I found myself unable to sleep many a night, going through Costa Rica issues of various types throughout our whole construction process.

I never had much luck looking for clothes in Florida, but in Tennessee, there were great deals everywhere. I found some cool bathing suits, including a splurge on a two-piece, and I hadn't worn a two-piece in years. I also bought a beautiful new piece of lingerie, which I hadn't bought in years either. I got a few other things that were low cut. This was all with mom's advice. I was becoming a lot more daring in my old age of 40. I was not sure what that said. The only thing I couldn't find by the end of the day was a black tube top I needed to wear under a wrap dress, which I wanted as a safety feature, in case my wrap dress fell down. All right, so maybe I was not becoming that daring. It was so much fun shopping with mom, and all this shopping got me more excited about our February cruise.

Chuck arrived home from his trip to the vehicle inspection site in San Isidro. The drive over the mountain to San Isidro in the Teryx was awesome. The only negative was that he did not pass the vehicle inspection on the first attempt. We had special tags on our Teryx starting with an EE, which translates to "special equipment" in English. That type of tag required a yellow flashing light on the roof. Luckily, he bought a light that plugged into the accessory outlet and could sit on the roof and flash yellow, so he passed inspection on his second attempt. The neighborhood guys were now calling the Teryx the "Disco Mobile" due to the yellow flashing light on the top. We would later learn at a police stop that this type of tag also required a heavy equipment driver's license. The inspection requirement for the yellow flashing light on top made more sense, but why a Teryx would be considered a piece of heavy equipment still baffled us. Luckily, the police let Chuck drive on without confiscating the Teryx, despite him not being properly licensed. They let our friend who was following him in his Rhino go as well, which apparently required a motorcycle driver's license, according to how his Rhino was tagged. There seemed to be some inconsistency in Costa Rica on handing out tags, and fortunately, the police were nice to look the other way that day.

Chuck celebrated his 45th birthday in Costa Rica. He spent the day doing a few errands and visiting our contractor. Our contractor thought we had to put up a gate with a wall to stop the theft and keep word from spreading we were an easy target. Chuck knew we didn't have the money for that right now. Plus, he was worried about people finding out he would be gone on the cruise, making us a bigger target, so they discussed getting a night watchman while he was gone. I felt really bad for him being alone and in the dumps on his birthday, of all days. I decided to tell him about my idea to take out the home equity loan.

At first, he didn't like it. The more he thought about it, he realized it made a lot of sense. He didn't like the idea of borrowing either, but most people had house payments. Our goal would be to pay it off in five years. I would be 45 by then, and Chuck would be 50, which was still an excellent plan. By the end of our conversation, he felt better. The possibility of finishing, not eating off the grill forever and moving forward had picked up his spirits. He was not as excited as I thought he would be, though. The fact we had to ask for help to make it all work out was bothering him. It was hard for me to swallow for a while too. Nevertheless, sometimes we had to accept help from others to reach our dreams.

We developed a strategy. First of all, Chuck needed to start designing the gate and figuring out where the gate wall would go right away. Secondly, we agreed to have our contractor hire a night watchman during our cruise, so we did not have to worry while we were on vacation. Bottom line, though, we did not want to tell people we were borrowing the money. Even though most people had mortgages, a lot of people still judged us for moving and investing in another country. We didn't see the need to give them something to talk about.

We had a number of positive things happen. We got our residency filing number, so now Chuck did not have to leave the country every 90 days. We heard that the box of door hinges and other items had arrived in Costa Rica and were ready for pick up near San Jose. Chuck scheduled a courier to deliver it to the B&B we stayed at in Escazu. He planned to pick the box up during his stay at the Escazu B&B, on his way back from the cruise.

Chuck went to work on a water line break. On the way home, he found Jefe at the neighbor's house, playing with his dogs. It was nice to have a social dog. Chuck also said that on the nature front, an exciting thing happened. They heard some squawking overhead, and he knew right away that it was macaws. He and some of the workers ran outside to look. It was a beautiful sight with four macaws flying right overhead. He was impressed at the sight, but he was very surprised at how impressed our crew was as well.

It was crazy how my life had changed in the past three months. Everything now revolved around my family. I got to talk to my friends, and I did things with my family, which was the opposite of how things were when I was in Florida. It was nice being around my family, but I did miss my friends. The cruise would be a good chance to reconnect with some of them.

Chuck spent some time designing the bar for the tiki hut. In most houses, people congregated in the kitchen, but in Costa Rica, people spent a lot of time outdoors. I actually saw the tiki hut as an important project for our place, because it was planned to have everything in it. It had beautiful views of the pool, our place, the ocean, and mountains. It had drinks. It had food with a grill and a big green egg. It had mood lighting at night. It had swings, bar stools and a table. It had music. I thought it would be the heart of Ocaso Cerro, and I could see lots of people having fun and good times relaxing, talking and enjoying nature. It made me wonder how many people would sit at our place and decide to move to Costa Rica. I didn't know if our place would influence others to that extent. However, I did hope that for the short time people came to visit us, they forgot the stresses of their lives at home and enjoyed the simple riches that Costa Rica and Ocaso Cerro had to offer. It was a vision that was growing closer.

Chuck posted progress photos. The bamboo provided the house a warm tropical and Costa Rican feel. The new light fixtures were awesome. All of the windows and doors in the B&B closed everything in and made it look like a real house. The wall paint colors looked great too, and the white paint made the columns stand out nicely. It was impressive to think Chuck had done all of that painting by himself, with each wall requiring a minimum of four coats of paint, especially knowing he hated to paint. I was very proud of him for what he had accomplished.

Pretty soon, I wanted to start telling other people, like my co-workers, about the B&B. I was excited to tell them, but I didn't want it to become a big deal either. I wanted to stay focused on work during working hours. Plus, I didn't want to make myself the target of layoffs, if people felt like I had another business to go to on the side. I was committed to my job. I hoped that Chuck and I living apart now proved that to my bosses. During the past four years, I had managed to keep the B&B quiet and very separate from my work life. In fact, two of my agents had not been aware of the B&B for several years, and it only slipped out to them by accident. It was hard to contain my excitement at times, but I had felt it was necessary to do so. Again, I thought my work life needed to have a clear line between the

B&B and work.

Chuck emailed me mid-morning with exciting news that our property taxes were paid. His email said, "Guess who paid them – me!" It was odd at how difficult some things were in Costa Rica, yet other things he thought would be hard, like paying property taxes, turned out to be so easy.

My dad came into my office that morning after breakfast with his "great idea." He thought Chuck and I should finish the place in Costa Rica, sell it, move to Tennessee, live in the house here with mom and build a place for him out back, where he could live and smoke without bothering us. I thought it was funny, because he was dying for us not to move to Costa Rica, even though he had never been there. I was betting once he went, he would love it.

Mom and I had a lot of fun one weekend night doing more girly stuff. We played with her makeup. The makeup actually looked so good hiding my sunspots, I ended up buying some before the cruise. She polished my fingernails and toenails. We looked through all her jewelry to find missing pieces that I thought I might need for our cruise. It was like going to a jewelry store. It was amazing to see how many beautiful pieces she had. It was nice to enjoy my mom time in Tennessee. I had missed out on this, since I had been away from home for a number of years, but I was glad to experience it now.

I received a few emails from Chuck the next day. He made it to San Jose to the B&B in Escazu in 3 hours, 15 minutes. It was an amazing time. The new highway was open, and it was great. There was a slew of traffic on the new road, because everyone was taking a look at it. He was ready for vacation and couldn't wait to see me. I emailed to ask if he thought he would recognize his sexy new wife tomorrow at the airport in Puerto Rico. He replied he didn't know he got a new wife and wanted to know what I did with the old one he liked so much.

I had to awake super early for my flight, because all the new girly stuff required extra time to get ready. The roads were covered with ice and snow, which made for a very stressful drive to the airport. Being on a plane during de-icing was a new experience for me, and going down the runway was a shock too. When the pilot initially said we would de-ice and it would be rough going up, I thought he had meant rough in the air going up. Now I knew he meant rough on the ground.

In Puerto Rico, I saw Chuck come down the stairs. He was very skinny, and his hair was cut strangely. It was long on top and short on the sides. He smiled at me through the glass and waved. We hugged and kissed before grabbing a taxi to our hotel. Riding to the hotel, we both smiled at the fact we were finally together again. Chuck and I went up to the room to find that our friends had left for dinner. The room was a bit of a shock. There was only a curtain separating the two bedrooms. The other odd thing was that the bathroom door was in the second bedroom. This was not what we had expected in a two-bedroom suite, for the price we were paying. I couldn't believe we had waited to see each other for such a long time and be alone, yet here we were with only a curtain separating our rooms. I guess my new lingerie would remain in the luggage tonight. However, Chuck pointed out we were alone for the moment and better take advantage of it before our friends got back.

16 A TEST OF OUR COMMITMENT

UPON ARRIVAL AT THE SHIP, we headed to the top deck to meet all of our friends. It was great to see everyone. Some friends, we had not seen in months, and we had not seen others in years. We had a great time at the sail away and enjoyed a nice dinner afterwards. It was so much fun to be able to eat with Chuck, like a normal couple. It was nice to go to bed together again, and it was even nicer this time, with our own room and full privacy. We were still laughing at the curtain between our rooms on that prior night. All of our other friends had a huge laugh out of it as well. It was almost embarrassing when they kept telling us to go to our room to be together alone. Oh well, it was obviously nice to be alone. It had been a perfect day, and we still had several days to be together. It was exciting to think of all the fun that was yet to come.

I felt bad for Chuck, though. He really missed Jefe. I had only met Jefe the one time, but Chuck was very attached to him. I remembered how upsetting it was to leave our other two dogs (before they died) home while we went on vacation. I knew Chuck had gotten close to Jefe very quickly, especially since he provided his only companionship. Chuck seemed pretty heartbroken. The thought of not seeing Jefe for two weeks had him upset. The thought of how Jefe would be handling it made him more upset, because he knew Jefe would be lonely. Chuck was very sweet to be worried. It reminded me why I loved him so much.

We spent our first port of call in St. Croix. Later that night, we had a fun time talking about the beer drinking pig excursion that we had seen signs for ashore. We couldn't imagine what that would possibly have been like. We came up with a word called "snorfle." We talked about how the pig would "snorfle" when one of our friends challenged the pig in a beer-drinking contest. In fact, we laughed and talked about it so much that I doubt if going on the real excursion would be nearly as good as the story we made up. It became the joke of the cruise for us to "snorfle" here and there. We created a lot of good memories that day. Happily our friends enjoyed their first day out on their first cruise, which Chuck and I had convinced them to take. It was nice to once again be spending time with Chuck. When we went to bed that night, I realized how happy and how lucky I was, not only to have such a great husband, but to also have many wonderful friends. We had yet another new place to look forward to tomorrow. What an amazing cruise this was going to be.

The next five days involved stops at different islands, including St Kitts, Dominica, St Lucia, Barbados and Grenada. Each day offered new experiences and memories we would cherish forever. Dominica was a beautiful island that reminded Chuck of Costa Rica, making it one of his favorites. St. Lucia was my favorite island, and I had been looking forward to returning. On our first cruise excursion there, the local lunch of hot bread and cheese made the cruise for me. On this cruise excursion, we were not close to that local bakery, but our guide had arranged to get us lunch. At the end of our tour, we drove down an alley to a van, parked alone, which actually was a little creepy. Our driver pulled a brown bag full of bread from the van and brought it back to us. Another driver had made the drop earlier. It was not piping hot, like we had received on our initial Cosol tour years ago, but it was still great bread. Our driver had delivered as promised in an unconventional way. It was a beautiful place with great friends in a van, sharing a few loaves of bread, some cheese, beer and rum punch along the way. That was a unique day we would happily look back on for the rest of our lives and a big reason why Chuck and I had not wanted to pass up the opportunity of this cruise.

It was nice to snuggle with Chuck that night. I was still in shock that we were spending lots of time together. I had waited so long to be close to him, and here he was. It was nice to know there was time on our side, with almost a week left to cruise. I felt very happy and loved on the boat, not just by Chuck, but also by all of our friends. They called us the honeymooners, despite our 19 years of marriage. I was happy we had come on this trip. We had thought a number of times about cancelling, once my employer said I couldn't telework in Costa Rica. However, we had given our word to our friends that we would go. Some of our friends were going on this as their first cruise, so we couldn't let them down. Plus, it was too good of an opportunity for us to pass up. It did mean that a lot of my vacation was going to be gone early in the year, and that would make it much harder for Chuck and me to be together as the year went on. Right then, though, it seemed like we had made a smart decision. We were going places and seeing things with friends that we might never have a chance to do again. Although the road might be harder for us later, life was about taking advantage of opportunities, and this was one we did not want to pass up for us or for our friends.

We were exhausted from so many consecutive exciting days ashore. Therefore, although Chuck and I were not big sea day fans, we were actually pretty happy to have a break from pushing ourselves to awake early and visit our next island. We were looking forward to sleeping in and enjoying some free unplanned time to explore the ship at sea that next day.

We took our time getting ready and headed out for the big brunch. Afterwards, we explored the ship a little bit and decided to check our emails. What a change of pace our relaxing day was about to take. Our first email from Jefe's dog sitter stated that he was doing fine. However, our next email was titled "Fire at Ginette's Place." This was referring to the B&B in Escazu where Chuck had parked our car and couriered the box that I had shipped him. We both held our breath as the Internet crashed. Our hearts were racing as we thought about what might be in that email. Finally, when we got back into the message, it said there was a fire in the garage at Ginette's place, which had caused damage. They were trying to contact us to find out what to do with our vehicle.

Wow, our minds were really racing now. Did it mean that the vehicle was fine and just needed to be moved somewhere else? Did it mean the vehicle was damaged and needed to be hauled away somewhere else? What had happened to our box that we had delivered to her place? Chuck had left it in the room next to the garage. Our vehicle was parked outside next to the garage. Beyond that, did everyone at the place get out all right? Were her dogs all right? We had no property insurance on our vehicle either. How much was this going to cost us? If the vehicle were damaged, how would we get it fixed? What would Chuck use for transportation while it was being fixed? All of our door hinges were in that box. What would we do for door hinges now if they were gone? Jefe's new doggy bed was in that box. Chuck's Christmas presents were in that box, and he didn't even know it. We certainly couldn't afford to replace a vehicle if it was gone. It was all very upsetting news.

We exited the computer room in a state of disbelief. All of our hopes felt washed away at that moment. We went back to our room and sat there, stunned. We thought we had done the right thing to park at Ginette's place versus parking at the airport. I had thought it would be a good idea to courier the items to her place from the shipper's warehouse, for Chuck to pick up there on his way home from the cruise. It all made sense up front as a safer and more efficient plan for us. Now it all looked like a bad mistake. We couldn't change what had happened, but would simply have to figure out how to deal with it. We planned to call Costa Rica from shore that next morning. For now, we hoped for the best-case scenario.

A friend called and wanted us to visit their room. They tried to keep us cheered up, but it was difficult to think about anything else. I tried to stay optimistic. After all, the email stated they needed to know what to do with the vehicle, so it shouldn't have been a total loss. I wished I had pushed Chuck harder to buy the auto physical damage insurance. He had been busy, and things in Costa Rica were usually not simple processes. Therefore, I had not pushed him hard on the issue. If we had been insured, then I would not have worried as much about the situation as I was now.

It seemed like the world was against us finishing. We had just gotten through obtaining money to replace the power lines, and now we had to deal with a car fire. Would we ever be able to finish? Had we made the right choices? Was this all a big mistake to go to Costa Rica? Chuck was even questioning why he had quit his job to start us down this path. That was not something I would question and was obviously something he had to do for his health. Tough times made us think hard about the choices we had made in our lives. They tested our ability to stay optimistic and on track. They were crossing points in our lives. We had to realize we could not change what had happened to us. Our challenge was to change how we reacted to it. Our choice was to deal with it or be depressed about it. However, it was far better to take the challenge head on. It was better to decide how we would deal with the consequences of what had happened than to dwell on the past and why it happened. If we got stuck focusing on the past, then our thoughts would bring us down like a vicious cycle that feeds on itself, pulling us down more and more into depression. We had to push forward, right into the gut of what happened, and take it on straight ahead. If we did that, then we usually found the problem was not as bad as we had thought. Sure, nobody was happy about having problems, but they did make us stronger. Having overcome those problems made us appreciate what we had much more. When two people solved those problems together, it helped to build a relationship and make it stronger. It was part of a bonding experience that made a successful marriage last many years. Chuck and I were certainly bonding more these days, with our continuous problems along our Costa Rican adventure.

Deep down though it was up to the individual to push ahead and keep the focus on dealing with the challenges thrown at them. It was always a benefit to have a good support system which could be from a spouse, family, friends or spiritually. The more people an individual had in their corner to give them support, the easier it was for them to stay positive and on the right track. Chuck and I were very fortunate to have a good support system. We had each other on the cruise, and we had a lot of friends encouraging us along as well, during the trip. As I mentioned, we tried not to focus on our problem and tried to stay as positive as we could during the remainder of that day.

It was a relief when bedtime finally arrived. The next day delivered factual answers, when the unknown became the known. We were problem solvers by nature. Once we knew what the scope of the problem was, we would be all right. We were smart, and we would figure out how to resolve it. All we needed were the facts. It was another hurdle on our big adventure. After all, if it were easy, everyone would be doing it. For some reason, we were being tested to see if we would be up to the challenge, so we had to keep going. I knew we were meant to make it, but yet again, it was going to be a little bit harder than we had planned.

I did not sleep well that night. My stomach was in knots. I was grateful when it was finally time to get up. Once we reached port, Chuck called Costa Rica. The electrical fire had started in the garage, moved to the kitchen, pushed into Ginette's bedroom and also burnt a small bedroom next to the garage. This bedroom was where Chuck had slept before the cruise and had left our box. The box had been destroyed. Our vehicle was parked right next to the garage, but was separated by a concrete wall that had provided it some protection. It had sustained some damage, mostly to the front. Some parts had melted from the heat, but it was still drivable. A driver used by Ginette had taken our vehicle to obtain an estimate for the repairs. He planned to call or email Chuck with the number, and Ginette would front the money for us. It would be repaired by the time Chuck returned from the cruise. We were probably facing at least a few thousand dollars for the repair, with used parts. Everyone had gotten out of the fire all right, including her dogs. She planned to find another place for Chuck to stay upon his return, and she was very sorry for everything that had happened.

Chuck was very upset. I actually couldn't decide how to feel. On the one hand, I was thankful that it was not a total loss. On the other hand, the idea that we had to spend thousands of dollars was depressing, because it was money I knew we didn't have. I actually was not as upset over the money as I was over the loss of the box, which had the hinges I had worked so hard on getting there, along with the doggy bed and the other items meant for Chuck. It was all replaceable, but it seemed like destiny was against us. Chuck was taking it very hard, because reality was setting in for him, hearing the actual facts.

The island of Curacao had been on my "to-do" list for years, and here we were in an unpleasant position, being forced to deal with problems back in Costa Rica during our Caribbean rendezvous. Our plan for the day was to take a group tour of the caves, along with a stop at the Blue Curacao Factory. However, after breakfast, I totally broke down in our room on the ship. I cried and couldn't stop myself. I did not want to be around anyone for the day. I wanted the two of us to stay on the boat. I didn't want to ruin everyone else's day, but Chuck knew I had wanted to see Curacao for years. He was not going to let me stay on the boat. We were going on the excursion. We made plans to sit in the back of the bus and stay to ourselves. This was an opportunity that we were not going to pass up. We came all this way, and we were going to make the best of it. If my crying bothered everyone else on the bus, then they needed to ignore it. We were certainly entitled to have a bad day, and our friends would forgive us. He was going to be sure that I saw Curacao.

I knew Chuck was right. I threw on my sunglasses to hide my red eyes, and we headed out for the day. A few people asked me if Chuck was all right, and I said yes. They didn't know I was the one having a breakdown.

As planned, Chuck and I sat in the back of the bus. I shed some more tears. Chuck held my hand tightly and smiled at me. Eventually, I got wrapped up in the scenery and was able to focus on the island. It was all I had imagined. The colorful pastel buildings of various shades were beautiful all lined up together, especially along the blue waterfront. As we drove through the city, it all looked cheerful. It was hard to be depressed while looking around at all the colorful buildings, so my mood continued to improve. We arrived at the Hato Caves. Little did we know, this was going to be a wonderful surprise. The rest of the trip turned out to be great as well, and I was thankful for Chuck not letting me pass up an opportunity that I had waited so long to see. My memory of the car fire would fade with time, but I would always treasure the memories of our day in Curacao. It was a lesson in carpe diem.

We checked email before bedtime to read that, remarkably, the door hinges were fine, with the exception of two. We also received confirmation the car would be fixed before Chuck returned. We headed off to bed with some hopeful news. Everything else in the box was minor, in comparison to the hinges. The car would be fixed. Overall, things could have been much worse, so we were lucky. We had also made the most of our time in Curacao and not let the fire spoil our plans. I was proud of us for pulling each other through that day, and I knew we would get through the fire situation as well.

We enjoyed a final port of call in Aruba, where I got to take my first parasail ride. Chuck agreed to dress up that night for a romantic dinner at the finest restaurant on the boat. Unfortunately, I didn't feel well at dinner and barely made it back to the room before I got sick. Thankfully, I awoke feeling better. We sat on the little sofa in our room, listened to some music, looked out at the water through our porthole and talked about the future. At times, we pulled up photos and spreadsheets on the computer. Overall, we talked about how we had gotten started, how far we had come and how far we still had to go. The fact was that we would make it, no matter what. We had to stay strong, and things would work out. We agreed that taking out the home equity loan at the bank was going to work out fine. Talking things through helped us both reenergize and focus. It had been a good cruise. We had seen several interesting ports. Obviously, the first week had been better for us, before we knew about the car fire. Even so, we had made the most of it. It was sad we would soon be separating from our friends and from each other. However, it had been a long vacation. It was soon time to go back to the reality of daily life. Jefe was waiting for Chuck, and my family was waiting for me. One day, we planned to be together in Costa Rica. For now, we planned to enjoy the short time we had remaining together, before our departure from the ship and San Juan.

After we departed the ship, we spent our last day in San Juan. It turned out to be a great city with lots to offer. We got ready for bed, and already I could feel my heart pounding and tears welling up inside of me. The fear of letting go of Chuck was coming up far too soon. We had shared a great vacation together, but it was only temporary. This trip had been over a year in the making. It had turned out to be more than I had ever imagined. We created many great memories. However, I hated the thought that it had taken two weeks of my vacation time. At this moment, I wasn't sure how I was going to survive the rest of the year apart. I told myself I had to breathe and take it one day at a time. I had to hold back the tears for now. The cruise was an opportunity that we decided had to be taken, and we would suffer through the rest of the year somehow. It seemed overwhelming that this could happen, but it all would in due time. I snuggled with Chuck, still thinking this would be the last night we had for a while. He fell asleep, but I still lay awake. The tears flowed a little, and I eventually drifted off to sleep.

Chuck walked me to my gate at the airport and sat with me until I caught my flight. I did my best not to cry as we parted, but it was very difficult for me to hold back. I had no idea what problems he would be returning to in Costa Rica, and I didn't know when I would get to see him next. I would not be going to Costa Rica until the end of May, which seemed like an eternity away. I told myself to be strong as I got on the plane and went to my seat, but my eyes were teary as I flew away.

Later, Chuck called to say he was in San Jose. He was tired but happy to be back in Costa Rica. The car looked good, from what he could see in the dark. He was spending the night there and would drive back to our property the next morning.

Soon after, came Valentine's Day. I believed it was my first Valentine's Day without Chuck during our 19 years of marriage. I usually received flowers this one day a year. I didn't mind living without the flowers, but to not see him at all seemed odd. I was always depressed when Chuck and I first separated. Being without him left a void in my heart. A lot of time needed to pass before I made the adjustment, and I got back to what felt like a normal life without him. I had to accept it as reality. I cleaned up and headed out for church.

After church, we had food in the church hall, along with the annual dessert competition among the guys. All the guys did a great job with the desserts. Chuck didn't cook many desserts. However, I wondered what he would have made to enter into the competition if he had been around that day. Whatever he would have done, I knew it would have been good. He was such a great cook.

I spoke to Chuck that night around dinnertime. He had made it home from San Jose earlier in the afternoon. He was tired but glad to be home with Jefe. The car looked pretty good, except they didn't have our fog lights in Costa Rica. They replaced the damaged parts and repainted it. He was impressed they fixed the car while he was gone. The front license plate was melted, so he had to call our attorney the next day to discuss how to obtain a replacement. All was fine at our place. Jefe had done well while he was away. There was no need for me to worry.

I missed Chuck a lot at night. I had gotten used to sleeping in bed with him again on the cruise, so it was hard to go back to sleeping alone. I didn't know when we would be able to live together permanently again, but I knew it would be a long time. I guessed that I had better get used to the separate living arrangements again. Overall, I thought that I had done well, in that I got depressed only once that day and allowed myself to cry only early in the morning, after I cleaned up. Going to bed alone made me want to cry again. If I just had a deadline in sight, I could get through this so much easier. I truly hoped that eventually we would have a deadline for me to move.

It was scary that Chuck was down to $600 in the bank. Our contractor only had about $900 left, and payroll was due in two weeks. We really needed the home equity loan closed by the end of the month.

Chuck took Jefe to the vet, and everyone loved him there. Jefe needed three shots, and Chuck bought six months of heartworm pills. The total vet bill was only $75, including the prior owner's balance of $27. He mentioned the door hinges still functioned after the fire, but they needed to be sanded and spray-painted. Unfortunately, the visible side was the side that got burnt the most. We were lucky though to have any remaining at all.

The stucco guys matched the colors he wanted for a great price. It was only going to cost around $1,800. Of course, that made him happy. Also, the crew had built the gate, which looked great. This surprised me. Although we needed it, Chuck was a little ahead of himself, since we didn't have the money to pay for it yet.

We finally got the home equity loan paperwork finalized. What a relief. It had been a long time since Chuck and I were this tight on money. I felt bad for people who had to deal with money pressures to live day by day. I didn't think people needed a lot of money to be happy, but I did think people needed a small cushion to be able to breathe freely. Hopefully, this was all we needed to get the B&B up and running smoothly. However, until that happened, I was going to worry constantly. Now, my parents were more invested in this whole Costa Rican adventure, since the home equity loan was on their house.

Some neighbors talked Chuck into taking a break from all the construction pressures to join them for some fun in the neighborhood. There was a small group on the hike. They hiked for 3.5 hours to reach the waterfalls and did 7 or 8 rappels. They were gone for over 10 hours. Chuck got home around 5:30pm. He was amazed at one of the ladies in her 70's who endured this amount of physical activity. The waterfalls were awesome. The highest waterfall/rappel was 115 feet, and all but one was over 50 feet. It was a trip for the adventuresome. He was tired and was grabbing something to eat before going to bed early. I was glad he made it back safely and that I had not been with him, since I'm physically not up to such a challenge.

I emailed Chuck about how jealous I was, seeing other couples together. I guessed eventually I would get over it, but right now, I missed him a lot. I missed our evenings in the kitchen, when he would cook. I missed waiting for our contractor to send us photos of the progress in Costa Rica, and I missed the times when we would talk about all of our plans for our place. I also missed going out on Friday or Saturday nights together, when we would pick a new restaurant or most of the time pick one of our old favorites. Hopefully, with a little time, I would get used to the new way things had to be for now, but I missed that part of our old life together.

Neighbors gave Chuck the name of an insurance agent. Chuck was convinced we should buy insurance on the house, but we were fighting over buying the physical damage insurance on the car. He thought it was too expensive. I clearly learned my lesson from the fire, even if he didn't. We were buying it on the car.

Earlier in the day, Chuck sent a few photos from his hiking trip. I would have been shaking like a leaf, rappelling in those photos. In Florida, I was scared of heights and couldn't even stand on the roof of our one-story house. I didn't know how I ever let Chuck talk me into buying rappelling gear in Tampa. I had to be out of my mind that day. Chuck could certainly talk me into doing some adventuresome stuff, but this was way outside of my comfort zone. It took my stomach to look at the photos. He was nuts to think about one day taking me on something like this.

Jefe had not wandered off in a long time. Our neighbor with the dobermans had asked what was wrong with Jefe, because he had not come by to play with his dogs in awhile. We figured Jefe was worried Chuck would go on another long vacation if he left. They were bonded now, and Chuck was very happy from his email. He was also very sweet, saying the weather was awesome and that life would be almost perfect if I were just there. It made me want to cry.

There was only one more week left until the bamboo ceilings would be done on the outside of our house, which was a huge victory. Plus, Chuck said the bats were now officially all gone. The crew pulled up the roof panels and cleaned out underneath. Fortunately, they did a good job flushing them out alive before they sealed up the roof, as only one dead bat was found. Yeah for no more bats or bat poop!

Now that mom was doing my nails, I liked it. I enjoyed my mom time. When she was doing them one time, she said, "See, we aren't so bad, are we? We thought you guys didn't like us because you never came around." I told her it had nothing to do with them. They knew how stressed out I got and how much I worked. They needed to take that and multiply it 10 times for how busy and stressed Chuck was when he was working. It was unbearable with the two of us together. It was not easy to balance out travel to see both of our families, travel with our jobs and travel for our vacations. Most of all, finding time away from work was the hard part. We literally forced ourselves to do it for vacations, but sadly, to visit family was not as high of a priority for us back then. I felt bad about that, now that I was here in Tennessee. I realized that we should have made it more of a priority to spend time with family. However, spending time with family was not relaxing, because we spent most of the time running around to meet them. I thought if people had congregated in one place to come see us, then maybe it could have been relaxing. In fact, I thought there should actually be travel rules to accommodate others who travel from out of state. People needed to make time for them and go to them instead of making them run around the state to meet them. Plus, travel was a two-way street. People needed to return the favor so one party was not always the one leaving their own home. It was nice to visit others, but it was also nice to be visited. Hopefully, when I got to Costa Rica, Chuck and I would be able to vacation back to Tennessee with a priority to visit family, and we would make some travel rules to make our trips more relaxing in the future.

Outside of having some playtime in February, Chuck spent time during the month continuing to paint, along with laying and grouting tile. He also continued to organize more things for the future of our project and spent a lot of time during the month working on his new duties with the homeowner's association.

17 A CLASSIC COSTA RICAN DAY

WITH OUR NEWLY BORROWED FUNDS, we were able to proceed at a faster pace on the construction. Our re-hired workers reported to the job site at the beginning of March. It was our old foreman and two other members of our former crew. Everyone was in good spirits. Our two normal crew members continued their work at our house. The new guys were assigned to finish trimming out the bamboo ceilings inside the B&B with black rope. Our foreman tested out a small section, and it proved to be tedious work. This was nothing new for our bamboo ceilings, as they had been the definition of tedious. Chuck's plan was to have all the crew finish the bamboo and then move on to stucco, which would take a month or so. During the whole month, Chuck would focus on tiling, with some time still spent on the water association work and continued supervision of our place, to keep the project moving along in other areas.

Chuck could clearly hear the surf at night, once all the city noises calmed down. It was amazingly loud. It surprised me, because our property was fairly high above sea level. However, I remembered once hearing a cow moo, all the way from the valley, so it made sense the sound of the crashing waves would carry as well.

On March 4th, Chuck's mom went into ICU. It turned into a rough month for her and the family. It was the beginning of a lot of back and forth between the nursing home and various hospitals. At one point, her doctor even suggested putting her into hospice. It was a lot of stress for everyone and hard on Chuck to not be there. His mom assured him she was fine when he called, but he knew she wasn't.

The bamboo and stucco work progressed slowly. As the weeks passed, the crew fell further behind schedule. Chuck finally told me that he did not think the pool deck and tiki hut would be done before mom and I arrived in May. This was upsetting to me for a few reasons. First of all, I had said a number of times the most important thing to me was the tiki hut. Secondly, my biggest fear was that if we didn't do the pool deck now, with a big crew on hand, we would run out of money for such a huge expense. But Chuck was set on having the stucco done first. I just didn't understand why stucco was such a priority to him. Third, I had my heart set on seeing the tiki hut and pool, to envision what the whole place was going to look like. If I didn't get to see it during my visit in May, then the B&B would be open before I saw it. It was highly disappointing.

In fact, it was so disappointing that I was contemplating postponing my May trip. I didn't think Chuck had a clue of what it was like not to be there to see the progress. He used to remember, but he had forgotten. He was talking like we were sure to run out of money again too. I didn't know what he wanted me to do about it. I had done all I could. I thought I had done enough that he could build the tiki hut, so I could see it.

Work continued to progress on the B&B in other areas. The electrician worked on ceiling fans. The wood guys arrived to install the B&B front doors. They did not finish in one day but got the main doors mostly installed. Chuck had designed bamboo door pulls that he wanted made for those doors. They got a hoot out of them. He believed they thought he was whacky, but I told him they thought that a long time ago, with all his crazy design ideas.

After I heard Chuck's story about how far behind schedule things were, I felt I was going to be disappointed when Mom and I arrived in May. However, there was really no way to predict when things would be done, if I wanted to reschedule our trip. Therefore, we decided to stick with our original dates and hoped for the best.

Chuck had a good time on his quad trip. He posted photos on the Ocaso Cerro Facebook page. It was amazing at how green everything still was in the dry season, compared to a year ago when we saw wildfires. He had pictures of the mountains, a view overlooking our place from afar and photos of a restaurant/bar where they stopped. It looked like a good trip with a small group.

Chuck posted updated construction photos, and I got to see some of the things he had talked about in more detail. The rope trim on the bamboo ceilings showed up well. I saw the doorstops that he had custom designed and installed last week. That photo caused my mind to race, thinking about how much work was needed to keep all the door stop holes in the concrete dirt free. The whacky wave pattern painted on the bathroom wall in Vista Mar was very cool. The colors were all blending perfectly. The B&B front doors were indescribable. I saw a white line where the paint met the concrete floors in some rooms. I was sure Chuck would have a plan to fix it. The outside bamboo ceilings on our house were really done! No wonder he was excited. They all looked amazing too. I said I would never look at the bamboo ceilings and enjoy them, due to the time it cost us, but I had to enjoy them. They were too beautiful not to appreciate.

I was excited to hear that Chuck paid the insurance agent for all of the insurance, with the exception of the theft insurance on the quad which was $1,000 every 6 months. Yes, apparently theft of quads was a separate coverage that was rather expensive. The homeowners insurance was $1,800, which included earthquakes. However, the earthquake insurance was still subject to approval. Landslide was impossible to obtain. I was proud of him for buying everything, especially the auto theft insurance, without us fighting over it again.

Mom and I discussed my annoyance with the phone calls I received from her and dad at the house every night, while they were working their second shift jobs. I knew they meant well, but I did not like being checked up on every night. It was distracting, and it kept me from getting things done. I wanted to be honest about it, even if it hurt their feelings. It was especially annoying when they had nothing to say, and it was obvious they were just calling to check up on me. If I didn't answer the phone, they kept calling back until I did, which was even more upsetting. After I said something last time, they improved but only for a short time period. I hoped they got the message and stopped for good this time.

I had an email waiting from Chuck on Friday morning, March 12th. He arrived back in the house at 12:45 am, and he was exhausted. He planned to write later with the details, but it had been a classic Costa Rican day. It made me smile to know he was all right. On Chuck's one-year anniversary, he ranked this day as one of the two most memorable events during his first year in Costa Rica. His email was as follows:

Made it to Constru Plaza around 9:30. Found an English speaking person and got the tile order put together. They had all but 4 boxes of the 1x1, 54 pieces of rope and any 2x2 tiles that I want to use for the base where there are concrete floors. They should have more in one month. Then went over to the bamboo lady and order the bamboo. Price is only $46 per meter not $66 as we thought and they have all of it! I call Eduardo and he comes 20 minutes later. Pretty excited at this point, then things go bad. Tried to charge the bamboo ($5,681) and it did not authorize. She then tried to run it in 2 charges. First one goes through, second one does not. I give her the Bank of America card and she charges the rest. Went to pay for the tile and ran into the same problem, able to charge part of it. So off to the bank to transfer the balance. Eduardo drives me to the bank in Escazu. Problem transferring because of the new passport. So I get in line to wait for customer service to update the passport info. 45 minutes later I get to try again and was able to transfer the money. We go to the bamboo place's warehouse to see how much bamboo there is – massive pile and over 6,000 pounds! Eduardo says no way in his van (I knew that already). He makes phone calls to various truck owners. Back to Constru Plaza to show proof of payment and the salesman was at lunch. Waited 30 minutes and finally get the receipt. We find out the tile weighs like 5,000 pounds. Eduardo makes more calls. He says don't worry he will get someone to get the stuff by the end of the day or tomorrow so we part ways. He did not want to get paid and said the truck, because of the amount and weight, would be $500. Seemed reasonable. I head to a place called Bali Imports that was recommended by the Constru guy for pebble type tiles. They have a decent choice so I get it and was able to use the CR credit card.

I head home and Eduardo calls like 30 minutes later. He has a truck and they are picking up the stuff and he said he would be there in 4 hours. It is around 1:30 at this point. I also then realize I need to have $500 dollars to pay them so I have to stop in Jaco to get $200 more dollars.

It took like 45 minutes to find it and wait in line. I have not had even a sip of water yet all day. Tried to stop at Steve & Lisa's restaurant but it was closed. I was not hungry anymore so I continue on and get home about 4:30. I unload the pebble tiles and call Eduardo around 5:00 to see where they are. He says they are almost to Jaco and they should be there in a little over 2 hours. So I run down to Real La Costa for a bite and meet up with the rest of the neighbors.

Wanted to eat before they arrived since they tend to chat and eat later. Some old Tico was sitting near me and kept talking to me like I understood him. I kept nodding and agreeing. About 6:30 I went back home to call Eduardo again. They are not even to Quepos yet. I have Gerardo and Carillo lined up to help unload. We wait and wait, I call Eduardo and they are near Dominical so I head back down to the restaurant to meet them. Everyone else is still there hanging out. Finally around 9:00, they show up. They follow me to the bottom of the hill and can't make it any farther since they don't have 4x4 and the steep grade caused the stack of bamboo to fall over. We stop and unload about half the bamboo in the road. I then tow the truck up to the base of our driveway. We unload everything else there and let them head back.

The truck had broken a leaf spring from all the weight. We then head down to retrieve the bamboo at the base of the hill. Many trips (driving backwards up the driveway to prevent the bamboo from sliding out the back) later we get that part to the house. We were so tired already. I took them back to the restaurant to buy them a beer for working so late and we had yet to get 75% it that was at the base of the driveway. We get back and bring up the rest of the bamboo as it is starting to sprinkle. By now it is 12:30. We decide to get the tile in the morning.

I brought the tile up in the quad this morning by myself. It took 3 hours. At least it is all here and appears that there is not one broken tile. Rick came by and chatted for about an hour. Gerardo finished the bamboo! I need to head to the hardware store here to order the remaining 24 meters of the tile. Don't get too good at shopping!

Once Chuck picked up all the missing pieces, the total on the tile was approximately $7,000, which was right on target with the budget. The total for the bamboo was about $5,700, versus the $8,000 we had budgeted, so we looked good there. Thankfully, we were finally under budget on something.

Chuck was worried about his mom and thought he needed to book a flight to the U.S. in April, to see her and me. We decided for him to fly to Nashville. From there, we planned to make the trip together, for a short weekend to visit his family. He booked his flight, and we were excited to be able to see each other soon.

Now that he had plenty of tile stocked, Chuck tiled all day long. He started on the tile in the Ocaso bathroom. In the shower, he completed all of the tile rope and laid about 2 ½ feet up the wall of the regular tile. It was looking awesome already. I wished I could have seen his face as he was looking at it. His vision to see things was coming together now, so I knew it had to be exciting for him. Plus, he was happy to be working and making progress. He loved having work to do. Although I knew, with so much to do, it was probably driving him crazy. I was surprised he was not working 24/7 now.

One of our workers invited Chuck to go watch a soccer match on Wednesday night. It was a new step in his Costa Rica experience to be mixing with the locals, and he was excited. He wasn't sure where the soccer game was, but he was all for it. I was anxious to hear what kind of an adventure that would be.

Chuck was forced to stop tiling and work for three hours on the homeowner's association water system. He got the new pump installed, so the neighborhood was back in water again. He was very happy. I was sure all the neighbors were happy too. Our water storage tank was still half full, so our place had been fine. However, the neighborhood had been out of water for over a week.

That next day, I found out they had a good time at the soccer game. Although Chuck and I had thought they were going to watch a live game, they had simply watched it on TV. It ended up being only him and one worker, as the rest of the crew was too tired from working out in the sun all day. At least our place was not left unguarded. I just wished I had known that earlier since I worried all night for no reason.

I arrived at my aunt's shop to have my hair done. As usual, she took charge. While she was cutting it, she decided we should change it a little. This time, I gave her free will to cut it however she thought it would look good. By the time she was done, a little turned into a lot. My other aunt thought I looked 10 years younger. Now, that was a statement! Apparently, I needed my hair changed a long time ago. Everyone seemed to love it. I liked it, but I also knew I could never dry it the way she had. I just hoped it still looked good when I tried to fix it on my own.

Chuck stopped working around 4:30pm and grabbed a beer, a chair and the iPod. He sat up on the Ocaso balcony for an hour. It was cloudy and cool. Jefe was lying down next to him. Work had consumed him lately. It had been a long time since he relaxed a few minutes and enjoyed the view. The howler monkeys had been really active recently, and he could even hear them over the iPod. The sunset was beautiful. It was hard to believe how neat it was at our place.

Later, Chuck sent me a few pictures to look at. One was of Jefe enjoying the view, which he must have made when they were relaxing together on the Ocaso balcony, and the other was of the view from there. It was very nice. It made me smile and want to cry at the same time. I felt lucky to have them in my life, proud of what he was accomplishing and sad to be missing out on the building progress first hand. In the email, Chuck stressed how much he was looking forward to enjoying some Mexican, BBQ and a real hamburger on his scheduled U.S. visit. Apparently, there was a downside to living in a construction zone in Costa Rica.

After church, I started working on my new computer. It felt good to have a fast machine. I was proud of myself for setting it up without any help. I depended too much on Chuck for some things I really needed to know how to do on my own. In some ways, living apart was good for me, because it taught me to be more independent.

Although Chuck had been told the crew would be off only a few days for Easter, our contractor was now stating it would be a full week. Chuck was panicked. We were hiring a watchman to be sure there were no problems. However, he wanted the gate wall done, and the gate put up at least temporarily, while the crew was away on holiday. We were now going to be really pushed for time to finish. The good news was that our contractor agreed the workers could watch Jefe while Chuck was on vacation.

Chuck was frustrated that the association water system was screwed up again. While trying to fix a leak, the association worker broke the line and a shut off valve to the line. He went to the next valve, which broke, and now the whole line had to be cut off. The guy did a good job. However, he needed to work on the roads for a while, once the water was working again, as Chuck really needed a break from dealing with water system problems.

On a bad note, the municipality dropped by to look at the lots next door and saw our gate wall. They complained about our lack of permit. Chuck thought we had some leeway on the percentage that could be added to a project without new permits. Although that might be the rule, our contractor said it was better to obtain the permit like they asked, so he called our architect to acquire it.

On a funny note, Chuck mentioned that Jefe visited the workers every morning around 5:00am. He poked his head into the workers quarters to wake them up. He waited for them to have breakfast to eat their scraps. The workers really liked Jefe, and Chuck even caught them filling his dog bowl with food at times. Jefe sat with them, waiting for scraps while they ate lunch and dinner as well. He sounded like a spoiled dog, but I had to admit he was smart. It was interesting to hear about his daily routine.

I was practically in tears at my desk one day, from my migraine. The constant headaches were irritating me. It was now the 3rd day for this migraine. It was becoming worse. The daily migraine medicine I was taking was simply not working anymore. I made an appointment with a doctor to ask for help. I hoped he could provide it.

Our Costa Rican architect resolved the permit for the gate wall with the municipality. He was surprised when Chuck said we would be done with construction in five months. He was thinking we would be done much sooner. Chuck thought that was excellent. On top of all that good news, we finally had a front door on our house. It looked great too.

Chuck had dinner at a neighbor's house. The food was great, as usual. The neighbors had promised me they would take care of Chuck, since I couldn't be there. They definitely were doing it, which made me happy. I also knew Chuck was happy to eat real food, given he still did not have a kitchen after almost six months of living in Costa Rica. We were lucky to live in such a great neighborhood, where people were looking out for him.

I liked that Chuck had signed his email, "Love, Chuck and Jefe." How sweet. When I wrote him back that night I told him to tell Jefe, "Mommy loves him." I was not a fan of large dogs, but I wanted to have a dog to love, especially one that Chuck loved so much. I hoped seeing Chuck soon would help rejuvenate me. I really needed it to keep my energy up and going.

My doctor appointment went well. He concluded I was having muscle spasms in my back and neck. Those were putting pressure on the nerves. He thought physical therapy might help with my migraines, but he warned me it was going to be painful. Maybe there was some relief in sight. I hoped it worked to improve things with time.

18 MAKE THE MOST OF EVERY MOMENT

IN APRIL, CHUCK FELT EVERYTHING was organized for his departure to see me in the U.S. The new entrance gate was up, so the property was now better protected. He was a little worried about our contractor, who mentioned he might check himself into the hospital for breathing problems. Apparently, his smoking habits had caught up with him. Hopefully, he was all right while Chuck was away. The workers were set to watch Jefe. He should have all he needed to be well taken care of, even though I knew he would miss Chuck.

I had everything organized in Tennessee on the day of Chuck's arrival. I couldn't wait to kiss and snuggle up in bed. I was so nervous that I was running to the bathroom with an upset stomach. How stupid! We had been married for almost 20 years. It felt like we were dating again, and I wanted him to like me. All my nervousness disappeared as soon as I saw him at the airport.

It was Chuck's first day in Tennessee. It felt strange to sleep in bed with him again, but it was nice to have him there. The first thing he complained about was all the covers on the bed. It made him hot, but I was cold without them. It was funny to go through our old fight routine of hot versus cold.

I was tired when the alarm clock went off, but Chuck was ready to get going. He hated to sleep in. I had forgotten our normal routine. He had to get in the shower first before drinking his coffee. Since we didn't really have everything secured in Costa Rica with a true bathroom cabinet, Chuck had a little baggy which he had been carrying around since November, with his toiletry items. It was worn out from six months of usage. I gave him a new baggy to take back with him and let him live baggy free while he was in Tennessee, although that took some time for him to become used to.

After I finished my workday, we headed out to do some errands. We stopped for various items that were needed for Chuck and the B&B. We stopped by a fast food place to grab a hamburger, which was on Chuck's wish list of items to eat in the U.S. We relaxed with a little TV. He hadn't had TV in Costa Rica since he got there in November, so he enjoyed watching it. We put our cruise photos in an album for Chuck's mom. It was fun, as it brought back memories from our February cruise. Before we realized it, the night was gone.

The next day, we headed out in my dad's truck for Pensacola, on our way to visit Chuck's family. It was a beautiful day, and we had lots to talk about. Chuck told me more about the neighborhood Thursday night dinners, including all the people he had met, the stories he had heard, what he ate and the places they had gone. He told me more details about Easter dinner at a neighbor's house. He went into more detail about his daily routine. We talked about different decorating ideas for the B&B, such as artwork for the walls, mirrors for the bathrooms and lighting fixtures. We had not had a chance to talk in a long time, so it was a lot of fun to just talk. It made the time go by quickly.

Before long, we pulled over to get gas, grab some food and switch drivers. Now that I was driving, it was my turn to talk about living in Tennessee. I talked so much and for so long, Chuck asked me if I had passed up the exit. I knew I hadn't been driving for that long. However, when the next exit sign came, it was our exit. I had talked more than I thought, and he got a big kick out of my surprise.

We spent a nice long weekend visiting with Chuck's family in Pensacola. We ate some good seafood, and it was a nice break for me to be away with Chuck. It had been a good idea to keep him company, and it had allowed us a lot of time to spend talking together. His mom was not doing well when we arrived, but fortunately, her health would significantly improve with time.

After our long drive back from Florida, we decided to relax at home. We enjoyed a bottle of wine while we watched TV and went over some things that were left to do on the B&B. It was nice to be together again, enjoying wine and talking about our dream coming to life. It made me happy. We used to do this a lot, on our dock at the old house in St Petersburg, but we really could do it anywhere. We had made a lot of progress on our dream since those talks on the dock, years ago. Here, we were still in the backwards phase of our plan, but I truly hoped we would soon be going forward. Eventually, the night was gone, and it was time for bed. Unfortunately, I would have to go back to work while he was here, but having him close by made me happy.

Chuck entertained himself all day while I worked. After work, we ran some more shopping errands on the way to meet some friends for dinner. One of our stops was the Goodwill store. I had told him that on a prior visit, I found a ton of great shorts for $2. He was impressed at the selection of clothes too, and found some great deals on shorts to take back to Costa Rica. We had a nice time catching up with friends at dinner, before doing some more shopping. A few of the stops were at dollar stores. I wanted Chuck to see how great they were in Tennessee. He couldn't believe it and kept saying the whole time that everything cost a dollar! He was very impressed.

Once we got to my parents' house, we sat down to relax. We enjoyed a few drinks from a bottle of rum we had bought during our February cruise in Grenada. It was as good here as it was there. We talked about how I didn't feel like I had a real home right now. I felt settled in at my parents' house, and it was comfortable to live here if I ignored my dad's smoking. However, it did not feel like my home. Our place in Costa Rica was still not real to me, since I had barely seen it, so it did not seem like my home either. To me, I felt homeless, even though I clearly had a roof over my head. Did Chuck feel like he had a home? He did not feel homeless, but Costa Rica really did not feel like home yet either. He didn't have a kitchen, and he wasn't sure it would ever feel like a home, even after he got one, without me there. I was not sure if once I go to Costa Rica to visit and actually helped Chuck cook in a kitchen, if it would feel like home to me or not. I hoped it would. Before long, it was time for bed. It had been another good day. It was nice to have Chuck here to drink with and do things with instead of being here by myself. I felt whole again.

It was the last day that Chuck would be here, which made me sad to wake up in his arms, knowing he would leave early the next morning. I always knew in the back of my mind, eventually our trips together would come to an end. It was inevitable. However, I reminded myself to enjoy the day and make the most of every moment.

While I worked, Chuck shopped for more things he needed. After work, we drove to my grandma's house. It turned out she was having a good day. For an almost 90-year-old woman, she was pretty much on top of things when she wanted to be. She asked Chuck a lot of questions about Costa Rica. She also wanted Chuck's opinion on Tiger Woods. He had played his first golf tournament that weekend since his cheating scandal, and she felt the media had given him a hard time for his personal life versus his professional life. She wanted to know how Chuck felt about it. Fortunately, I had already forewarned Chuck that she was a big Tiger Woods fan. Grandma was satisfied with Chuck's response that he had no TV in Costa Rica, so he had not been up on the media to know what was going on with Tiger Woods.

Chuck and I had a great dinner at my favorite Mexican restaurant. We finished the night relaxing and enjoying TV. It was a restless night for me. My mind raced, to be sure we didn't oversleep, and I was also sad at the thought of Chuck leaving. It had been a good trip, and we had accomplished a lot. I was especially glad he was able to spend some time with both his family and me.

I was pretty tired when the alarm went off at 3:30am. Mom talked most of the way to the airport. It made the time go by quickly and kept my mind entertained answering questions. Normally I tend to cry at the airport, but this time I didn't tear up. Knowing that Chuck was happy to go to Costa Rica to work and that I was doing all right in Tennessee made it easier on both of us. Plus, mom and I would see him in Costa Rica in six weeks, so that made it a lot easier. Chuck and I had the flights for our August trip booked to meet in Tampa for our anniversary, which helped ease my mind again. By all means, it was still hard to say goodbye, but this turned out to be one of our easier separations.

Chuck smiled as he went into the airport. Even though he was sad to leave me behind, he was really excited to return to Costa Rica. I would always remember that face and how much it meant we were doing the right thing. He was off to accomplish a lot of work for me, so things would be nice when mom and I arrived. When we got in the car, mom said that he was the sweetest person ever and that I could not have found anyone better for me. I certainly agreed.

I felt lonely with Chuck gone that night. I couldn't stop the tears. I knew he had to go, and I knew he was happy when he left. I kept remembering how he looked and what all he had to accomplish, but it didn't stop me from missing him already. I did so good that morning that I thought I could handle it pretty well all day. Maybe the heart still always got sad, no matter how hard the mind tried to reason with it.

It was after 9:00pm when Chuck arrived home. He was walking around the job site to see what work had been done while he was away. They had finished a lot of stucco and cleaned up debris. The electrician had done some work. The A/C guy had installed two big exterior units and put in some interior brackets. The wood guys had installed two cabinets and countertops but appeared to have put the countertops in at the wrong height. They would have to redo those. Despite being at the wrong height, the countertop looked awesome. His Internet was still down. Most importantly, Jefe was happy to see him.

It was not long before problems arose. The stone Chuck planned to use on the house exterior walls was no longer available. The pool tile we had wanted was gone as well. The A/C guy was supposed to come back two days ago and still had not shown up. We had two upper windows in the B&B that were leaking. The window guy was supposed to show up, and he was another no-show. A problem Chuck did not notice until later was that the kitchen sink he bought was too big for the B&B cabinet width. On top of all this, our contractor mentioned there was a problem with the brackets for the balcony railings. Apparently, they were being stored offsite, and the roof had caved in there. Some of the brackets got damaged and needed to be repainted. It was not the best of luck. Chuck was worried about what they were going to look like afterwards. I told him not to sweat it. Eventually they would probably have needed to be repainted or touched up anyway someday. It was just happening sooner rather than later.

Chuck sent some photos. One showed that the B&B finally had power. It was a beautiful picture of a lighted grand hallway. Another was of Jefe, "the eye-slapper." Chuck had been telling me how hilarious it was to watch Jefe's tongue go back and hit him in the eye as he ran alongside the Teryx. It was the funniest thing to see.

I made it out of town for my business trip all right. I went to bed exhausted. It was strange to go to bed without emailing or talking to Chuck about the events of my day. I didn't like it, and there would be more days to come before I was back in Tennessee to talk to him again. I wondered if he had been emailing me while I was away, so I would get to read his emails when I returned. I hoped he was. It was difficult to be apart all the time and not know how he was doing. Since he hadn't heard from me either, I wondered if he was worried about how I was doing.

After returning from my business trip, I was excited to have emails from Chuck waiting for me. He was relieved that the damaged railings looked great after being repainted. The weather had been unusually hot. He survived the hottest day of the year at almost 85 degrees close to bedtime. The biggest news was that he had picked out the granite countertops for the B&B. He was worried about our contractor, who got really weak when looking at the granite. Apparently, he still hadn't gone to the hospital to be checked out, despite promising he would for weeks. Chuck didn't know how to talk him into it, either.

I loved that Chuck had written me every day while I was away. Even though he didn't get a response from me on those days, it was still like he was carrying on a conversation with me. I felt like I had not missed out on any of the progress. However, now that I was back, Chuck thought it would be more fun to not tell me much about the progress on the B&B going forward, so I would be surprised when I arrived in May. It would be a nice surprise, but I wasn't sure I would be able to wait it out.

Chuck had a bad day. After hearing his story, to only call it a bad day is an understatement. We had a worker injured on the job site last Friday. He just found out that the hospital told our injured worker that our WC (Workers' Compensation) policy expired in November. We thought separate WC coverage did not exist in Costa Rica and was instead a portion of the paid employee wages that our contractor sent to the government every month. Unknown to us, our Costa Rican architect purchased the WC policy in our name when he obtained the building permit in November

2008. It was a one-year policy, so it expired in November 2009. Neither our contractor nor our architect ever said anything to us about a WC policy expiring. We were now responsible for all the medical costs of our hurt employee. Obviously, we would have purchased the insurance, had we been properly informed that we were responsible for it. Unlike in the U.S., where the contractor as the employer would be responsible for the WC, we learned that in Costa Rica, property owners were responsible for WC on everyone working on their premises. Chuck was waiting for news from the eye doctor and paperwork from our attorney in San Jose, so he could go to the municipality to try to correct the situation. I was sure that this was going to cost a lot of money, but I would just be grateful if our worker got his eyesight back. Plus, we needed to purchase a new WC policy before someone else got hurt on our property.

When I was finally about to sleep, I had nothing but bad dreams, like a worker cutting his leg off while chopping at our property, a stucco guy stepping off a balcony, a stucco guy falling off scaffolding and our foreman falling off a ladder when an earthquake hit. It seemed like the scenarios kept coming with one nightmare after another. In my dreams, telling the crew not to do any dangerous work still had my mind racing with ideas of them going off and doing dangerous things, despite what they were ordered to do. Maybe having a career in risk management allowed my imagination to run wild with all kinds of scenarios that might not come to a normal person. I finally got out of bed around 3:00am. I emailed Chuck and our contractor that I was getting no sleep over this whole thing and for them to please not let anyone work the next day at our jobsite. I felt a little better that my plea might make our contractor listen to me, but I knew Chuck would not want to give in to any lack of productivity at the jobsite.

I finally got up around 4:00am and sent yet another email. In this email I offered a compromise that maybe the crew could mop the bottom main level only of the B&B. Chuck had been complaining about how dirty it was. I figured they couldn't get hurt too badly passing off buckets of water from one to another and using a mop. After all, cleaning floors was a national sport in Costa Rica, so the workers should prefer that over sitting around, bored to death. Chuck would be happy they were at least accomplishing something productive. I felt pretty good that it was the least hazardous thing they could do. With a compromise solution proposed, I was proud of myself and managed to finally get some sleep. I only had a few hours before it was time to awake for work, but it was better than nothing.

Once I cleaned up, I checked my emails for a reaction. Chuck promised the crew would do only safe low impact work that day, so I did not need to worry. He also said that the monkeys had been hanging around outside the tower of our house. There was a tree with berries in it that they really liked.

He was trying to make me feel better by the lighter tone of his email. It did put me at ease, but I still hoped that after receiving all my worried emails last night, maybe our contractor would talk Chuck into sending the workers home. At lunch, I had another email from Chuck. They decided to send everyone home for two days with no work. For more good news, our foreman talked to our hurt worker, and his eye was all right. He was ready to come back to work when everyone else returned in a few days. What a relief!

Our Costa Rican architect did his part with the municipality on our admission of liability and worked with our current insurance agent to secure the details for a new WC policy, effective the next day. Unfortunately, our insurance agent gave Chuck bad news on our personal policies. We had been declined for earthquake. Our agent was very upset about the earthquake declination and was writing a letter to someone higher up for reconsideration. In the meantime, we were receiving a refund on the car insurance for a reason Chuck was not clear about, but it would require my appearance in San Isidro to pick up the money. He was fine with that since we could stop at the Rum Bar along the way for good pizza. One interesting bit of news was that our contractor mentioned there may be an opportunity for Chuck to help take over his business, as he was interested in getting out. His health had not been good lately, and he was getting older. The opportunity was good news on one level, which really excited us. On another level, being a contractor was a total headache. I told Chuck it might be worse than being an architect. Chuck certainly was capable, but we had to finish building our place first. We would cross that other bridge of opportunity when we came to it.

I was worried if Jefe would like me or be jealous of me. Chuck said Jefe loved everyone, so I did not need to worry if he would like me. Plus, Jefe would pick up the vibe between us, and of course we would be vibing! I thought that was sweet. I was very lucky. I wished I could kiss him at that moment.

Chuck was worried about running out of money again, but there was nothing we could do about it. I was worried about that too and had been for a long time. I didn't feel like we had a good back up plan in place at all. It would be a huge mess if we ran out of money again. My salary alone couldn't keep as many guys on the monthly payroll as we had before, now that I was making the monthly home equity loan payment. I hoped Chuck was figuring out a backup plan now, before we ended up in the hole again. It was stressful to think about money, so I tried to focus on other things. What was this secret construction work Chuck was doing? I hated not knowing everything that was happening in Costa Rica.

19 GET READY TO BE BLOWN AWAY

MAY ARRIVED, AND CHUCK WAS overwhelmed at the amount of work that needed to get done before mom and I arrived. One day was especially brutal. He grouted Cano's shower, which took him six hours of working non-stop. He ate lunch before cleaning up Cerro, which involved moving about 18 five-gallon buckets of stucco to the electrical room. It took him over two hours to move the buckets, which weighed about 80 pounds each. For most people, that was a full day of work. However, he spent more time tiling and painting in Vista Mar. He was killing himself to have things ready for our visit, but I knew it made him happy.

The granite for the B&B arrived. It was awesome! Other than the granite guys drilling the hole for the bathroom sink of Ocaso in the wrong place, all the granite looked perfect. The kitchen was beautiful. Now that the kitchen was completed, Chuck had ice for his drinks!

It finally seemed like things were going along smoothly for us, after having so much stress recently. However, it was depressing to watch the news, which showed the lives of people in Nashville and surrounding cities brought to a halt, devastated by floods in early May. I felt very lucky to personally have things moving along in Costa Rica so well and for my job to be going well too. I missed Chuck a lot, but I knew eventually we would be together. Although things did not always go as we planned, we had a lot to be thankful for in our lives. It was important to remind ourselves how lucky we were.

After breakfast, I finished getting ready and checked my emails. Chuck had sent a few photos of squirrel monkeys. They were in a habit now. He enjoyed watching them outside the office window while he drank his morning coffee. They were also coming by the family room every morning, down on the ground, and peering in the doors. Thankfully, he had the doors closed. One photo showed a monkey standing up on his hind feet, looking in the house. Mom was confused by where the photo was made. It didn't make sense to her, because there was concrete on the ground. Yeah, right! Chuck had poured concrete he had not told me about. We wouldn't bust his bubble, since he was doing secret construction work that he had been keeping as a surprise.

It was my aunt's MBA graduation, and we couldn't have been more proud of her. The key speaker at the ceremony gave advice on how to succeed. It included dream big, always do the right thing, look at the glass as half full and act now. Later, mom said those words described exactly what Chuck and I were doing with the B&B in Costa Rica, especially the dream big part. It was completely how I felt. Although I didn't think we had always done everything right, we had tried. My whole family felt inspired by the message that day.

The squirrel monkeys were there again, and they were in the tree next to the spa when Chuck came through after quitting work. They did not move, so he walked to the edge of the pool. They jumped out to the end of the branches to take a look. He went inside and headed upstairs for a shower, and they had traveled over to the trees outside our family room. They were looking in the upper windows at him when he got out of the shower! He hoped they were still around when mom and I visited.

On Mother's day, Chuck emailed that I needed to check Facebook for his late night visitor. It turned out to be an anteater that had somehow gotten inside. Chuck had chased it into the laundry room and boxed it off from the rest of the house. After taking a few photos, he returned to bed, leaving the back door open. Apparently, Jefe had tangled with one previously and left it alone, as he knew it had claws. By morning, the anteater had found his way outside. It was difficult to believe Chuck had actually slept, knowing it was inside the house downstairs, but he said he was tired, despite how noisy it was down there.

Chuck sent a message later, on Mother's day night. His mom and lots of others at the nursing home loved the singing telegram we sent her for Mother's day. He had forgotten to mention earlier, there was a surprise waiting for him this morning. He had to clean up anteater poop in the laundry room, yuck. And finally, Jefe needed a mother and wished I could be there. Ahhh, I wished I could be in Costa Rica too. I kept hoping it would happen soon.

The countdown continued to get closer to our Costa Rica vacation. I couldn't wait to go, although I was already becoming a little depressed at the thought that I wouldn't be able to stay. It was a bad thought to have when I hadn't left yet, so I had to put it out of my head.

Overall, Chuck sounded happy and frustrated at the same time. All the work was getting to him. He needed a break. He was working long hours, 7 days a week. He didn't have a TV or anything other than short periods of

Internet to take his mind off of the construction. Chuck wanted it to be perfect for mom and me so badly that he couldn't stand it. He kept saying there was no way to explain how much work still had to get done. He was overwhelmed and really worried about running out of money.

I felt a pit in my stomach now, thinking about all the work Chuck said had to be done that was beyond my understanding for him to describe. It scared me to think, yet again, we were not going to make it with the amount of money we had. I feared the end was drawing near to laying people off, like the last time I had visited Costa Rica. I knew Chuck was thinking the same thing as well. He tried hard, and I wanted him to be happy. I was doing fine here in Tennessee, even though I missed him deeply. It was hard to think of living apart for another year, but I knew I could do it on my end. I hoped he could get the B&B running, so he felt better on his end, to help get through living separated for another year. It was going to take at least another year before I could live in Costa Rica, and that was if we were lucky.

The crew called Jefe "backhoe," because he used his nose to backfill the dirt into the hole when he buried his stuffed squeaky bone. He got incredibility dirty doing this, and it was very funny to watch. Chuck also told me another cute Jefe story. The piece of foam Jefe slept on got wet from a driving rain. A small piece he chewed off was spared, since it was sitting on top of two tires. On top of that was a piece of cardboard, a rag and a tool left there by our foreman. Jefe refused to sleep on the wet foam, so he pulled the small foam piece down. He was curled up real tight to fit on it when Chuck woke up. All the other stuff that had been sitting on the foam was scattered about all over the patio around him. He looked cute on it that morning. Chuck knew what he did to reach that small foam piece would have been funny to watch. Jefe also spent most of the morning chasing the monkeys back into the trees as they tried to come down. Chuck thought they were taunting Jefe. They were very mischievous monkeys.

Chuck heard that our contractor was feeling better but still in intensive care! He finally got well enough to make phone calls from intensive care (apparently they allowed that in Costa Rican hospitals), to help get Chuck the things he needed to prepare for our arrival. It all seemed rushed, but things were coming together at our place. After some time went by, our contractor was able to leave the hospital. He told Chuck he felt better, and he looked better to Chuck. He had a lot of issues, and the doctors wanted to do surgery. However, some complications prevented it. He was going to try to quit smoking again. Hopefully, he would be properly motivated to succeed this time around. We were very grateful he was doing much better.

In the U.S., I continued to struggle to finish my work before vacation. I tried to stay upbeat, but it was hard being apart from Chuck. It was particularly difficult one day in late May. Work was frustrating. The rain seemed to pour harder, and I heard about a death of one of my co-workers. Her death was something I couldn't stop thinking about all day. It showed that you never knew when your life could end. I felt like quitting my job and flying to Costa Rica immediately, to be with Chuck, but those were irrational thoughts. We had to stick to the plan where I made money here and Chuck worked on the construction. For now, we were doing the best we could to make the most of every day apart so that our lives would be fuller and richer, once our plan brought us together in Costa Rica. It was a sacrifice for our future that I hoped we would both live to see.

That day turned out to be a difficult day for Chuck as well. Needless to say, it was not what I wanted to hear. Our contractor had called him to say we were out of money. This was despite Chuck having sent money just two days ago. Apparently, the accountant had not been keeping the bills up to date. They sent Chuck the updated spreadsheet. He couldn't share it with me, to avoid spoiling the surprise on my visit, but he was calling to give me the bad news. Also, our contractor was not feeling well. He wanted to talk about having very little involvement in our project, as he wasn't up to dealing with it anymore. He was checking back into the hospital soon. Now things were really going downhill. Chuck had been worried about him surviving our project, and now our contractor thought he might not make it. Chuck told him we would sit down on Sunday, when mom and I were there, and talk out what to do as the next steps. Now, I was freaking out! My bad day just got worse.

Chuck and I talked some about money and where things stood. He thought we needed $40,000 to finish the job, which meant we were about $11,000 short. We would find out later, this estimate was way under what we needed to finish. He thought I would be surprised at how much work they had done. I was not sure what to believe, though, since he also talked about how much was unfinished in his next breath. He sounded very excited at times, although we didn't know what we would do about the money shortage. It was scary to put it on the credit cards, but that might be our only choice. He was not worried about getting open and having business anymore. He had seen other places around us, and they all seemed to do fine, including the places with poor reviews.

My dad called while I was working. He had a bright idea for me to use one of his trucks when I needed a vehicle, so that I could use the money from the sale of my car for our construction. I was not sure I could part with my car. We had sold our house. Everything that was in it was gone. Our dogs here in the U.S. had passed away. Chuck was gone to Costa Rica. The only thing of mine left in the U.S. was the car. Plus, I didn't know how long I would need to live here. My planned one-year stay could turn into needing the truck for two or three years. Of course, my parents wouldn't mind a longer stay. If I needed to sell my car, I knew I would do it. I was not looking forward to it, although I knew Chuck would say we needed the money.

Chuck called a few days prior to us leaving on vacation. He had a meeting set with our contractor for the morning after I arrived in Costa Rica. It was like déjà vu. Chuck thought it was different this time, because we didn't have to lay people off right away. I was not sure about that yet as I feared we would have to lay people off. He also mentioned that he lost more weight. He was down to 156 pounds. Although I should have been happy for him, it annoyed me. I was here, stressed and gaining weight, while he was there, working and losing weight. I started to feel like I was sinking into a hole of never making it to Costa Rica and wishing I had never heard of it. I hoped that seeing everything there would bring back the feeling that this was all going to be worth it one day, because right now, the stress was getting to me again.

The day before our Costa Rica departure, Chuck emailed that he spent all day cleaning, washing sheets and moving furniture. "Get ready to be blown away!" Thinking about Chuck's email made my imagination run wild, picturing what the place would look like and hoping that I would have a tiki hut. I didn't want to have my hopes up. However, I knew he would not say it was that good if it wasn't going to be really great.

We arrived in Tampa a little after midnight and caught an early morning flight out to Miami, where we made our connecting flight to Costa Rica. Mom was proud of her new passport and ready to leave the country for the first time. It was exciting when we touched down in Costa Rica, because we knew Chuck was waiting for us outside the airport. After picking up our bags, we headed out to look for Chuck.

As soon as I saw the big glass windows at the exit, I spotted Chuck waving to me. He looked great. We hugged and kissed. We drove out of town on the amazing new highway. There were beautiful mountain views everywhere. We stopped on the way to Jaco at a bridge in Tarcoles, where there were huge crocodiles, the size of cars. Mom was amazed. We saw some beautiful sarongs for sale at a stand along the bridge, perfect to hang on some big walls of the B&B for decoration. We didn't buy any that day but would do so later. We stopped for a few more photo ops along the coastal highway past Jaco. Mom loved the tree fences. Because things grew quickly in the tropics, Costa Ricans often planted trees to use as their fence posts. Before I knew it, we were in Dominical. The drive had gone smoothly. I meant that literally too, as the road between Quepos and Dominical was now paved. The government had done much to improve the roads since we first purchased our lot in 2005. The drive from the airport to our place was easy now.

Finally, after a stop for lunch and groceries, we arrived at our place. I saw the tiki hut and the concrete poured around the pool. What a surprise! There was furniture inside the B&B. The new living room suite looked great in the family room. Our old entertainment center, which had been broken some by the movers, was now in one piece with our old Sony TV in it. Our old dining room table with all the chairs was sitting in the dining room, and it looked beautiful. Chuck had put some of our new outdoor wood furniture together for the sunset deck. The handles on the front door of the B&B looked great. The retractable screen doors took some getting used to. Hopefully, guests would catch on to the concept faster than mom did. It was all so much to take in at that moment. The pool deck and the tiki bar were the real surprises for me, and seeing them made me want to cry. This whole time, I had not understood why he wouldn't pour the pool deck. It meant so much to me that he did all of this and wanted it to be a surprise. He had said, "Be prepared to be blown away," and I definitely was. Jefe was a huge hit as well. I wasn't sure he would like me, but he loved me.

We had a good time unpacking the groceries and looking around more. Mom's room, Ocaso, had the most awesome bed I had ever seen. Chuck had designed it, and it was all-encompassing. Mom and I both loved the room's orange paint color and amazing views. The bathroom looked great, with the waterfall faucet and vessel sink. The lime bedroom, Cerro, was all its own, with a wonderful bed. The bamboo floors were beautiful. The wood guys had done an awesome job on the baseboards, the cabinets, the wood doors and the furniture. We went through the other bedrooms, which were all nice, but not as far along as the other two. However, they would also be unique when completed.

Mom and I were excited to call the U.S. and tell everyone what we had seen. Chuck mentioned he revealed photos on Facebook already, that prior night. We had waited all that time for our big surprise, and everyone else had seen it first on-line, while we were traveling. He was sneaky. Now I knew why he was always asking me what time we were leaving for the airport.

We finally unpacked our luggage. I put Jefe's dog bed by the front door of the B&B. We were surprised when he climbed into it. He was adorable. He seemed to know exactly what it was. He left a number of times that day but always returned to his dog bed. I was happy now that we had carried it all the way from the U.S. He loved it, and the color matched the B&B great.

We settled down to a nice dinner of chicken soup. It was Chuck's first meal cooked in the new kitchen. It had taken some time for us to scrounge up the kitchen items he needed from various boxes, but I was glad we did it. After dinner, we sat in the family room to enjoy looking around at things some more. It was dark outside, and the lights in the room made the B&B

feel warm and inviting, maybe too inviting for some unwanted visitors. Chuck glanced over at the dining room when he thought he saw a snake's head outside. Sure enough, it was a snake, dangling his head down into the lights outside the dining room screen door, looking for prey. It was the first time all the lights were on in the B&B, so the lights were obviously attracting lots of attention. Mom was not excited to hear about our first snake sighting on the first night of her first visit to Costa Rica. Needless to say, she wanted all of the doors shut in the B&B before she went to bed that night, but she quickly got over that fear in the following nights.

Since I had very little sleep in the prior 48 hours, I was exhausted and planned to sleep well. I also realized it was my first time to sleep in our new house. We had stayed at a neighbor's house when I was in Costa Rica during my last trip. Plus, I was sleeping on our old mattress with my old pillow in our new house. It felt great, and it was wonderful to snuggle up to Chuck again. I missed him at night. Since I was not used to him being around a lot recently, it was strange to have him there, yet it was comfortable at the same time.

We awoke early to the noises of the howler monkeys and birds. I was still tired, but I was excited to get ready for the day. It was different to shower on the rough concrete floors, pink from fungus. Chuck cleaned them, but it was hard to clean concrete. At least now, he had a kitchen and didn't have to clean his cutting board with chicken goo in the shower anymore. Poor Chuck had lived like that for six months or more.

After breakfast, our contractor showed up for a late morning meeting. We talked about our new game plan. It included the fact that we were almost out of money, so it was going to require a tight ship to finish. Given our contractor had been sick, it was surprising for me see how good he looked. Things went pretty well while we sat outside and talked about the progress. Mom took a good photo of us with our contractor, sitting on the balcony during our meeting. Our contractor said he was concerned we would not make enough money with the B&B at first, due to the poor economic situation in the U.S. He wanted Chuck to help run his construction business and relieve some stress for him, which he needed for health reasons. We weren't sure exactly what he was offering. We hoped the B&B would do well, but it did make me feel that somehow things were going to work out for us in Costa Rica. We had made the right choice, even though this road was not the easy one at the moment. Maybe there would be other opportunities for Chuck, but for now, we all had to focus on just finishing the B&B, with our contractor taking less of a role in the job, due to health reasons. I felt better now that we had a new plan.

Once our contractor left, we all got to work. Mom helped with the kitchen. We worked on cleaning the cabinets and putting in shelving paper. Chuck worked on installing towel bars and other things that we had brought from the U.S. in our luggage. It was hard work but fun too, knowing we were accomplishing things. Before we knew it, the day was gone.

It was odd to be waking up so early. The howler monkeys were howling, and the birds were chirping. It was exciting to be alive in Costa Rica. All the noises were cheering us to get up and get going, because there was so much to do. My mind was also racing with all we needed to accomplish. I didn't want to leave things undone. Mom and I needed to do all that we could to help Chuck. However, Chuck was incredibly cute sleeping. I loved to watch him sleep. He was exhausted from all the hard work he was doing daily. I felt bad now, being upset last December that he didn't hear the people steal the power lines, that night in the pouring rainstorm.

Chuck awoke when he heard some monkey noises. Sure enough as I watched, the monkeys came through the trees. He commented they would climb down to a small palm tree and onto the ground. It was a little routine they had down. When they didn't see anything through the family room doors into our house, they climbed back up the branches to look into the windows of Chuck's office. I ran up to the office, but they didn't like seeing me too much. When they saw me instead of Chuck, they started making lots of noises. By then Chuck was out of the shower and heading out to get coffee. They followed him through the trees as he went downstairs and over to the B&B. I had wanted to get mom up in time to see them. However, Jefe scared them off too quickly. I hoped they would return another day.

After working some that morning, we headed over to the Tilapias El Pavon in Punta Mala for lunch. Even though I had told mom about the tilapia farm before, it impressed her more in person. After lunch, I started unpacking some items for the kitchen. Everything had to be washed again. It was a lot of work to find things, since Chuck packed to fit the most items in a box, which mixed things up. Thankfully, we had a list of items with the boxes numbered. By the end of the first day, I was pretty successful, with only a few broken items. I told mom a number of times that Chuck should kill me for having so many dishes and glasses. Every box I pulled had a different kind of stemware in it. Some, I didn't even remember buying, so it was kind of like opening up Christmas presents.

The dishwasher was not cleaning the plates well, and it was leaking. Chuck came to the conclusion that we had bought regular dishwashing liquid at the store instead of liquid soap for a dishwashing machine. It made perfect sense. After all, it was written in Spanish, so we really hadn't been able to read the label. We used some of his old dry detergent, and the dishwasher worked perfectly. Oh well, another lesson learned.

We headed up the mountain to another neighbor's house for dinner. It was a scarier drive than the prior night, and this drive freaked mom out. We had a nice evening at their house, talking about things, such as why they moved to Costa Rica, what they liked about it and what they didn't. Once again, mom mentioned she would never live there. I knew she was being honest, but I wished she would stop saying that to people. It was rude. Anyway, they had a good Internet connection, and we watched a live video, showing a robot working to stop the leak on the Deep Horizon oil well. Mom was impressed. She was also impressed when they mentioned they had a visit earlier in the week from a Dell computer technician. That a technician came all the way up the mountain to their house actually blew us all away. Mom worked for Dell, so it was a huge deal for her. We left their house a short time after 9:00pm. That time would later become important.

It had been a good day, and I was happy. We had all accomplished a lot, but I was stressed, given we had a lot more to do. I was never going to complain to Chuck about my desk job again. (Well, maybe that last statement was a little harsh. I was not going to complain about it for a little while.) It was fun being in Costa Rica, but it was also overwhelming. I cherished my time with Chuck and that feeling of living together happily in the moment. It was nice to fall asleep to the sound of the rain hitting the metal roof, wondering what adventure the next day would bring.

20 LIVE HAPPILY IN THE MOMENT

THE FIRST DAY OF JUNE started out with us enjoying some time on the sunset deck, when we heard some macaws. We looked up, and there were a pair of blue macaws flying by, off in the distance. Chuck had spotted macaws at our place a number of times now, but it was rare to see the blue ones.

We made a few touristy stops with mom and were surprised when asked if we had felt the earthquake from that prior night. It was a 6+ on the Richter scale that happened around 9:25pm. Mom was highly disappointed at not having felt the quake, since we had apparently been in the car. I was shocked she was upset. She had certainly gotten more adventurous during this trip.

Before we knew it, the day was gone, and it was time to clean up for dinner at a neighbor's house. Jefe was in luck, since he was going along for a doggy visit as well. We played Mexican train (a domino game) for a while and afterwards, ate dinner. We had spaghetti with hamburger buns, covered with garlic, butter and cheese, then toasted in the oven. Mom loved the food. It turned out she was more impressed than I thought, as she attempted to cook this meal later in Tennessee. Mom really liked our neighbors. Of course, when they asked mom about living in Costa Rica, she gave her usual comment about how she would never live there, but she surprised me this time by adding that she felt better about us living there now.

We headed off to bed having had a good day. It felt natural for me to be there, but I had to push away the thought that it was only temporary. One day we would be able to live there together permanently. When that day came, I knew it would be truly amazing. For now, I had to live happily in the moments that Chuck and I had together, without thinking about the future. I drifted off to sleep in happiness once again.

Yet another morning arrived where I awoke to the jungle noises, as I called them now. Mom was also captivated by the sounds in the morning. After breakfast, we drove to Golfito to look at appliances. When we arrived at the duty free stores in Golfito, we were surprised to learn they had increased the ticket amount to $1,000 per person. We found the items we needed in Golfito. We ate lunch and headed out to meet our insurance agent. We stopped by the government insurance headquarters to work on our appeal for earthquake coverage again.   However, with the recent earthquake a few days earlier, they were busy with bigger issues. Our agent hoped to return to us with good news, once they had time to consider our request. We stopped at the Rum Bar for mom to enjoy our favorite pizza and headed to bed early.

That next day, we went to our contractor's place early to borrow his truck for our return drive to Golfito. Mom enjoyed the ride over, as she got to see the small town of Ojochal. Mom was even fascinated by the Costa Rican garbage containers. She couldn't believe what a small amount of trash Costa Ricans generated. They were good at recycling or reusing things, so they generated very little trash, especially compared to us in the U.S. It was such a learning experience to venture outside of your own culture. I could see mom learning new things. I think she was developing a much better appreciation for how others lived and for how spoiled we were in the U.S. on some things. Plus, we could learn from other countries. I really wish everyone had such an opportunity. I believe it would benefit society overall.

We made the same drive back to Golfito, the duty free port. We went through the normal Golfito routine of buying things. It involved finding the salesperson from the previous day to say we wanted the merchandise for the price they quoted us. They took our quoted ticket to a window. Once there, we showed our paperwork to prove we had passed the required waiting period to make purchases, and they confirmed we were not over our quota for the specific product we were buying. They completed the paperwork and allowed us to pay. We took that ticket to another window, where we picked up our merchandise. They brought it out and unpacked it for us. They allowed us to inspect it for defects and showed us it worked properly by plugging it in for us. After we agreed it was not defective, they re-boxed the item and asked us to sign off to show it was inspected. Mom thought we were crazy for sticking our hand in the refrigerator we bought to see if it was cold. Eventually, she laughed, because she realized what we were doing. It shocked her that this process was going on at the store for everything that was bought. However, she agreed it made sense. After inspection, we were responsible for carrying our purchased items or paying someone else to carry them for us to the next store to repeat the same process for the next item we wanted to purchase. As a side note, it is best to be cautious when getting others to carry your items, especially of middlemen. They get you to hire them, but they hire someone else to carry your items, expecting you to also pay that person, without telling you until the end.

The other drivers constantly driving toward the middle of the road freaked out mom. It was a frequent occurrence in Costa Rica. Part of it had to do with many people walking along the side of the road, given sidewalks were uncommon, and part of it had to do with the jungle, which sometimes encroached upon the roads. Hence, a number of Costa Ricans tended to drive toward the middle of the road to avoid pedestrians. Mom recognized this, but it still was upsetting to her that the drivers frequently forgot to get over into their own lane when there were cars coming toward them, despite no pedestrians being around.

When we were about halfway home, a policeman stepped out from nowhere with a radar gun and waved us over. I was sure we were speeding, but he let us go without a ticket. I figured he felt bad giving Chuck a ticket after seeing mom hanging outside of the window taking photos and after learning she was on vacation from the U.S. As a side note, he was a traffic policeman in Costa Rica, but there are other policemen who you may see that cannot give tickets. There are always police stops in Costa Rica along the way for one thing or another, such as check points for immigration status and check points looking for illegal drugs or alcohol. However, Chuck and I always seemed to get stopped by the police somewhere other than the typical stops. In this case, though, we were clearly speeding. I guessed you just had to be prepared to deal with the police when traveling there. Mom actually liked this about Costa Rica. It made her feel very safe, and I have heard that comment from other people as well.

It was nice to clean up and be going out to a fancy restaurant in Ojochal with Chuck and mom. I knew mom would be surprised. From the moment we walked into Citrus, she couldn't believe this place was off of a gravel road in the middle of the rainforest. The service was good. The food was great. The atmosphere was excellent, and mom thought the dessert was the best she had ever eaten. Mom was a dessert expert too, as she eats it at almost every meal, including breakfast. She had a good time at dinner that night and was completely impressed. She was also getting a better picture of why people would go to Costa Rica to stay with us and of how lucky they would be to have so many great dining choices nearby. It was another happy day of memories.

I washed Chuck's laundry for him, but it was odd to have no closet or furniture to put away his clean clothes. I obviously had seen the boxes next to our bed with the stacks of folded t-shirts and shorts on them, but it never hit me that it was his make shift closet. When I asked him what he did with his underwear, he told me it was in the box that I had been piling my dirty clothes on all week. I felt terrible. I was proud that he now had a kitchen and that he was going to move to the B&B, where he could have a bedroom with storage.

After dinner, while we watched photos on the TV mom had taken during this trip, Chuck and I enjoyed our bottle of wine together, using some of our old Mexican stemware. It was nice to have some of our old stuff out of storage. He played with my hair on the couch, and we relaxed on my final night in the B&B. I wished we could stay like this forever. I was a little sad, but it had been a great trip. We had completed all we set out to do, and I was re-energized. It was almost time to go back to the U.S. to accomplish all I needed to do, so Chuck could stay here to do his part. We were both lucky to have found each other and be on this new adventure together. It was hard living apart, but we would tough it out, because we had a strong marriage that was made to last.

As we got ready to leave the next day, Jefe decided to go with us. Chuck had a hard time getting him out of the Xterra. Finally, it was time to say goodbye to Ocaso Cerro and head out to San Jose. It was difficult watching Chuck shut the gate that morning, as we waited in the car. I fought to hold back the tears, knowing it would be a long time before I returned.

Mom was impressed by our shopping experience in San Jose, including the escalator that took the magnetic wheeled shopping carts, the helpful employees in the stores and the security in the parking lots. We spent that night at our favorite B&B in Escazu, Casa Laurin, and went to the airport the next morning. Mom almost cried when Chuck said goodbye, but for some reason, I was at peace with things.

Back in Tennessee, I spent days getting things caught up again. After the next crew payroll, Chuck was going to be down to only $500. It was scary that we were almost out of money again. I decided to call on a credit card offer that I had. At least for now, it gave us the money to continue with finishing things.

I missed Chuck, but life was good. I kept dreaming about the B&B, our house and the future! Going to Costa Rica had recharged my batteries, and having a finish line in sight had made a huge difference for me. Now that mom had seen all Chuck had accomplished in person, she was more impressed with him than she had been before, but I knew all along how special he was.

Mom had her foot wrapped one morning. Her foot, hip and sinuses were all bothering her now. None of these had bothered her in Costa Rica, even though it was raining there, which typically made them worse. I told her I thought it was healthier there, and she tended to agree. Chuck used to tell me that I needed a doctor's note to work there, because it made me healthier. There was really something to being in Costa Rica that was healthier, and it was interesting that mom felt it already just from her one visit.

Chuck started on tiling the pool. It was brutal working in the sun. A few weeks into the month, he posted some photos on Facebook. One was a great photo that included the finished stucco on our house, some tiling on the pool and some thatching on the tiki hut. The other one showed another angle of the pool tile with the ocean in the background. Boy had he ever tiled a lot of the pool in such a short time. It was amazing. He thought it would take five to six weeks to finish. Little did he know. It would take tremendously longer.

Almost three weeks into the month, Chuck called to catch up. The palm guys had finished the thatch on the tiki bar. It looked like it had a bad hair day. There were things sticking up and out everywhere, but they said it was normal. They would return in a month to trim it up with a haircut once things had fallen out with enough time. It looked awesome. The pool tiling was not going well. He needed cloudy weather with no rain, which limited when he could work, and the tile saw was shattering the glass tile. Finding the rest of the matching bathroom tile was still a disaster too. He was terribly depressed and worried about money. He only had $300 in the bank. I felt bad that he was there working very hard, and I couldn't be there to help. He thought I had the bad end of the deal, living in Tennessee with my parents and working a stressful job. He had the good side of it, living in Costa Rica and being physically active and healthy. In reality, we were both doing our parts and suffering in our own way. One day, we would be together again, and we would look back on this as a journey that was worth it. I didn't regret it in the moment. It had not been easy, and I had certainly screwed up some things lately at work that I normally didn't do. I knew this journey was wearing on my mind, but I also knew we were following our hearts. It was peaceful and happy to be in Costa Rica. That was where we both belonged. He just needed to keep doing what he was doing. I had to find some way to obtain the money we needed.

I completed the last wire transfer to Chuck in late June. It was a little depressing to think that all of the money I had placed on the credit card was now gone. But it was also exciting to think it meant we were close to the end of construction. Since the wire transfer took time to arrive there, I worried about Chuck driving to San Jose for tile with only $300 in the bank. It was a long drive, and I feared he might have car trouble. Thankfully he made the trip fine.

One day, ICE tried to turn the power off for the B&B. Chuck had paid the bill via the Internet, but it had apparently not shown the amount properly. Our contractor called ICE. He straightened things out to keep the power on and hopefully fixed things going forward.

As the month came to an end, Chuck was still working on pool tile, and the crew had moved on to laying stone for the pool deck. Jefe had his first sleepover. Chuck said Cindy had followed Jefe home from the neighbor's house that prior night, and they were very cute sleeping together that next morning.

21 ONE DAY AT A TIME

THE YEAR WAS OFFICIALLY half over. I had survived living in Tennessee without Chuck. Sometimes, it seemed like forever, and at others, I couldn't remember where my time had gone. I wondered if Chuck realized the year was half over. We kept pushing the opening date for the B&B back, despite being positive of the new date we picked each time. Regardless of the date, the important part was that we did a good job for our guests when we opened. I knew that would be the case when the day arrived, and I knew that day wasn't meant to be in the first half of 2010!

It was not long after dinner when Chuck called. He promised to be careful on his second San Jose trip for the tile and to email as soon as he got back. Chuck thought the crew might need two more weeks working on the stone for the pool deck and another two weeks on the stone for the B&B walls. That meant they might finish mid-August, but I didn't see it happening that quickly.

Chuck gave me information on a DHL drop-off point nearby our property where I could send him new wet saw blades made specifically to cut glass tile. We hoped they would make it easier for him to tile the pool. At the shipping store, I ran into a problem when the U.S. DHL people couldn't find the Costa Rican drop-off point in their system. They did not sound very convinced I should be sending it. If Chuck had not gotten architecture drawings there before, then I would have been nervous too. However, I knew in Costa Rica the DHL people would find it. I filled out a customs form stating a value for the shipment, and they printed out a bill of lading for it. Chuck was expected to pay the amount declared by Costa Rican customs officials when he picked it up. By 7:00pm that night, it was processed in Nashville, on its way for San Jose, Costa Rica over the 4th of July weekend. I hoped it arrived as planned. Although I knew nothing ever really worked the same in Costa Rica, it usually still had a way of working out in the end.

Chuck arrived back to the B&B from San Jose around 2:30pm. He had bought bathroom tile but had to switch from the planned color. He was in a good mood. At least, he was until he received a balance sheet from our contractor, showing we were $9,000 in the hole. After that email, he knew we were in trouble, and he needed a drink. I told him to focus on the tiling, and we would figure out something to do about the money.

It was all overwhelming. We constantly struggled to move forward, only to be beaten back down with bad news and yet another obstacle to overcome. I recalled a flood victim had said on the news one night that you had to take things one day at a time, because to look at the overall picture was heartbreaking. You simply had to survive it day by day. I decided that was now how I had to look at things. One day, we planned to start paying back all of these things we owed. I hoped that day would come very soon, but for now, we had to still take spending it in stride, one day at a time. Somehow, I had to find the money to get us out of the hole and moving forward again. We were still more fortunate than many other people, and I was thankful for the opportunity given to us to work toward our dream.

After I spoke to Chuck, I checked my emails again. I had a response from a friend in Florida who I had emailed earlier that day. He wrote back to say I had used the word hope in almost every sentence I had written. He commented it was good to be hopeful, because hopes and dreams were what made life worth living. I had to smile. Wasn't that true? My friend didn't say to slow down. However, I realized that I needed to, as all my comments were about my hope for the future. True happiness came from living in the moment. In my opinion, most of us tended to live with too much chaos in our lives, always rushing to get us to the future without enjoying the present enough. I was anxious to live in Costa Rica, but I was enjoying spending time with my family. I needed to appreciate those moments more while I was having them in Tennessee.

I did not sleep well that night. I was constantly stressed over Chuck's email statement that we were desperate. A friend owed him money, and since we were desperate, he was going to beg him to get paid. I didn't like to feel desperate. I tried to think what it would be like if we had still been living in our old house in St Petersburg and never gone down the dream path to Costa Rica. Would I have money like I used to have and not need to worry? I quickly realized that would not be the case. Chuck might have had a heart attack by now. We would have been worried about the Gulf of Mexico oil spill coming into our back yard. We still would have had things to worry about. In the long run, Costa Rica was going to all be worth it. We had to get past this little hump and take it one day at a time. Unfortunately, rationalizing things out still did not help me sleep.

Early that morning, I cleaned up my car and had it ready for sale. I hoped someone would buy it, and fast. Now, I felt desperate for money. I almost cried, thinking about getting rid of it. In the end though, I reminded myself it was just another material thing that I had to let go of to get to a happier life in Costa Rica, so I was fine with it. I only hoped it went to a good home.

There was a big July 4th neighborhood party in Costa Rica. Chuck enjoyed the food. He and Jefe got wet on the ride home, so they were "2 wet puppies." He was not sure what we would do, but he was sure we would get through it somehow. I was happy to hear he was doing better. He had company, and he was working hard. He was happy making the most of his life in Costa Rica without me, just like I was doing here without him. However, we both missed each other. We were both worried like we should be, but we had to keep our stress under control.

Chuck wired more money to our contractor, which left him with just enough to buy the remaining materials we needed. He planned to talk to our contractor about laying off the crew the next week. It was hard to be motivated, with the sky falling in on him.

Selling the car was a definite positive for us. It was a relief to have the money, and I felt good about it going to a nice home. Chuck was happy to hear the good news. It now seemed feasible that it would all come together, so we could be open by September. After the B&B opened, we could tackle the other bills from there, such as corporate attorney fees and property taxes coming up later in the year. This was going to be a challenging time for us.

A few weeks into the month, Chuck sent an email about his day. He had a long hard day of grouting. He spent 11.5 hours and went through 11.5 bags of grout. Obviously, his hands ached. He was completely amazing. Chuck took progress photos. The bedroom armoires were beautiful. The whimsical bathroom mirrors looked like Mickey Mouse ears to me, even though they reminded Chuck of the Flintstones. They were not at all what I had expected to see, but they were a conversational piece no doubt. Another photo showed the blue tiled curved pool, the white coralina stone deck, the tiki hut with its textured roof and Jefe walking up the stairs. This one blew me away. I absolutely loved this photo. It visually took my breath away to see it in my mind the way I knew it would one day be with landscaping in the background and water in the pool. Plus, the fact Jefe was in the photo made me smile.

Chuck went back to work cutting the glass pool tiles with the special wet saw blades I sent to him. Unfortunately, because we had unmeshed paper fronted tile, the water from the wet saw made the tiles come off the paper if they got too wet. It was tricky work. He felt sick and was lonely. He was so sweet to say he was lonely. It broke my heart that I could not be there to take care of him when he was sick.

I woke up around 6:00am with my mind racing. My right side had started to hurt more that night. It had been that way for a while now, building up worse with time over money issues and time drawing close for our crew to be laid off. It was all stress related.

A few days later, Chuck emailed the deed was done, and it had gone pretty well. The whole crew had suspected the layoff was coming for the past two weeks. Also, the person who owed him money said he was sending him a check for a portion of it. I was glad he had some good news on such a bad day.

The next day, I emailed Chuck with some questions. He emailed quickly to stand by that he had VERY bad news. The time was 5:04pm on his email. Did he hurt himself like cut his hand off? Did our contractor die? Did one of our workers die, because we laid them off? Did one of our workers become upset and shoot our contractor? Did something happen to Jefe? Was there a huge earthquake? Did the pool collapse and slide down the hill? Did a roof collapse? Did the road collapse? Did we have a fire or a theft from the house? Was the car stolen? My mind was racing with scenarios as fast as I could think, which made my chest pound. I could hear my heart thumping in my ears. Was I the queen of worst-case scenarios? I had to tell myself to calm down. I waited, wishing Chuck could type faster and thinking if he lost a hand, it would take him forever to type an email. Why we were living apart like this? Was it really worth it? Please let things not be as bad as the capital VERY he typed.

Eventually my email pinged. The time was only 5:13pm, but it felt like hours had passed. I held my breath for the worst. There was a big accounting error in March that was corrected. After all of that, he was only talking about money! What a relief. I opened the balance sheet and it showed we were $6,300 in the hole now. Certainly not good news, but not news anywhere close to the devastation I had been envisioning. Plus, if there was one mistake, there could be more. The entire spreadsheet needed to be checked. Fortunately, by the time I was done rechecking everything, we were getting money back.

Chuck was already in bed before I had completed my review, so he awoke to the good news. He emailed I was the best! An $8,000 swing in our direction was amazing. He knew it took a lot of time and effort to sort through everything. Now he felt like we might have a chance after all. This was another reason he loved me so much! He felt motivated now and was off to work. It felt good to make his day after knowing he went to bed feeling down the prior night.

There had been a big electrical storm on Tuesday night. It was the biggest storm Chuck had ever been in before, and it was scary. Jefe was shaking like crazy and running around like a mad dog. The lightning was everywhere. As soon as Chuck saw a flash, he would instantly hear the thunder, which meant it was right on top of them. It also was like he could see the bolts coming to the ground. He had never seen anything like it.

Since the electrical storm, the gate no longer worked, along with lights in several rooms of the B&B. Also, the Internet was not working. He already called the electrician, the gate guy and the Internet people. He hadn't even driven out of the gate himself for the first time yet, before it tore up already. It was hard to believe we had yet more problems to struggle through.

He was working on the pool tile still, but it was so much work. He had read the glass tile research information I had emailed him. We were doing most of the stuff in the articles already. He did learn that once wet, the paper would stick better to the tile, so now he had developed a three day process for laying it. On the first day, he wet it to let it re-dry so that it would stick better. On the second day, he marked the tile to clearly show where to cut it and used the wet saw to make the cut. It was sticking better, without falling off, now that it was pre-wet the first day, and he laid it out to let it dry again after being cut the second day. On the third day, he put up what he cut from the prior day and pulled the paper off. The cycle of prep work began for future days. He needed good weather and shade to proceed, but following this process, he was able to lay about 12 square feet of tile per day.

Chuck hired back a few of the crew. Their words were "Pura Vida" when he asked them to return to work so quickly. The gate guy fixed the gate. It took him two hours at a cost of $60. I went to bed feeling much better, knowing the gate was working again.

Mom filled me in on what happened all week in Tennessee, while I was out of town for work. It was strange to think that in four days I had to know what had gone on in Tennessee while I was away, yet when I was living in Florida, I missed out on weeks of activity without it bothering me. How things had changed in my life now.

Chuck and I talked for about 45 minutes to catch up on things. In the overall conversation, Chuck was depressed about finishing. We had spent much more money for things than he had budgeted, like spray for the bamboo, stuff for the tiki bar and sealer for the coralina stone. I tried to be positive, but he seemed to be depressed, no matter what I said. If we didn't make money with the B&B, then I was never going to pay off our debt to get to Costa Rica. It was too overwhelming to think about, though. I felt confident it would work, but a lot of it was up to Chuck. He had a lot of pressure to get it done. I felt bad about that, in times like this.

In a little over two weeks, Chuck and I planned to meet in Florida for our anniversary. I still felt like something bad was going to happen in Costa Rica while he was gone to Florida. I wished I could shake that feeling, and I wished I could shake off some of the weight I had gained. I got on the scales. I knew I was becoming pudgy, but I had gained six pounds. That was the kind of weight someone gained after pigging out on a long cruise. I had told Chuck I was gaining weight in an earlier email, and he said don't get pudgy! He needed a slim, trim naked sex machine ready for him when he got to Florida. I certainly was not going to be trim by August vacation, but I knew he wouldn't care. He was going to be happy to see me, no matter what.

22 THE MAGIC OF PURA VIDA

I LOVED THE MONTH OF AUGUST. It marked lots of special occasions, like our wedding anniversary, my parents' wedding anniversary and my mom's birthday. This year, it was more special, as Chuck and I would be celebrating our 20th wedding anniversary together.

I made a brief comment in an email to Chuck that I might cook mom's birthday dinner. He wrote back that I needed to plan time out to cook for the entire day! His email made me laugh. I was a slow cook. But did he really think I needed an entire day to cook only three items? In retrospect, I did mess up making a no bake dessert recipe once for Bunko. Maybe that episode had something to do with why he thought three items were a lot for me to cook.

I also had to laugh at Chuck's comment that he spent time grouting and he expected to have the pool walls done in two days. He had just commented that prior day that his hands were raw, so he planned to take a break from grouting. I knew he wouldn't take a break. He was like the energizer bunny.

Chuck was in a good mood another day. The wooden bathtub was going to look unreal. The crew was still sanding it down. After it was smooth, they had to put a clear waterproof coat on it. At $130 a gallon, he was hopeful we only needed one gallon. Our contractor was doing really great. He had given up some bad habits and was taking better care of himself. Chuck was amazed that he could be so much healthier. It didn't surprise me though. I knew how much healthier Chuck had become after he left his desk job and started working in Costa Rica. It was a reminder that how we decide to live our lives impacts our health.

We talked about the clear rope lights for the tiki bar. Chuck tried to find some wire ties that were clear in San Isidro to help hold up the lights, but he struck out. Our electrician refused to use the white ones Chuck bought and insisted Chuck keep looking for clear ones. I thought it was funny that the crew took so much pride in our place that they told Chuck what to do.

We talked about our upcoming Florida vacation. It was going to be a lot of fun. Chuck surprised me at the end of the call, when he mentioned he was concerned how Jefe would hold up while he was away on vacation in FL. He referenced mom's Internet research from May, which mentioned separation anxiety as a common trait for Weimaraners. Apparently, Chuck admitted he worried about Jefe's separation anxiety, even during a normal day when he left to do errands. I had no idea he had even read mom's email on her research. He was very sweet to worry about leaving Jefe behind all the time, and I felt bad that he was so concerned.

Chuck had a big day tiling on the pool. He worked until noon, even though he was in the blistering sun. He laid 33 pieces on the main floor and 15 sections that he had cut previously for the trough walls. He tiled around one wall opening in the trough and one section that needed to be re-done in a corner. He finished cutting and laying the edge pieces for the shallow area too. After lunch, he vacuumed the B&B and did some touch up painting in Cano and Vista Mar. He cut holes in the armoires in Cano and Cerro for the refrigerator plugs. He brought the other two refrigerators over from our house, so they were all in place. He marked and cut 11 more sections of tile for the trough wall, to be ready for the next day. He made some twice-baked yucca, since he couldn't buy a big baked potato in Costa Rica. They were great! He ate one with some leftover cilantro lime pesto pasta from two nights before. Wow, what an awesomely productive day he had. I was once again totally impressed with how hard he worked and amazed to think how different his Costa Rican work days were from his prior work days in the U.S. He worked hard at both, but I knew he was much happier in Costa Rica.

I had a surprise email regarding our Costa Rican residency. There were a few items that were needed from us. They wanted copies of our entire new passports and a completed travel registration form with the U.S. Department of State. At least things were still moving forward.

To celebrate mom's birthday, I took her and my aunt to a little teashop for lunch. It was a nice drive there, through the countryside. It surprised us to see their sandwich in a bowl. Now I understood why it said on the menu that it had to be eaten with a fork! It was nice to be home in Tennessee to share such a special time with family.

After dinner, I looked for news from Chuck. We had a major ant invasion going on at the B&B that had him worried. He had to drive 20 minutes to get cash to buy bug spray, because he spent all his cash earlier, when he was buying wire for our electrician, due to the phone lines at the store being down and unable to take credit cards. If the ants weren't gone by Monday, he planned to arrange to fumigate the B&B. On top of that, he thought we had a water leak, because the water pump was running nonstop. He needed to contact our contractor about it. Finally, some surveyors were working around property lines outside our gate and down the driveway. They marked the edge of our driveway and the south boundary of the lot to our south with ribbons. He was not sure what to think. He emailed the lot owner to the north of us, and he did not know anything about it. It was odd. On the positive side, it was a beautiful sunset and might be the official return of sunsets over the ocean.

The news on the surveyors definitely had me worried. I was also worried about how our contractor could possibly find the water leak underground. I had been awake all night worrying about things, with my stomach in knots. Why did we constantly have problems?

I received an email from a friend who I had told earlier what a stressful week it had been for me. She commented it was difficult enough to start a business from scratch, but it was very difficult to imagine how hard it was to do it in a foreign country while living apart from your spouse and trying to live at home with your parents. Wow, it did sound overwhelming, the way she said it. We sure did sound a lot braver than I thought. I kept telling myself we had to get through this somehow.

By early afternoon, our attorney responded to my email regarding the surveyors. We did not need to panic. The national registry clearly showed we still owned our property. The municipality in Costa Rica would sometimes send out surveyors to check what we declared before them to be sure it matched reality, so this might be a simple procedure. It made me feel better to hear this from our attorney. I still wondered if this was going to lead to a problem in the future, but at least for now, I could relax. However, I was going to mark my calendar to check the national registry frequently, to be sure we stayed owners, in case the surveyors were up to anything fraudulent.

Chuck responded that the ants were under control. He also found the water leak. Luckily, it was only a pipe right outside the main house. It scared me that we had a leak at all, but I was grateful that he found it. It was a relief to have our immediate problems resolved.

Finally, it was time for vacation. We met at the Tampa airport and spent the night at our friend's Clearwater condo. We were exhausted, but it was great to be close together again.

The next day marked our 20th wedding anniversary, August 18th. Time had gone by quickly. I certainly found it hard to believe, considering we had lived apart during the year. It was not at all how I would have envisioned our 20th anniversary year, but we had made the best of our time apart.

We spent our anniversary day enjoying some typical Florida fun. We walked the beach and ate lunch at Frenchy's. We listened to our friend Tony D play the guitar at Caddy's. We enjoyed some chill time after dinner at the condo. We talked and talked that night, which made it so much fun. It was a great way to spend the day and catch up on things with just the two of us. Plus, we were looking forward to the rest of the week, when we would get to spend time with our friends. It was a perfect 20th anniversary!

As soon as we were ready the next day, Chuck was watching TV. He was very funny. He loved to see TV, now that he had the opportunity to catch up on all he had been missing. He was particularly in love with the food network and HGTV, since these were the two main channels we used to watch. I enjoyed watching him watch TV.

We had a great lunch at our favorite Mexican restaurant, Carmelita's, and we shopped a little. Most importantly, we faxed the updated stamped page on Chuck's passport to our Costa Rican residency attorney to show he had left the country. Despite the fact he was legal to stay in Costa Rica for more than 90 days with the file number showing we had applied for residency, a current stamp was needed to proceed with our residency paperwork. This was contradictory, but we had learned sometimes things just didn't make sense in Costa Rica. After completing our errands, we spent the day with friends.

We slept in a little late on Friday. It was nice to be in bed next to Chuck. I missed him being so close. We had fun holding hands and talking that day. Chuck said that even when things seemed to be going really bad in Costa Rica, one of our workers could look at him with a smile and say "Pura Vida." After that, everything was all of a sudden better. He didn't know why, except it made him realize that the problems he had while living a simpler life in Costa Rica (although we hadn't quite gotten there yet) were nothing compared to the problems he had while living the rat race in the U.S. Plus, he always eventually figured out a solution to his problems in Costa Rica, so things got better. We needed to get me to Costa Rica and open the B&B to make it perfect for him there. It made me smile to think that he at least had someone else to give him some encouragement in Costa Rica. Also, whenever I needed some encouragement here in the U.S., I planned to think of this story and say to myself, "Pura Vida." One day, a simpler life in Costa Rica awaited me too. It was a peaceful bliss that worked like magic.

We ate at more of our favorite restaurants, enjoyed listening to more guitar music, and spent more time with various friends throughout that afternoon and evening at the beach and in Tampa. I wished we could be like normal couples, going out together on dates to meet friends like the old days or staying at home, cooking dinner together in the kitchen. I looked forward to reaching that point one day in Costa Rica.

After eating breakfast on Saturday with our friends, Chuck and I reviewed our B&B budget. We still had to pay for the landscaping, gravel, pool equipment installation, signage, bathtub, crew salary and sealers. Once again, our best-laid plan did not work out as we had hoped. Something had to go, and it was probably landscaping. We finally agreed on our starting price points for our rooms. It was a huge accomplishment for us to have these few details out of the way.

We finished our day at a friend's house party. We arrived about 3:00pm and ended up staying until close to 10:00pm. We had fun eating, drinking, talking and playing in the pool. It turned out to be a great memory of our 20th wedding anniversary. It had been a great stay in Florida.

I awoke a few times that night to look over at Chuck. I watched him lying asleep next to me and implanted in my brain what it was like to snuggle up against him. I knew it would be a long time before we got to be in the same bed again. It made me smile, but it made me sad at the same time. But there was no time to be sad. I needed to sleep. I forced myself to close my eyes to sleep again.

We didn't have much time to sit together in the airport. It was all right, because I felt the fear of him leaving welling up inside me. I was fighting the tears. If he stayed long, then they would flow well before he left. He kissed and hugged me hard. I told him three months would go by quickly, but he shook his head no. I knew it wouldn't, but I had to pretend it would to get through it. He looked back smiling and waved at me as he headed out of the terminal. I waved back, and I walked off. It hurt to know he was hurting inside as much as I was. He wasn't hiding it anymore either. He was lonely in Costa Rica. I got to my gate and immediately felt the pain inside me. I tried to read my book, and after remembering Chuck's earlier "Pura Vida" story, I relied on its magic to help me feel better. Periodically, I thought of where Chuck might be along his journey. Before long, my flight was touching down in Nashville.

I stayed busy unpacking, checking emails and paying bills. Again, I did my best to hold back tears. We had a great trip, so it was fun to tell others about it, but it was hard not to think about how long it would be before I saw Chuck again. It was around 4:30pm when Chuck called my cell. He had no problems with his flight. Everything at the house was good. Jefe was fine. I told him I missed him already, and he missed me too. It made me sad in one way, but happy to be loved so much.

It was going to be a rough night to sleep without Chuck. It was the first of many nights to go. In fact, I had 89 nights to spend alone until I saw Chuck again. It made my stomach flip flop to think about it. At least for now, I tried to obtain some comfort from marking numbers off the countdown.

I found myself becoming very depressed. In fact, I was crying when Chuck called. The neighborhood guys had talked Chuck into going charter fishing with them as their fourth person. They did not catch many fish, which was disappointing. However, they saw quite a few whales, which turned it into a worthwhile charter, so he was happy.

Our conversation was even kind of funny, in that we talked about who had it better – him or me. I thought he did now that the house was better organized. At least, he got to live at our place to see what we were working so hard to finish. Plus, he had Jefe. He thought I had it better, because I had family and friends close by to keep me company. It was strange how we had different perspectives on things. It was not that long ago when we both felt the situation was reversed. I didn't want to live in his living conditions or work as hard as he was working every day. He didn't want to live in Tennessee doing a stressful desk job, like mine. We each thought our own situation was better than the others back then.

I tried to be optimistic as I got off the phone, but instead, I found myself in tears again. Leaving Chuck in Florida broke my heart. I was trying to be strong, but it was difficult. What I needed at the moment was time to pass in order to heal. I tried to count my blessings, that we were both healthy and much better off financially than many others. In retrospect, hopefully we were over the half-way point of living apart. If this was truly the case, then I felt I could cope with things. It was the unknown deadline that was making it difficult to handle.

Toward the end of the month, Chuck cut the last of the pool tiles (he hoped). The end was in sight on the pool. Our new maid was coming Monday, so he was excited. He told our two remaining crew to work through the end of the next week. He was lonely there, too, without me. But he was sure we could survive this time apart. He thought I should not focus on being apart so much and try to stay busy. Staying busy was what I had to do.

I needed to find a way to relax. I needed to get into a better mood, or it was going to be a long struggle over the next nine month minimum I knew I would be living in Tennessee, apart from Chuck. It was better to learn to live in the moment happily than to go through what I was doing to myself now. I had become unhappy, and I realized it was within my control to fix things. I had to force myself to snap out of it!

The nursery guy visited the B&B before he designed a landscape plan. Chuck made it clear we did not have a big budget. He said some things were not expensive. For example, he suggested a Travelers palm for $25 that in two years would be huge. We loved tropical plants, so the thought of owning a Travelers palm had us both excited. The landscaping options in Costa Rica were mindboggling. It was going to be hard to wait for the landscape proposal to be completed. We just hoped we could afford something nice on our small budget.

I knew this journey was going to be hard, but it was turning out to be harder than I thought. I heard a number of people say they didn't think I could be apart from Chuck for so long. They just didn't understand; we had no choice. We wanted to be together, so we could both be happier. After all, our journey wasn't about building a materialistic B&B; it was about us being together in Costa Rica to meet people at the B&B, where we could live a happier and healthier lifestyle. The bottom line was sometimes we had to do things we didn't want to do, like us living apart. We had sacrificed our time together, and I hoped it was going to be worth it to help us reach our end goal.

Given all we had been through on this journey to date, our relationship and appreciation for each other was stronger as a result. I knew I appreciated Chuck more already. I was resolved to making improvements in myself during this separation period, so I would be a better person when we were back together. I knew I would never learn to cook, though. I didn't have that in me, so I would always be Chuck's assistant in the kitchen. However, I decided my new goals were to work out more and learn Spanish. These goals gave me something to focus on besides being apart from Chuck. Once I got my new routine established, I thought the time was going to fly by much faster.

Chuck emailed two more easy days of grouting until the pool was done. All he could do was think about me. He missed me and looked forward to being together. Since things were getting close to completion, he saw what living in Costa Rica together would be like, and it was exciting. The maid was scheduled to arrive the next morning at 7:00am. After things were clean, he planned to start decorating. It was good to know that Chuck had a nice day and that time was going by fast for him. He envisioned a good life there together for us, which was wonderful.

The month ended with Chuck officially completing the grouting of the pool. It was a huge victory for him. For me, it was great to end the month happy again instead of sad, as I had new goals to focus on instead of focusing so much on living apart from Chuck.

23 EACH DAY IS PRECIOUS

YEAH! SEPTEMBER WAS FINALLY HERE! Chuck emailed that he couldn't explain how much he missed me. It was such a sweet email. It felt great to be loved so much. He never used to say such things to me. I wondered if these sweet emails had something to do with why I thought about sex more than ever. Would my thoughts stay, once we were living together again? Was this some kind of phase where I wanted it more, because I couldn't have it? Was it an age thing that everyone went through? Was it having so much sex when we were together for our short spurts, that now I wanted more? Whatever it was, I knew I had never appreciated our sex life enough until we were living apart.

Based on my new personal goals, I finished my first day of completing 10,000 walking steps and started my Spanish lessons. I decided to use our old Spanish CD's. Hopefully, I remembered parts and at least completed them all this time around. A friend was sending me their Rosetta Stone CD's too. Maybe between the two sets, some Spanish had to sink into my brain.

Chuck finally received the landscaping design. It came in at $9,400, well over our $3,000 budget. The plan had 2,663 plants. A great plan was possible at $7,500 that would attract lots of wildlife and include a section of fruit trees. As a percentage of the entire project, it didn't sound like much, for a plan that would knock it out of the park. Chuck really wanted to do it right and spend the $7,500. I knew it would be great if he loved it. But where would we find the money? Fortunately, my parents agreed and loaned us the money to proceed.

It was a two-hour ordeal, but the wooden bathtub was in place. Chuck loved it. It was very quiet with the crew gone for good. He found my Tennessee hat and purple blanket while looking through a box that day. It made him sad I was not there. We needed to be together. He loved me very much, and he knew Jefe loved me too. His words were so sweet they made me cry.

Macaws love almond trees, and Chuck found out we had several already on our property. We talked about money or our lack thereof, which was a little scary. He mentioned how our new maid was such a hard worker, but she liked to do things her own way. She refused to use the commercial grade mop bucket he bought and the broom he had. Instead, she liked to mop with her broom. She used a towel with a hole cut in it that she slipped over the broom handle. She pulled the towel off and washed it out in the sink. He was surprised, but it actually worked pretty well as a mop. He wished I were there to help him unpack and decorate. We were supposed to be doing it together, and it stunk that we couldn't. It was depressing to realize we would need some money for startup supplies for the B&B, such as room safes and stock for the mini refrigerators. We had to figure something out, but I didn't know what that something would be, since we were maxed out for money options already.

That night, I realized we should be able to access our equity in Costa Rica for a loan. It seemed stupid that with all our equity there, we should be living paycheck to paycheck. I did some research on-line, and it appeared feasible.

Later the next day, Chuck posted some progress photos on Facebook. The bathtub was incredible. The pool looked great totally tiled, and the stone on our house was awesome. There were no words to describe the tiki hut. I knew it would be my favorite spot. Chuck had hung our fish sculpture in the middle of the ceiling. It was the biggest surprise. The rope lights set it off too. I looked forward to sitting at the tiki bar and enjoying a margarita there one day.

Chuck was very excited about the possibility of taking out a new mortgage to finish our place in Costa Rica. However, even if the construction was done, our place was not truly completed until I got there. He was very sweet. Since the crew was now gone, he was lonelier without them, as they had at least given him some companionship during workdays.

I spoke to a mortgage lady in Costa Rica, but it didn't sound too hopeful. The banks did not like that our place was a B&B, and they did not like that it was too close to the end of construction. Later that day, I read that Moody's upgraded Costa Rica's financial rating, which meant it should be easier for people to obtain loans and invest there. It was now a preferred investment destination, based on debt reduction and the financial stability of the country. Maybe that good news would help us obtain our loan!

It was nice to hear that Chuck missed me. Of course, I missed him too. It made me smile to think he loved me so much. I was doing better now, staying focused on my new personal goals. However, some days were still rough. I got lots of well-wishes from my clients to keep up my spirits that eventually I would be in Costa Rica. They all wanted to come visit me there. I had so much to look forward to when I arrived. Thinking about that day brought tears to my eyes at times. I just wished I had a deadline to live there, as it would make waiting so much easier.

I went with my parents and my aunt to play bingo. We got some instructions, which only proved that the game was way more complicated than I had ever thought. We were overwhelmed in the Speed bingo. It was hard to believe a bunch of elderly people could keep up with it. Eventually we figured out the rhythm of the game, but it kept us all on our toes the entire night. It turned out to be a great family night full of laughs. Chuck had fun playing games, even though he didn't like to admit it. I hoped he went with us someday to the bingo hall. I knew he would get a good laugh out of it.

When I answered the house phone one night, I heard a faint familiar voice say my name. However, I didn't recognize who was calling and finally had to ask. It was Chuck. I had no idea he would be calling me from Costa Rica on my parents' house phone, but it was still embarrassing not to recognize my own husband's voice.

There was a vicious storm raging outside. He was watching a movie when the power went out. It had been out for hours now, so he was bored. The B&B had a roof leak from rain driven by the strong winds up under the flashing. He planned to call our contractor to have it fixed. Jefe was running around scared, terrified of the storm.

I felt bad that Chuck was alone in the dark. Plus, poor Jefe was stuck outside now, all wet and scared. I wished I could be there with them both. It made me want to cry, but we had to stay strong for each other. Our day to be together would come. I felt a special need to pray that night before I went to bed. I asked God to please watch over Chuck and Jefe during this storm and give us the strength to get through living apart to one day soon be together in Costa Rica.

It was unusually late at 11:00pm when the house phone rang. It was Chuck again. Something terrible had happened that he needed to tell me. I closed my eyes while visions of stolen power lines, lightening strikes and other bad thoughts ran through my mind. My heart was pounding. I was not prepared for what I was about to hear.

As was usual in our neighborhood on Sundays, many of the guys had gathered to watch the U.S. NFL football games on TV. During the game, the heavy rains had flooded the streams in the neighborhood. Two of our closest neighbors had been swept downstream on their drive home. One was just found dead. He was one of Chuck's closest friends, and the boyfriend of our maid. Her son, who was only 20, was also in the car and was still missing. This particular neighbor had warned Chuck specifically

155

about that stream being dangerous before and told him to be careful driving through it. It did not make sense that he would cross, if it were unsafe. It all seemed unreal.

I was hopeful they would find the missing son alive, but Chuck did not hold out much hope. Chuck and two locals had searched the entire bank and didn't find him on the smaller stream. Past that point, the stream dumped into a wider river that ran out into the open ocean. Chuck was pretty sure he was gone. He was going to clean up, since he was covered in mud, and try to get some sleep. A search party was leaving at 5:00am in the morning.

I was thankful Chuck had not gone to watch the football games. If he had gone, though, he promised me he would not have crossed the stream, had it looked dangerous. With the heavy rains that night, he was pretty sure it would have been bad. People made mistakes, and this one had a high price. I was going to continue to hope for good news about our missing neighbor.

I wasn't sure what to do. All my thoughts were of our neighbor's girlfriend and what she must be going through. It had to be a nightmare for her to lose him and to not know where her son was. I went to bed, but I knew sleep would not come.

The last time I saw our neighbors was when we ate dinner at their house during my visit in May. We had a great time there. Mom enjoyed the night at their house more than at any of our other neighbors' houses. She was so impressed by the food that she came home and tried to make it in Tennessee. Remembering the many times we played Mexican train, including that night which was mom's first time to play, made me smile. We had looked forward to entertaining them at our place once construction was done, in order to return the favor for all the dinners we owed them. I felt sad we never got that chance or the chance to say a final goodbye.

It was strange at the thoughts that had gone through my head. If maybe they had left a little later, then their lives could have been saved from a fallen tree that had blocked the road just 10 minutes after their departure. I wondered how many people had things happen where timing impacted their lives for the worse or maybe even better, yet they never realized it. There were those things that could change the course of our lives forever, but I tended to think of them more as things that changed how we lived and not those that could kill us. Did they think twice about crossing that stream? I supposed we might never know that answer.

The consequences of their actions affected many other people as well. Not only did his girlfriend have to cope with his loss and the potential loss of her son, she eventually also had to deal with how it changed her future. I wondered about his family in the U.S., who were unaware of the terrible phone call they would receive. His dogs had no idea they would never see him again. His loss had an effect on us. He was such a close friend to Chuck. He was also our closest neighbor. His girlfriend was our maid. Chuck ate dinner at their house often. They were a lot of company to Chuck when he was already lonely in Costa Rica without me. One of their dogs was Jefe's girlfriend. If they left, then Jefe would also be lonely. His loss had an effect on the homeowner's association. He played a big part in running it. He left a big void and big shoes to be filled by someone.

By 2:00am, I was cried out. Exhaustion hit me, and I finally managed to sleep for short periods of time. I was awake, waiting for the alarm to go off at 7:00am. The night had gone on forever. By now, the search party was underway in Costa Rica. I waited all day, anxious for Chuck to call with good news. As time wore on, I realized that it would obviously not be good news. Late that afternoon, news came from Chuck that the search was unsuccessful. The stream that took their lives was only three feet wide and three inches deep when he saw it that afternoon. What a difference 10 inches of rain in 4 hours made in people's lives. It was still hard to believe they were both gone.

Chuck gave me more details about the night of the accident. According to a local Tico who radioed for help, the truck first washed only a short distance down the stream. The son was standing on the roof of the truck, close enough to jump to shore, with our older neighbor still inside the driver's seat. When Chuck heard the call for help relayed to him, he rushed out in what he was wearing, which was shorts and his crocks with socks and a bright yellow poncho. He got there in time to meet two other Ticos, but the truck had washed further away already. They jumped in our Teryx and rode with Chuck along a narrow path on a Tico's land, adjacent to the stream. Our neighbor's body was found in a tree. They walked down the banks to look for the son, in case he was laying ashore somewhere. Chuck never thought about snakes, spiders or anything as he walked around with shorts and his crocks through the jungle, since he was frantic to find our other neighbor. They were all making so much noise that they would have scared anything off before they walked up on it. After searching for a while, they realized he was probably gone and finally gave up.

Chuck drove by to look at the stream again. It was hard to believe that a truck could go down it. The positive part of us running out of money to lay off our crew was that he had not gone to watch the football games that day as usual since he had decided to not leave the property unguarded for a long period of time. Otherwise, we both knew he would have been there. That thought had already crossed my mind a million times since he had given me the bad news. All I wanted to do was to hug him. He said he really needed a hug right now too. I felt terrible that I was not there for him. It was something that I would always regret, as I knew he needed me badly, but our situation simply didn't allow it. All I had to offer were words of comfort.

In the end, I decided it was destiny for this to happen to our neighbors. I didn't know for what reason. They were good people. One was older but always willing to help others. One was younger with a life full of so much promise for the future. It did not seem fair to have bad things happen to such good people, but I accepted it was God's path laid out before them. I was grateful Chuck was not on that path.

Not long after we talked, Chuck emailed. Our contractor called to say his ex-wife had died. Chuck thought he sounded drunk, and who could blame him after news of all the deaths. He loved me and missed me terribly. It broke my heart to hear it. I was grateful we had a friend from Florida who was going down to visit Chuck in a few weeks. He really needed a friend there more than ever.

My aunt mentioned she wished we would sell our place in Costa Rica after we got it established. I admitted it had crossed my mind in the last 24 hours. It was dangerous in Costa Rica when there were heavy floods, but that was true in the U.S. too. People died when Nashville flooded in May. Every place had its own dangers and problems. I still felt like it was our neighbors' destiny to leave this Earth, and I didn't think anyone could have changed it, just like I still felt we belonged in Costa Rica. We simply needed to find a way to finish and get me there, so we could be together. This whole experience only proved to me that each day was precious, and we had to make the most of it. I wanted to be with Chuck. We had to figure out a way to make it happen, and we would.

Chuck emailed around lunchtime that the body was found. It was an amazingly far distance away from the little stream where they crossed the road. Thankfully, it brought some closure for our neighbor.

The pool people showed up today to install the equipment. However, Chuck didn't know he needed to buy things for them. Apparently, the pool guys made a list of things they needed bought but failed to tell Chuck anything about it. They planned to return after Chuck bought everything on the list.

Chuck received a quote of $1,600 for the B&B signs we needed. He had enough money to pay for the signs, the landscaping and his expenses through the end of next month. I hoped we had enough to get the B&B going, to at least start making some money. At this point, I was still questioning if that was going to happen.

During the day, a friend wrote on our Facebook wall that the new international airport planned in Costa Rica near our place was being squashed. I googled it, and sure enough, they had killed that original idea. Instead, it was revamped into an idea to change the current smaller airport in Palmar Sur, closer to our place, into an international airport. Since it would be on a smaller scale, the cost was cut in half. In the future, the original idea would come back into play with many Costa Rican politicians pushing for it and additional environmental studies being done on its impact. If it will happen or not is yet to be determined. All I know is that change is inevitable, so my guess is that it will happen one day. Hopefully, when it does, steps are taken to protect the environment as much as possibly to balance things out for the benefit of all.

Chuck spent a lot of time making tons of B&B photos for the website. He thought it was looking really good. I peeked at them on our temporary pages. The photos were stunning. Chuck had done an awesome job. He had gone all out to stage things nicely. He had the dining room table set, flowers in vases, margaritas and books on the patio tables. The views almost didn't look real, but I knew they were. It didn't seem to me that anyone could look at our website and decide to stay anywhere else.

A neighbor's wife offered to stay at our place while Chuck went to watch the U.S. NFL football games with the neighborhood guys. It was a great game, too, that went into overtime. He was glad it did not rain. I thought we needed rain for our new landscaping, so I didn't know why he was so happy about the lack of rain. Eventually, it hit me. Chuck had made the same Sunday drive that our neighbors had tried to make last Sunday when they died crossing the stream. It gave me chills to actually think about it. I was glad that I didn't know he had gone until after the fact.

Dad and I had a good dinner at a Japanese place in town. My fortune cookie stated, "Your present plans are going to succeed." I emailed Chuck, and his comment was that he guessed it was too late to think bigger. Since my present plan included a successful B&B, moving to Costa Rica, finishing our house and selling my book for $1,000,000, I was not sure how much bigger I could go, except to win the lottery. I just hoped my present plan succeeded.

Once the landscaping was done, Chuck posted photos. He had warned me already the plants were tiny, but some were almost invisible! Was there a money tree planted in there somewhere? We sure needed one. There was no money tree according to Chuck, but there was a miracle fruit. Maybe it would produce some miracles!

On another good note, he asked our maid if she wanted to stay in the neighborhood or if she wanted to move away once the house she lived in sold. She told him she would prefer to stay in the neighborhood. That was great news. We hoped we could keep her.

The pool guys showed up to do their part. They told Chuck to fill the pool, and they would return on Monday to finish the spa equipment, along with the pool wiring. Our contractor told Chuck he thought we were probably going to owe a lot more than the normal $125 typical hookup fee. That was fine with us, as all the work had to be done. Thankfully, it was all fitting into the equipment room nicely, despite their original complaint of wanting another room built with more space.

The pool was full, but the pool guys did not show. The pool dropped 1 inch in 2 hours. Chuck figured out the skimmer was leaking. There was a missing plug at the bottom! He stuck a stick down into the soft dirt. The pool photos Chuck sent were amazing. I actually gasped as I saw the first photo. My gasp startled me. Then it made me smile. It was much prettier than I was expecting. It had been a bad day, so those photos made me realize that all this sacrifice was going to be worth it. I needed to put things back into perspective.

Chuck picked up our friend at the airport in San Jose and had a good shopping trip afterwards, buying needed supplies on the way home. The bad news was they arrived home in a downpour, to find a major water leak into the pool's electrical panel. I was thankful my prayer they would make it home safely was answered but sad that they had arrived home to a problem. At least Chuck was not there alone this time. After all, our friend had gone to help him. I told myself not to worry, but it was very hard to sleep.

Our electrician made an emergency call to disconnect the power. They discovered the next day that the landscapers had broken a line with their shovel and never said anything. The rain had funneled down the cut pipe all the way into the electrical panel. It was not the welcoming he was sure our friend had expected. In my opinion, it was like saying welcome to Chuck's world, where life was a roller coaster ride with ups and downs and unexpected turns.

After solving the electrical panel problem, they shopped in town and worked on the tiki bar. When the weather broke some that afternoon, Chuck took our friend for a ride in the Teryx around the neighborhood. Our friend loved that part. He found it hard to believe how lush things were and that people lived up in the mountains. He especially found it hard to believe the spot where our neighbors had gotten swept downstream could be raging enough to kill two people. By the end of the day, they had grilled some wings and built much of the block for the big green egg in the tiki bar.

It was nice to know Chuck was enjoying his company. I appreciated our friend venturing down there, and I hoped the weather cleared up for him to see how beautiful Costa Rica was in the sunlight. I was relieved to know they had resolved the electrical panel problem. I knew it meant a better night of sleep for me, and I certainly needed it.

It was shocking to hear the St Petersburg Times newspaper in Florida was considering writing a newspaper article on us and our Ocaso Cerro dream. We needed some good publicity, and we were honored they would consider us. I knew people were interested when we talked about our dream, but it was different to have someone in the media actually confirm it. They were also interested in hearing about the book I was writing. I didn't want to get my hopes up, but it was exciting news.

24 THE POWER OF A HUG

CHUCK AND OUR FRIEND went on a ziplining excursion. One platform was in a tree over 500 feet tall. Chuck thought it was cool to stand on the platform at 300 feet and still see the tree continue 200 feet above. The tour company, Osa Mountain Canopy, told them they were building one of the longest ziplines in the world! It was obvious they had enjoyed the trip from looking at their faces in photos Chuck sent.

After Chuck dropped our friend off at the airport the next day, he told me he missed me terribly, and he planned to post photos soon on Facebook. He was also proud of the progress I had made on my Spanish lessons, as I had told him I finished the entire 2nd set already. My heart swelled, and it made me smile to hear those words. I knew he was especially sad to be home alone, now that our friend was gone. He posted ziplining photos, photos of the tiki bar interior build out and the big green egg stand they had made. The tiki bar interior was complex. It even had holders to hang the glasses in underneath the bar! It was all much more than I had expected. They had done a great job.

The credit card billing systems I had researched were not going to work for the B&B. The companies wanted high minimum monthly bookings or large commissions. As a small start up, we simply did not fit those guidelines. We were running out of time to find a credit card system before our November opening date.

I decided later in the afternoon I would make one more attempt to call the mortgage broker to whom our attorney had referred us. I was shocked when he answered. If we became residents one day, then it was possible we could jump through a lot of hoops to obtain a Costa Rican mortgage. However, as nonresidents, it was impossible to do what we wanted to achieve. The options we had wanted as nonresidents went away after the world financial crisis. Right now, we could get a hard money loan at 14%

to 18% interest for two years, with a balloon payment at the end. Since we wanted a conventional loan, I thanked him for his time. At least now, I knew where we stood.

Chuck had worked on tiling the tiki bar for seven or eight hours. He was running out of tile, and he had no money for more in the bank. My bad news on both the mortgage and the credit card information was too much for him. He thought that it was all a big mistake and that we should just give up. We were never going to open. I almost cried on the phone. I wished I could give him a hug, because I knew he needed it badly. He deserved a chance to vent, as it was only natural. He finally calmed down a little bit and agreed to make a list of the things we needed to open up the B&B.

The list totaled almost $6,000. I developed a plan of attack as best as I could, and I sent Chuck what money I had for now. Some things we had to have, but others simply had to wait. It took saving into November, but it was the best plan I had to offer. It was all we could do.

I had a difficult time sleeping that night. I hated not being able to hug Chuck to make him feel better. We were not used to being with our backs up against the wall like this. It felt like we kept pushing harder and harder to squeeze out a little more money. So far, we were finding what we needed to get by, but it was never enough to finish. Was it ever going to be possible for us to make the turn to climb back up?

A $50,000 guarantee was required by another credit card company to use their ecommerce services for our B&B website. Chuck was frustrated to have reached another dead end. It looked like we might have to be a cash only operation. However, what was really important was getting me to Costa Rica in the long run. Living apart was too hard. Chuck signed his email, "Love, Chuck and a sleepy Jefe." It made me smile that he was at least doing better. He really did miss me. After reaching another dead end on the credit card issue, I requested advice from our mentor. Her recommendation turned out to be the name of our own bank in Costa Rica. I had not thought to try them, but they turned out to be the answer to our prayers.

Chuck grouted the egg top and bar, which took until noon. He worked on hooking up the sink, the drain for the icemaker and a door for the locking liquor cabinet in the tiki bar. The guy came with the gravel for the driveway but got stuck close to the gate wall. They had to call a backhoe to lift him out. It took a while, since the backhoe ran out of gas down the hill. They had to siphon gas from his truck for the backhoe to reach our house. Despite the pool guys saying they were waiting on our electrician, things were not ready for him when he came. It was very frustrating. He called them, and they were on the same page now, hopefully.

I did not sleep well again. I started thinking about our lack of money and missing Chuck. I finally came to the realization that we needed help from friends. In the middle of the night, I emailed a friend about our financial situation.

In response to my request for help, our friends were offering to loan us money, so we could open the B&B and finish our house. It was a bit of a dilemma if we should borrow enough to finish our house too. There was the possibility it might put me further away from getting to be with Chuck in Costa Rica, if my job didn't let me relocate there. It meant I could be stuck in the U.S. for years more to pay back the extra money. Regardless of what we decided on the house, it allowed us to open the B&B, which was such a relief that I couldn't begin to put it into words.

Chuck did not seem happy at all about going into more debt. All he wanted was for me to be in Costa Rica. I wanted that too, but it was not possible now. Maybe a good night of sleep and a clear head would help us figure things out more clearly.

Thankfully, Chuck was back to his normal self the next day. After thinking it over, he agreed borrowing more money was a good idea. He thought the tiki bar was totally awesome. He had been sitting there and watched 30 monkeys go by through the trees. It was an amazing site. Jefe was going crazy, but the monkeys simply ignored him. The pool water was still crystal clear, despite sitting for almost two weeks with no running pumps. Chuck started shouting there was an earthquake! Jefe got excited. It turned out to be a 5.9 magnitude quake centered 26 miles north of San Jose.

After the earthquake was over, we talked about Chuck's new garage design and potential caretaker's quarters. Did our maid want to live there? She had gone through so much with the loss of her boyfriend and son, so we hoped she wanted to stay. It was small but new and clean. It gave her a place to live once she moved out of her existing place and allowed her to keep her job. Plus, she was like part of our family, so we didn't want her to move away. With our new funds, we hoped we could keep her, now that we could afford caretaker's quarters as well as finish the B&B. We also agreed to borrow the money to finish our house, since it allowed for more B&B revenue and made sense in the long run.

Going forward, Chuck thought we had to have two guys working on the bamboo ceilings inside our house, as it was very noisy work, so we needed to finish it before lots of B&B guests arrived. We planned to open the B&B in November with three rooms, since Chuck lived in the fourth. The remaining construction on our house needed to wait until we knew I was able to relocate my job to Costa Rica.

I felt much better now that we were on board with a plan. Plus, Chuck told me I didn't have to pay the loan back by myself, since he would be making money too. It made me smile to think about the change in his attitude from that prior day. He was back to his old normal problem-solving Chuck. He obviously needed time to come to terms with going into more debt. After all, most people in the world had debt, especially at our young ages. We needed to put things into perspective. We simply needed to get the B&B open and get me to Costa Rica. All this debt talk was secondary. I knew we would pay it off someday.

I wished everyone understood how important it was for us to follow our dream, but that was simply not going to happen. Some people thought we were crazy to throw away what we had in Florida to go through what we were doing now. They seemed to think that we were trading in our materialistic things in Florida for materialistic things in Costa Rica. They didn't understand we were trading in a lifestyle. The B&B, while materialistic, was a business to attract people who went on vacation and wanted to stay in a nice place. It was difficult some days, when I could tell people were listening to me talk about our journey but didn't really understand what we were doing. Lately, though, it seemed I was talking to fewer people who didn't understand it and more who did. I wondered. Was it because we were getting closer to the end of our journey, so they could see physical results (i.e. on Facebook or on our website)? Was it because more people were burnt out on their jobs due to the poor economy, so they were willing to think outside of the box now? Maybe this cultural shift was responsible for the popularity of shows like House Hunters International where people dared to follow a dream for a different lifestyle. I didn't know the answer, but I liked that fewer people seemed to judge us for following our dream and more were excited to go along for the ride.

The pool guys showed up again. They still did not finish. However, Chuck was finally able to filter and clean the pool. It was awesome! The spa waterfall was nice, and it flowed over the infinity edge great. We needed to decide on the woodwork we wanted done in our house, for our contractor to review. It would be January before they could get wood out of the kiln, if he was willing to build it. Personally, I wanted to stick to our original plan, which did not include all the woodwork right now. Chuck was pushing for it, though, as a last chance to use our contractor before he closed down his woodshop business.

Chuck spent three hours in town doing errands. His meeting went well with the attorney. The attorney advised us to set up a new corporation for the B&B business for about $450. After that was done, we needed a tax accountant to do some paperwork to apply for our business license. The license required an inspection where typically, the only problem to obtain approval was handicap accessibility issues. Chuck planned to call our Costa Rican architect the next day to confirm we were all right, because we were positive he had told us we did not need to worry about any handicap codes the multiple times we had asked him. According to the attorney, it was not a big deal for us to go ahead and start operating without the business license. The great news was that we were considered a commercial property. Therefore, we did not have to worry about the luxury property tax, which applied only to residential properties.

Our Costa Rican architect's response regarding the inspection requirement for handicap accessibility was simply to return the handicap code to Chuck. Chuck was upset, since the law was comparable to U.S. handicap codes, meaning we had no bathrooms that were even close to complying. Regardless of what we had been told, permitted and built already, the fact was we were going to have to comply now. That was how things went in Costa Rica. We had yet another hurdle to jump, and this was a big one.

After brainstorming, we came to the conclusion that we could build our caretaker's quarters or cabina as we would call it now, so it would be handicap accessible. It allowed us to comply with the codes to obtain our business license. Our architect seemed to think the municipality would give us the business license with only a drawing of the cabina detailing the handicap information. I wasn't sure they would be that lenient. However, our attorney said we didn't need the business license to open. At least we had a plan now that seemed like it would work, and it kept the original design of the B&B intact. Cabinas were good rental income, so maybe it had worked out for the best in the long run.

Chuck was set to have TV installed and hoped to have it in time to watch the big Auburn game that night. The TV guys installed the equipment, but they were upset about his signature on the contract not matching his passport. After multiple attempts, Chuck told them he had enough and walked off, ending the dispute. The satellite had to download the account information, so the TV guys were to return in 1.5 hours. They came back 3.5 hours later to let him know the contract address listed the incorrect city. They needed to return with a new contract another day. Chuck was highly upset at being left with only the information channel on TV. While the TV guys were doing their thing, our electrician worked on the pool and got things nearly done around noon, when the pool guy arrived. There were many problems the pool guy could not fix, so the main pool guy needed to come back another day. We still had no TV and no functioning spa. Chuck did not think we would ever get open. Even Auburn's win didn't seem to override the other disappointments of his day.

I awoke in the early morning hours and found myself crying. I missed Chuck. I was thinking about a moment from church earlier. A simple gesture, when a husband reached over to touch his wife on the back during the sermon, had made me miss Chuck even more. I longed for the last time he had touched me. I wanted just a simple touch on the back, a hug or to hold hands for a few moments. I needed the connection to be there again. How did people in the military live apart for so long? My tears flowed as I lay in bed. Did we ever get to live again in the same house, like a normal couple? I had to get a grip on myself. I had to look forward to travelling to Costa Rica on my next trip in November. At that time, I was going to hold his hand constantly, for the entire week. I needed to make up for a lot of time that week, to get me through times like this, when we were apart. I settled myself down and finally went back to sleep.

The TV guys arrived with the revised contract, but things did not go well. First, one of the guys was not paying attention and walked through a retractable screen on the front door which was shut instead of the door where the retractable screen was open. They finally got the TV working, so Chuck thought he could watch the NFL night game. He was wrong. The TV started acting funny. Basically, our old TV was now shot. We needed to decide what to do about it. Our choice was to buy a new cheaper TV for use in the B&B or to use the new one we had already bought for our house, since it might take forever to finish.

The experienced pool guy arrived and fixed everything in about five minutes. It was a surprise and a relief to finally have the spa and pool all in working order. Chuck was pushing again to have our contractor to commit to the woodwork in our house, which I didn't think we could afford. He wanted to spend more on landscaping too. That was yet another thing I did not think we needed to spend money on right now. Plus, it was not a good time to plant, before the dry season. I felt like we were not on the same page at all anymore.

I hoped Chuck was safe on his trip to have the car inspected. I realized I had to focus on my job here, or I was going to drive myself crazy worrying about things in Costa Rica. It turned out he had a great day. He passed inspection with the car, and afterwards he got lots of good deals shopping in town. On top of everything else, it was a beautiful day of weather. He deserved to have a good day. I wished he had more of those.

Beginning the third week into October, Chuck started work on our house again. It was exciting to finally make some progress on our house. He painted and ordered more bamboo in preparation for our ceilings to be finished inside.

One day, we heard about the theft of electrical lines in the neighborhood again. Chuck figured this meant that the thieves knew we had protected our lines, since they had left us alone. He was actually relieved. However, I was still not so sure it meant anything except that we were lucky this time. I hoped Chuck was right.

I ate dinner and watched some of the TV show, "60 minutes." It was a story about how bad the economy was for a lot of people. They called some of the people the 99'rs, because they had been on unemployment for

99 weeks or close to it. Their benefits were running out. The majority of them had college degrees. A number had masters, and a few had PhDs. After watching this story, I felt fortunate my family and I had not been hit hard by the poor economic situation. Chuck agreed we were lucky. Even though we were in debt and living apart, we still had a lot to be grateful for and a means to work our way out of debt. Many of the 99ers had lost so much that it would take them a long time to recover to their prior standard of living, if ever. We realized how important it was for us to be happy with the simple things in life and really mean it, for everything else could disappear one day.

Chuck and I laughed about how we had both spent most of that day painting. It made me feel good to know we had been doing the same thing, even though we had not been in the same country. It was funny how something simple could be so important to both of us these days. If I lived in Costa Rica, there was no way Chuck would have painted. He hated to paint. I was sure he would have commented about how slow I painted but that I did a great job. It brought tears to my eyes to think how I would have loved to have that conversation, since it would have meant I was in Costa Rica.

Chuck got the new TV set up in the B&B and took a dip in the pool, since it was a beautiful day. We had eight macaws fly by at low altitude over the pool, and two more fly by the front of the B&B. Later, he counted at least 20 macaws flying by overhead. They all grouped up in a circle before splitting off again. It was exciting to watch.

Chuck was ready to go all out with the woodwork in the entire house again, but I was able to talk him out of it. We came to an agreement to do a few smaller tasks for now, like the baseboards for the bedroom, the closet and some items in the laundry room. We agreed to hold off on the kitchen. After all, we really had to have the cabina done for our business license, so we had to keep the money in the budget for that to get finished. We also agreed he would buy a few more landscape items now, just to fill in some empty spots. We felt it was a good compromise solution on both the woodwork and the landscaping.

It had rained solid all night and day in Costa Rica. Chuck ordered some more palm trees and got a lot of painting done. He was thrilled that the final pool installation bill was only a little over $500! The sign guy was going to get started on the sign the next day. The palm guys were going to deliver the plants at a cost of over $500 for eight trees. The bamboo people were making their delivery the next day as well. We hoped it would be all the bamboo we needed for the ceilings.

I completed the final CD in the last set of the Spanish lessons I had, and I planned to work on my book notes more, now that I had extra time. Chuck was very proud of me and hoped I made a million bucks with my book, which I thought was cute. He wanted to know the name of the book, but I refused to tell him. It was all in the title, so he hoped I had a good one. I thought I did.

Chuck had a challenging day. Other than a three-hour stoppage, it rained hard all day and night again. There were lots of mudslides along the coastal highway. A few were on the highway, down past our waterfall. There was also a big outage toward Dominical, where they might close the road. He had heard a truck driver had been killed by a fallen tree. The nursery had called to cancel their delivery. The bamboo guy made it. However, while coming up our steep driveway, the bamboo fell out of the back of his truck, turning the delivery into an ordeal. They had to carry the heavy bundles of bamboo up part of the way. The driver then tried to back the truck up close to the tiki bar, and somehow, he got stuck. Chuck had to tow him out before he slid down the hill sideways. This was the fourth person to become stuck in our driveway, so it was not a good idea for them to try to back up in that small area. Jefe was in the doghouse. All his cooped up energy from the rain came out when his girlfriend arrived. They got into the shallow end of the swimming pool with muddy feet. Chuck yelled at them both, and they ran off. He had not seen either of them since.

After lunch, I found an email from our legal attorney with an update on our residency status. I dreaded to look at it, anticipating a problem. I opened up the email to see the following: "Congratulations!! Your Residencies have been approved." I was immediately shocked. Was this a joke? I had been prepared for the worst, but we were approved. We needed to pay the rest of the fees owed, sign up for the CAJA to prove health insurance and get photos made for our national ID residency cards, called cedulas. The CAJA was $70 a month for both of us at our ages, and it got cheaper once we reached over 55 years old, which was the reverse from what you would expect.

Within minutes of receiving my message, Chuck called me in shock. He was excited. It had gone so smoothly up until this point that it was surprisingly easy. In fact, it had been too easy, which made us both worry the road ahead would be a rough one. We needed to figure out how to prove our income requirement was properly exchanged each month from dollars into colones, to avoid problems renewing our cedulas in two years. As a side note, the dollar amount required varies, depending upon the law in effect at the time you apply for residency. For us, it was $2,000 each month.

It had been an exciting day for me, having completed my first charity walk in downtown Nashville and now hearing news we were Costa Rican residents. The rest of my night turned out to be eventful as well. I went to the company family fun day that mom's employer hosted. While there, mom and I got lost in a corn maze, since I had no sense of direction, and neither did anyone in our group. The ride home was exciting but not in a good way. We were hit from behind at a stoplight. It was an accident, and the other guy admitted it was his fault, but I was not happy to have wrecked my dad's truck. It was his pride and joy that he was constantly updating with aftermarket parts, for me to have a truck that would turn heads in town. Not too long after the cops arrived, it was strange to look up and see my dad in the big rig sitting right next to us, stopped in traffic. He happened to glance over at me. I smiled and said, "Hi daddy, sorry about your truck." I had no idea then what a disaster the whole thing would turn into, as getting the truck repaired would not go well at the body shop.

Chuck was sorry to hear about the accident. He was just glad nobody got hurt, and it was not my fault. He had met with one of the crew we wanted to hire back. He would prefer to return to work at our place over his current job, which was great news. It made me smile when I saw Chuck signed his email, "Love, Chuck & Jefe, El Residente" in honor of our newly earned Costa Rican residency status.

It was late in the day before I remembered Chuck and I had made the drive to Tennessee from Florida exactly one year ago. We arrived before dark on Halloween. It was hard to believe, but our one-year anniversary away from Florida had officially arrived.

25 WEATHER, WILDLIFE AND LESS PEOPLE

IT CONTINUED TO RAIN into November. Chuck was sick of the rain. On his way into town, the road was now partially washed out, so traffic had to take turns sharing the one lane that remained. It did not appear anyone was working to fix it either. At the bank, he was surprised at how quickly the paperwork to request the credit card machine for on-site processing at the B&B went. All of the people there recognized him now, so they were being more helpful. He got home only minutes before the landscape people arrived unexpectedly. After they were done, it all looked so much better than previously that it made him want to buy more landscaping. Our maid and her daughter had ridden into town with him to do some errands. She commented it was difficult living in the neighborhood now, due to bad memories, but Chuck reminded her there were good memories too. We were hoping she would stay in the neighborhood once we offered her our cabina as an option to live in, but Chuck was waiting for me to be there to make the offer.

The constant rain had me worried about landslides. Chuck thought the waterfall on our lot meant we had some rock bed underneath our hill, which was good news. If we could make it through this year in a record rainfall with no problems, then Chuck thought it would be saying a lot for our hill holding up in the future. I was going to continue to say my prayers that everything stayed safe.

It had been raining nonstop since Chuck and I talked last. He spent three hours with the accounting lady, talking about the homeowner's association books. While he was there, the main coastal road to Uvita collapsed. He hoped there would be a work-around before he had to pick me up in three weeks at the airport in San Jose. He got the wireless Internet to work throughout our property and got the SSL certificate for our Internet website as well. He had made some progress with the website reservations people too. I was saying my prayers for things to continue to remain safe at our place and for some sunshine there.

It was still raining in Costa Rica, but the rain had let up enough that Chuck was able to run into town to drop off the insurance paperwork. Both the coastal highway and the Pan American Highway were closed, so truckers were parked everywhere. A few of the neighbors had to detour to reach home. It apparently took one neighbor 6.5 hours on a detour for a typical 20-minute drive from Uvita. Chuck was very lucky he did not become stuck in Uvita, since he had made that drive the day before the road collapsed. He was going to look for something to watch on TV and head off to bed early. I was thankful he was home safe, even though he and Jefe were bored.

The weather in Costa Rica was worse the next day, with darker clouds, harder rain and intense winds. What was going on there? After work, I watched the national news. It talked about a tropical storm headed toward Haiti. Now, that explained it. From looking at the satellite, Costa Rica was in the outflow of the storm. It was only moving at 5 MPH, so it was still going to be a while before it moved away. A neighbor who kept rain statistics told Chuck there was a rain total from Monday morning to Thursday morning of almost three feet in three days. That was a lot of rain, even for the rainforest.

There was a break in the water line. Since our property had water storage tank, Chuck was fine at our house, but he was in charge of getting things fixed for the association. Also, the road had dropped 30 inches up the hill past us, by a neighbor's house. He was not sure what was going on up there. Obviously, it did not sound good. Although he heard there were still lots of road closures further up the coastal road, he had heard tractor-trailer trucks late that afternoon, passing by us again on the main road, which was a good sign. We hoped the rain stopped soon.

After talking to Chuck, I listened to the Hemingway's Whiskey CD that I had finally taken the time to buy. It was nice to chill out, listening to music and drinking some wine for a change. It felt good to be migraine-free too. I was stressed about my grandma, who had returned to the ER that day, and about the heavy continuous rains in Costa Rica. It was all out of my control. I had to force myself to relax and look forward to seeing Chuck in a few weeks. I hoped Chuck and Jefe stayed safe. I also hoped Grandma made it through the night all right. She had told me she would have to get better before she could die and that she felt worse in the hospital than before she went in. But I didn't believe that at all, because she looked significantly better.

It was still raining in Costa Rica the next day, but it had finally slowed a little bit. Our contractor made it back home after he crossed a river, which terrified me, given the recent death of our neighbors. He told Chuck he was cautious, though, and went only after he watched three other people make it.

Chuck worked some more on getting things ready for the workers to start. He wasn't sure what he was going to do the next day if it was still raining. I asked him if he wanted to spend time reading part of my book, since he was bored. I was surprised he liked the idea.

According to our neighbor who tracked rain totals, this was going to be a record year, with a total already close to 252 inches from January 2010 through October 2010. These numbers didn't include the current deluge in November, with a four-day total of 49.5 inches from Monday through Thursday. It was hard to imagine that much rainfall.

Even though he had not read much of my book, Chuck thought it was awesome so far. It made me feel great. He was thrilled that the sun was coming out too. The updated rain totals showed 56 inches of rain since Monday. It was amazing to comprehend what kind of damage almost five feet of rain in such a short time period could do. With the sun out, Chuck decided to explore the neighborhood. Our road was partially blocked, but the Teryx made it through fine. Our road was scheduled to be fixed later that day; however, the area up by the condos was going to take a while to fix. He sent a few photos of the damage. Jefe enjoyed the exercise around the neighborhood. Chuck was going to work on tiling before watching the football game that afternoon. He was excited to have a break from the rain.

That night, we had a spa party at my parents' house. We had good food, good laughs and good company. It was great to spend time with mom and all of my aunts and others who came. I looked back at the night and realized what a great opportunity it was to have this time in Tennessee, even though I missed being with Chuck so much.

November 6th marked Chuck's one-year anniversary of living in Costa Rica. He agreed to answer my interview questions about his first year there. Time had flown by in some ways, but it seemed like forever when he thought about me. What he liked most about living there was the combination of weather, wildlife and less people. The recent rains were the result of an unusual storm. Overall the weather was almost perfect. The wildlife was abundant, and it was nice to be in a less crowded environment. The thing he liked least was worrying about petty crime. It was hard for him to decide on his most memorable day, so he picked two. The first was in September when our closest neighbors died in a tragic auto accident. The second was in March when he went to San Jose to purchase flooring, including its late-night eventful delivery. His biggest surprise was what a great dog Jefe had turned out to be, after such a rough beginning, with him running off all the time. He had expected living in Costa Rica to be different, so it had not been a big adjustment for him. However, the language barrier was a challenge. Learning the language better would help, but he would always be a foreigner. There was no way change the fact he was a minority in Costa Rica. His favorite food in Costa Rica was ceviche. Since he could not pick being separated from me, his biggest challenge had been living on a construction site with the mud, dust, bugs and no kitchen for months. It was a great interview, and I enjoyed hearing his answers.

After undergoing his second surgery for sinus cancer, my uncle was fighting to recover at the hospital. He told me Chuck and I were crazy for undertaking our Costa Rican adventure, but he wished us the best of luck. We thought we were crazy sometimes too, but we were determined to make it work out. After all, it took a little craziness to make the world go around at times. Maybe one day, we would turn out not to be as crazy as a lot of people thought. We had certainly spiced up our lives and had many experiences that we had learned from to make us stronger individuals.

Chuck spent a lot of time moving things around in our house, getting it ready for the crew to start with the bamboo the next week. He dealt with more neighborhood water and road issues from all the rains. He worked on the website some and uploaded it, including the reservations page. He sat out on the sunset deck and read the rest of my book while he watched a beautiful sunset. Chuck didn't read much, so it was sweet of him to read my book. He didn't have a lot of changes either. He really liked what I had written, which was a huge compliment coming from him. He liked the title, too!

A co-worker called me for work advice and asked me afterwards how things were going in Costa Rica. She mentioned how much she loved to see our progress. She hoped that one day she and her husband could stay with us. She thought a lot of my co-workers were living vicariously through me and my dream. If I needed anything done on my desk while I was gone on my next trip, she wanted to know, as she planned to do what she could to help out. She was looking forward to the next update, after I returned from Costa Rica. I really appreciated hearing those encouraging words. I told her she made my day, and she commented that you never know how what you do may be blessing someone else. She was along for the ride and loving it!

Chuck drove into town. The road had washed out in two places. Two huge landslides were almost cleaned up. On the plus side, there were now nice new vistas of the ocean, since the road slid all the way down into it. Waiting to take turns on the roads took some patience, but overall, he had a pretty good day. After his drive into town, he spent a lot of time dealing with water and road issues for the association. The water was now working again. The roads in our neighborhood were finally in much better shape. He painted a second and a third coat in the office. He tiled the baseboard of the balcony upstairs. The best news of the day was that the roads further north would be all right from the airport, as a neighbor had made the drive fairly smoothly. We were in good shape for him to pick me up when I arrived at the airport in a few weeks, so I didn't need to worry about that anymore.

It took me a minute when I awoke to realize it was my birthday. It felt great to start the day with lots of happy birthday emails. Chuck emailed to say my birthday marked the first official landing of macaws on our property. A pair landed in the almond tree by our gate. He attached a few photos. One showed the macaws eating nuts, and the other photo showed a macaw as it was just landing from flight. They were beautiful. What a great birthday present to start my day! The birthday celebration continued all day, including my favorite Mexican dinner.

Our workers showed up for their first day back on the job and got a lot accomplished. It was great to have some crew on the job site again. Chuck went to the duty free stores in Golfito with some neighbors. He got the mini fridge for the tiki bar and four safes to help get the B&B ready for opening. He was excited that he did not have many more nights without me there. How sweet.

I made the drive from Nashville to Atlanta uneventfully. I found myself laughing that I was one of the people who fought hectic commuter traffic daily when Chuck and I lived in Atlanta. It was pure madness, but this was normal life to a lot of people. It was a huge contrast to see this traffic, versus the uncongested world of our place in the Costa Rican rainforest. I actually enjoyed sitting in Atlanta traffic, thinking about it and watching it all play out in front of me. There was energy being in the mix, but it was not something I would enjoy on a daily basis. I was thankful for my telework job. Fortunately, I found my way through all the heavy traffic to the hotel near the Atlanta airport.

Our Ocaso Cerro signs arrived that day. Chuck had been a little worried, since they called to install the sign without letting him proof it first. Obviously, there was some sort of problem, since he had not told me he liked them. Instead, he commented he would wait to see what I thought. Everything was still on schedule for Chuck to pick me up at the airport the next day. We were both excited.

I awoke tired but still excited to be on my way to Costa Rica. Thankfully, there were free carts in the San Jose airport, since I had four bags to carry alone. It was great to kiss and hug Chuck. We drove home in heavy traffic and held hands along the way, catching up on lots of details. We called in a pizza from the Rum Bar to take home. Our Ocaso Cerro signs along the road were great, but I did not like the one next to our house. It turned out Chuck didn't either, but he had an idea already to fix it. We arrived at the B&B to find all was fine. Everything looked beautiful to me, especially the tiki bar. We ate under the tiki hut, so we could spend some time with Jefe. The photos had been great, but everything was better in person. I was able to see where Chuck placed all the decorations, which were not obvious in the pictures. We were both tired and went to bed in Cerro. It was chilly, which made it nice to snuggle up to Chuck in bed.

I enjoyed looking around at the house more in the daylight, especially outside. The black bean and egg wraps Chuck made for breakfast were amazing. After breakfast, I saw the trees moving. It turned out to be the little monkeys. They came up from the jungle, passed the waterfall beside our house and crossed over behind it to the front of the property.

While we were working the B&B, the sun came out for a second, and I heard a noise that had me baffled. I was looking for raindrops but saw nothing. Chuck explained that the sun was heating the aluminum roof, causing it to expand and sound like raindrops hitting it. It was amazing to be in Costa Rica and listen to all the different noises that I was not used to in the U.S.

Later in the afternoon, we saw the howler monkeys eating berries and leaves in the trees. Chuck had a scope that zoomed right in on them. I had seen the howlers before, but I had never seen them eating up close. It was so much fun to watch nature in action.

Our electrician came to the B&B once and joked that Jefe's new dog bed was nicer than his bed at home. I hoped Jefe learned to like it, because he wasn't going for it so far. It was nighttime as we enjoyed our first margaritas at the tiki bar and watched Jefe take to his new dog bed. The softness had finally won him over.

We headed to San Isidro to do errands, including obtaining a piece of paper, called a personal juridica, that Chuck needed to activate his new cell phone. The first time he went to the government office to obtain this paper for the bank, he waited in line for an hour to learn stamps were required before they could help him. He then had trouble finding the stamp window. It was a small window in a yarn store located a long walk away from the government office, so it was easy to understand why he had trouble finding it. He knew exactly where to go on this trip. The personal juridica was required for owners to show they still owned their corporation. Places (i.e. the government ran phone company ICE in our case) required it to be currently dated at set periods, such as 30 days, to continue to prove your authority over your account.

At the ICE office back in Dominical, we were able to have Chuck's new cell phone activated with the new personal juridica. As an added bonus, we were able to get his voicemail menu reprogrammed in English. ICE also gave us the utility bill the bank required to complete everything we needed to set up our personal bank accounts. With the info from ICE, we got all four personal bank accounts set up with relatively little problems at our bank, outside of some minor Spanish translation issues. It was a rare day in Costa Rica, where everything seemed to work out.

It was wonderful to awake in Ocaso that morning. In fact, our neighbor from the U.S., who had visited that prior day, had said it was his favorite room. Despite being small, it had a lot of punch. Chuck and I talked about what made that room feel so special. All the rooms had great views; however, the high bed in Ocaso and bright orange walls made the room feel cozy and inviting. I wanted to stay in bed there all day and watch the birds fly by below, but we had to get going.

We arrived at the duty free shops in Golfito with no problems. On this trip, we were looking for a refrigerator for our house and splurged on a nice one. It was our first time to arrange for transportation, so we hoped all went well with the delivery the next day. On the way home, we stopped at the CAJA (i.e. social security) office to pick up some paperwork. Normally the CAJA representative came to our house during the month to deliver paperwork for Chuck to complete, showing how many workers we had and their hours. Each month, Chuck turned in the paperwork and made the CAJA payment. The paperwork also included proof of benefits to the workers, in case they needed them. Strangely, the representative hadn't shown so far that month. Chuck was told at the CAJA office he was delayed due to car problems, and the paperwork would arrive soon.

Our crew was making progress on our house. They had finished the family room ceiling, including spraying it and putting up the rope trim. They were laying the bamboo ceiling in the hallway and would soon be ready to move onto the kitchen.

We had friends over for dinner. It was a very nice evening in the jungle. Once, Jefe decided to carry off his dog bone pillow from his new doggy bed. I put it back in his bed. I hoped he learned not to play with it, because I knew Chuck would never go to the trouble to put it back. I wished I could stay in Costa Rica, but I knew I couldn't. It was going to be time to return to the U.S. soon. I had to live in the moment for the happy times we had while we were together.

It was time for our return trip to Golfito. The fridge looked massive, and I wondered if we had made a mistake. The delivery guy was a friend of our salesman and was charging us $100. We waited outside the car with the fridge. He finally arrived some 30 minutes later in a big box truck. In a matter of seconds, he and some other guys tossed our fridge on its side and laid it in the truck. Even I knew, you were supposed to stand them upright at all times. He closed the doors, took the warranty information to get past the police checkpoint, said, "Ojochal" and took off in the truck. We stood there in shock. We jumped in our car, but he was long gone by the time we paid our parking fee.

I tried to remain positive, but I thought we would never see the delivery driver again. Our whole idea of going on a slow drive home following each other was shot down the toilet. Chuck drove fast and furious, but we never saw the guy. At one point, traffic stopped in both directions like there was an accident ahead. Chuck wanted to know if I saw a fridge lying on the road anywhere. I laughed, because I had been thinking the same thing. We finally concluded the guy had to have stopped somewhere. On the bright side, at least we didn't have to worry about the fridge becoming wet from rain in a box truck. We drove all the way past our road to Ojochal without spotting him and returned to the entrance of our road to wait.

A neighbor drove up and asked me if everything was all right. He laughed at my story. He said somehow things never go as you planned in Costa Rica, but they had a way of working out. It was déjà vu. Chuck had said that a few minutes earlier to try to comfort me, and you know what? Only minutes later, the delivery driver came honking by at us. It was a small victory! No, he didn't turn around or pull over but instead stopped in the middle of the road past us. As a side note, I have no idea why Ticos do not pull out of the road when there is a perfectly good spot to pull over, but they do not.

He followed us up our driveway until he could not make it anymore. Apparently, the four wheel drive requirement he had confirmed he met at least three times that day and twice the prior day was not true. Chuck told him to back down, but he was scared he was too close to the edge. As another side note, I also do not understand why Ticos like to drive close to the outer edge of our driveway instead of the middle, like they tend to drive on most roads. The delivery driver had a tow strap, so we towed him up the rest of the way. It was a heavy fridge. Thankfully, with the help of our crew, they got it into the house. Most importantly, the fridge worked great a few months later, when Chuck plugged it in for the first time.

We awoke to Thanksgiving morning, or Dia De Gracias. It was our second Costa Rican Thanksgiving. I painted the Ocaso Cerro sign next to the house to hide the white background. It was always a compromise in Costa Rica, and this worked out well, by the time I was done. While I worked on painting the sign, Chuck worked on cleaning the patio deck. His work turned out great as well. We made a good team. I wished we could both be living in Costa Rica. I knew I would have to work full-time at my normal job during the day. However, it would be nice to have the weekends and nights to accomplish things together at the B&B and around the house.

We had a great U.S. Thanksgiving with all the trimmings. The sweet potatoes with marshmallows over the top were my favorite. The sweet potatoes in Costa Rica were not like U.S. ones. They were not the same color and not as sweet, but they were awesome. It was great to see everyone, old and new. Some people loved Costa Rica. Some people were getting disenchanted with it, and others (like me) were still trying to get there. It was this mixture of people, all doing their own thing, that made the world go around.

That next day was a hectic one, full of errands. At the bank, things went great once again. It took hours, but we achieved all our goals. We organized a few things around the house and later enjoyed some time with Jefe by the pool. We spotted tons of stars. It was nice to relax and enjoy our place.

It was a wonderful experience to get a feel for the B&B rooms at night. Ocaso took my breath away. I felt like I was on top of the world, floating on the balcony, looking out at the night below and the stars above. Cano was much different from Ocaso, with a more natural feel. It provided views of the trees to the back of the property, meaning lots of darkness with little light pollution at night. The view from Vista Mar felt grounded. It felt more down to earth with my feet on the ground, even though there were still views of everything along the coast below. Vista Mar offered the most privacy and seclusion. Cerro was where we had been sleeping, so its view was no surprise to me. Overall, each room felt unique, which I definitely liked.

It was finally the day of our tiki bar party, and I was excited to be entertaining again. I felt out of place, though, because I didn't know where to find things to help Chuck get ready. I recalled one time Chuck scolded me for using the maid's exclusive paper towels. Apparently, the quality level of paper towels and toilet paper was an issue in Costa Rica. Chuck tried to buy the best, but the grocery store didn't always have it. Therefore, the maid had some saved for cleaning that was off limits. I made sangria and cleaned the tiki bar, doing what I could to help out. I reminded him of a few things, like to check for toilet paper, which turned out to be a good idea, since he was out. The list of things Chuck did was endless, from cooking gumbo to fixing the toilet to hanging lights. We were ready by party time.

Only a small group showed up for our tiki bar party, but it was a lot of fun. Guests arrived close to 3:00pm and left around 8:00pm. They saw how much Chuck and I missed each other and joked about leaving the lovebirds alone at the end of the night. The tiki bar layout inside worked out to be great. I was surprised how many people were interested in mixed drinks. We had to brush up on our bartending skills. We also realized we needed to invest in some more outdoor lighting close to our gate. Overall, our tiki bar party was a memorable evening for us. It had looked like rain all day, but the weather held out. Immediately after everyone left, the rain started. I had said my prayers, and they had worked. Chuck and I were both amazed at the timing.

I awoke to see Jefe lying in his doggy bed out front. He was a happy dog. I was going to miss him so much. It was my last full day at the property, and it was a busy one. I already felt myself becoming upset about leaving, but I tried my best to push it away.

While in our house painting shelves, we had our second hummingbird fly right into the glass doors. In talking to a neighbor about it, they mentioned four toucans had died from flying into their house, so they had to put a fern up in one of their windows to stop the toucans. It was sad. I was thankful that our hummingbirds had not died. Typically, Chuck had the doors opened so the hummingbirds could see the screens. We also planned to put in hummingbird feeders, to attract them away from the doors. After the painting was done, we went over our list of what to include in the information books for all the guest bedrooms of the B&B. Now, we needed to take time to write it all out over the next few weeks.

We used the pool and spa for the first time together, and I was finally able to relax in the wooden bathtub in Vista Mar. After having fun, we enjoyed a great dinner outside with some champagne a neighbor had given us as a house-warming gift. It was a good celebration on my last night.

After packing up that next day, the time to leave grew closer. At breakfast, my tears flowed. I tried to relax and enjoy the time we had left together, like Chuck wanted. However, it was very difficult. Jefe had run off in the early morning hours, and I did not know if he would return before I left. Finally, time to leave arrived. Jefe came back right when we were taking the luggage to the car. I got to say my final goodbye, even though he was wet and covered head to toe in red mud. It made me laugh to think about him out playing in the river all morning. He was a happy dog and had no idea I was leaving. I knew I would miss him dearly.

The drive to San Jose was uneventful. With flight delays and heavy rains, it was a long, tiring drive between Atlanta and Nashville. I made it to bed by about 2:30am the next day, exhausted.

I went to work drained. My desk was overloaded. I recalled telling mom I was so tired I could not see the computer screen. She realized I had failed to turn on the office lights. Obviously, I was overly stressed to have gone until 2:30pm, not realizing the lights were off. I survived through the end of the workday, but I had one more stop. My grandmother had returned to the ER that morning, so I made a quick visit to the hospital before heading off to bed exhausted.

26 POWER OF POSITIVE THINKING

I WORKED HARD ALL DAY again. However, I struggled to keep my parents out of my office. I was doing my best to bite my tongue, but I was close to a breaking point. Now until year-end was crunch time at work. I needed to adjust to the heavy workload and pressure, and I needed my parents to adjust as well..

Jefe had been needy lately. Chuck thought it was because he missed me. However, he did not miss me nearly as much as Chuck did. I missed them both. Although I had been too busy since leaving Costa Rica to become depressed yet, I was sure it would hit me eventually. I still had to unpack my luggage. I had not brushed my hair since I got back from vacation, three days ago. I had simply pulled it up into a ponytail daily, but I couldn't take it anymore! I had to unpack my luggage to find my hairbrush.

The bank was set to inspect the B&B as part of the credit card approval process for our Internet site. Before I knew it, my workday had flown by. However, the bank had not shown up or called. I was shocked. We had assumed it was a done deal, given the constant reminders from the bank staff during our many visits there the prior week. In Costa Rica, though, most things did not work out on the first attempt, so sometimes we got our hopes up too high. We needed to get things worked out soon, or we were going to be looking at a 2011 opening for our first customers. Chuck was even more disappointed, since he had cleaned for the visit.

Our crew made a lot of progress on the bamboo ceilings inside our house. Chuck ordered more bamboo to keep them going. The bamboo delivery did not go well. The guy backed off the hill, so Chuck had to tow him out.

Since it was my first weekend after returning from Costa Rica, I had more time to miss Chuck and Jefe, and I found myself starting to become depressed. I decided to work on organizing my life. I completed some sections of the information books for the guest rooms. I sent thank you notes to people in Costa Rica for house warming gifts and dinners. I also completed more work on my book notes. I tried to stay busy to distract myself from missing Chuck.

We needed to open, or we were going to miss the Christmas traffic. He missed me and wished I were there. It sounded like he needed a hug. I knew he must be happy Auburn won their big game, but I knew it would be more fun if he had someone with him to celebrate. I prayed that night for the bank to come out early the next week and for sunny days to return to Ocaso Cerro.

I awoke the next morning missing Chuck deeply. My heart was broken, and I knew his was too. It was not the same when we were apart. I kept thinking I just needed to make it until June, but what if my job did not let me move in June? It was more than I could bear. I had to take it in small strides and hope for the best. For now, I had to stay busy instead of feeling sorry for myself. After all, I was sure Chuck was up and tiling in Costa Rica already, so I had to do my part here.

Our contact lady at the bank was on vacation, so Chuck still did not have any news about why nobody showed up for our inspection. He finished laying the wall tile in the entire master bathroom of our house. Although it still needed to be grouted, it was a huge accomplishment for less than a week. We hoped for good news from the bank lady upon her return to the office.

I was exhausted by the end of my workday. Chuck called late in the night. He had gotten an email from the bank to say they were coming out for a visit the following afternoon. I was going to say my prayers for good news from the bank.

Close to 5:00pm, Chuck sent news that the bank staff did not show. It was disappointing but not unbelievable to be stood up again. He planned to call another bank to start the process over. I was furious when I went to eat dinner, but it turned out Chuck had spoken too soon. The bank people arrived at 5:20pm for the inspection, and they loved our place! It was going to take a few weeks for the paperwork to be processed. We had to pay the $600 bank fee, and it was up to our Webmaster to work with the bank on the website and finish setting everything up on-line. He was thrilled. What a roller coaster ride we were on from one moment to the next!

It was going to be a long day, as my cold continued to hit me hard. I tried to get some things accomplished, but I had a lazy day. Chuck had a lazy day too. He grouted the shower floor in the master bathroom of our house. After that, he swam in the pool and listened to music. He was excited that the guy from Auburn won the Heisman trophy. Jefe was sleeping in his new bed, now outside of our house instead of the B&B. His bone pillow with his name on it was still around too, even though I figured it was long gone. Chuck planned to start cooking breakfast for dinner so that he could get some practice in before customers started to arrive. He thought we needed to officially announce we were open for business, despite not having the credit card processing ability, and I agreed.

Chuck met with our attorney again regarding obtaining a business license. After we obtained one piece of paper, we were ready to proceed with the license inspection request. Our attorney did not think the inspectors would come out until next year. We hoped to have the cabina permit by then in order to make it easier to get our license approved. After meeting with the attorney, Chuck signed up Ocaso Cerro on TripAdvisor and BedandBreakfast.com. It felt like we were getting closer to having the B&B open.

Chuck knew I was not comfortable spending the money, so he finally told our contractor we had to put the kitchen millwork on hold. We needed to get the cabina done and get the B&B open to start making some money first. Our contractor was actually fine with the decision. We agreed the next day would be our big grand opening, as there was no reason to delay it. I was not certain what that really meant, but it was what we were going to officially call our B&B grand opening. It sounded exciting to have a date!

I mentioned to mom that December 15 was our official opening day. She thought it was funny there was really no big reason for the moment being that day other than we decided it was. Mom said on Facebook Chuck had written the following: "The day has finally come. We are officially open today. Now we just wait for people to find us!" My aunt laughed about it. She said people weren't waiting behind the trees in the rainforest to jump out when we declared we were open. Obviously, she was right, but I wondered how long it would be before the guests started to arrive.

It was nice to see all of the wonderful congratulation wishes on Facebook and in my email that day. It felt like we had accomplished a lot. I hoped our first guests would have a wonderful time. Chuck and I talked about our big opening day and how exciting it was, and we got a good laugh out of it too. Chuck realized he was not prepared for guests. He didn't have bottled water or toilet paper. How did he forget to buy an important item like toilet paper? We had our big official B&B grand opening with no toilet paper on hand. How crazy! Our place really needed a woman on site, and I wanted so much to be there.

Chuck's day in San Isidro was a challenge. He went but did not accomplish all he needed to get done. He did not obtain the WC insurance policy he needed for the cabina. This was his main goal after our Costa Rican architect called the prior day in a panic, needing the policy so that he could obtain our permit before year-end. Chuck found out that our insurance policy for our house would be changed to commercial and would cost significantly more for the increased exposure. Our agent also mentioned that if we ever put in a trail to the waterfall that we would need an endorsement to the policy. I wished there was an insurance manual I could read, or even better, a policy I could translate. I felt like there was so much we did not understand in Costa Rica. It was scary at times. Chuck had his hands full just surviving day by day right now, but I hoped one day we would have time to figure things out properly.

The big news of the day was that the bamboo ceilings inside our house were officially done. It was the end to a major part of our construction. Our Costa Rican architect showed up at our place looking for the WC policy that Chuck didn't obtain on his trip that prior day. He sent Chuck to the municipality anyway. The engineer had thankfully signed off on the drawings, as it was his last work day until the New Year. Chuck had a hard time communicating with the guy at the municipality, since he spoke no English. Luckily, our architect decided to stop by and had a good relationship with them. They worked it out so our insurance agent could fax over the WC policy once it was in place. Chuck simply had to return to pay the fees. The permit was ready if we could show our policy and pay. We were all waiting for our attorney to finish his part in getting the WC policy placed. Chuck was hopeful for good news soon.

It was slow to get started in any business. Chuck's architecture office in Tampa was slow to start too, but with time, things built up and took off fast. We knew it might be a while before our first guests arrived at the B&B. I was still sad I would not be there to see it all happen, but I didn't mention anything to Chuck. I knew he would love for me to be there too.

Chuck pulled weeds for two hours. He then spent some time putting up some of the tile base. Afterwards, he laid the wood floors in the office tower of our house. His knees and back were killing him from all the up and down work. He never heard a word from our insurance agent. The crew had removed almost all of the worker's quarters. They were leaving the roof up, since the cabina would fit underneath it. This way, they stayed out of the rain and the sun while they built the cabina. I begged him to please be safe on his quad trip and to email me as soon as he got back. I really worried about him while he was gone on these trips and also worried that the quad would break down, but he deserved to have some fun. I hoped all went well.

Chuck went on his quad trip with the neighborhood guys. The trip had been fun until the Teryx messed up. It had engine trouble less than a mile from a neighbor's house. The guys towed it to their place. He had no idea what was wrong, but it was probably going to be serious. He planned to have a mechanic from San Isidro make a house call to look at our Teryx and a neighbor's recently wrecked quad.

Chuck wished I were there. The holidays were going to be tough alone.

He wasn't much of a Christmas person. However, I thought we could create our own Costa Rican Christmas tradition together. It had to be something simple. What might that be? Chuck liked to create things, and I was sure he would come up with a great idea.

Chuck finally got an email from our insurance agent. He had already emailed our new WC policy to the municipality and our architect. Apparently, he didn't understand he was supposed to copy Chuck on that email too. Chuck now needed to pick up the cabina permit. He had driven by some other hotels and B&B's that day, and their parking lots were full. He was disappointed we still had no guests. I reminded him we were late getting open, so we had to be patient. Most people still didn't know our B&B existed.

Chuck got the Teryx sent off to the mechanic in San Isidro. Afterwards, he bought a ton of stuff for the cabina and spent $200 on wire shelving for our master closet. Once he got home, he started installing the bamboo floors in our master bedroom and worked on installing the master bathroom sink and faucet. The crew dug the first part of the footers for the cabina. He made some tortilla soup for dinner that was yummy. It made my mouth water to think about it. I really missed his cooking.

I did not sleep well that night, because I was worried about potential problems, like running out of money and getting guests. Chuck thought we would both feel better once business was going. He wished me sweet dreams. Just hearing those words made me smile, and I immediately felt better.

Our crew installed a new directional sign along the road to our place. Hopefully, this made finding our property clearer for people without reservations who might be driving by. It was still disappointing we did not have our first guest yet, but we kept trying to convince ourselves it would take time. Once guests started to arrive, things were going to work out just fine.

Chuck worked more on installing the bamboo floors in the master bedroom, along with getting the payroll organized and weeding for a few hours. He received tamales from our maid and workers, which is a traditional food for Christmas in Costa Rica. They were awesome. The crew finished digging the cabina footers. It had been a lot of work, since the ground was hard and a lot of concrete had been poured in the area they had to dig through. On Monday, the crew planned to start tying the rebar for the footers, so it was important they got the delivery from the hardware store immediately. I was surprised, but they delivered on Christmas Eve.

Later the same day, Chuck spent three hours at a Tico's house who had invited him over for Christmas Eve. He had not been sure what to expect. He was the only Gringo. It was a group of about 25 people in total, made up of the Tico's family and some friends. The women stayed in the house and cooked the food. They ate chicharones (i.e. fried pork rinds), which was one of Chuck's favorite Costa Rican foods, along with yucca and some other items. The women cooked the chicharones in a big cast iron pot. Chuck mentioned the women had the pig head at the table, hacking it into pieces to boil for soup later, which was a little too much for him to see while he was eating. The kids mostly stayed inside. There were only a handful of guys who stayed in a shed out back, where Chuck stayed. I was curious to know what they talked about. He didn't remember exactly. Since they only spoke in Spanish, he wasn't always sure what they were saying. From what he recalled, they talked about their horses, their pigs and where they lived. It sounded like normal conversation to him. He really enjoyed his visit.

I awoke to a White Christmas here in Tennessee. I sent Chuck a copy of the Ocaso Cerro Christmas Cards I had mailed to everyone, and he liked them. Later in the morning, I sent him a photo of the wall of Christmas cards we had received. Throughout the day, I sent him photos from inside some of the cards. One of our friends still didn't understand Costa Rica wasn't an island and sent their card to the "Island People." I knew Chuck would laugh at that one. I didn't want him to feel alone, so I hoped this kept him a little entertained during the day.

I emailed Merry Christmas to our contractor later in the day and copied in Chuck. In my comments, I said I hoped next year would be my first Costa Rican Christmas. Chuck wrote me and said no more Christmases apart. Next year would either be my first Costa Rican Christmas or his first Christmas somewhere else with me. It made me smile. I hoped he was right about next year being my first Costa Rican Christmas.

After dinner, I sent Chuck some photos we made while opening presents, and later I called him. He finished installing the bamboo floors in our master bedroom. He went to Christmas dinner at a neighbor's house. They ate the traditional food of turkey, ham and all the sides. Overall, it sounded like he was doing all right. I was glad he had been able to get out of the house for a while. Jefe had done a good job guarding the place while he was gone.

Chuck was sniffling and admitted he had cut some wood for the baseboard behind the bed, which created enough sawdust to cause his allergy to react. I reminded him to please be extra careful that night if the power went out. I was worried about something bad happening, especially since it was one year ago when we had our copper power lines stolen. It was a high crime week in my eyes, so I begged him to please be very sensitive to things for the next week, particularly that night. I didn't mention it to him, but it was not a good day for him to take an allergy pill, which would make him sleepy. Maybe I was being paranoid and nothing bad would happen. I had definitely been saying my prayers all week.

I lost track of how many times I awoke that night and said to myself I hoped all was well in Costa Rica. It was a relief the next morning to see Chuck had power, given his Skype was on-line. It at least appeared he had made it through the night, and my prayers had been answered that all was well.

I spent time following up on a few items that needed to be done, like dealing with our TripAdvisor listing. It had been a few weeks now since Chuck had entered our Ocaso Cerro information, and there were still no details up yet, other than our pictures. Furthermore, our location was showing up with restaurants located 2 ½ hours from us, so it seemed we were not listed correctly. Chuck's request to correct it had been rejected. It appeared they did not quite understand that in Costa Rica, addresses were not exactly black and white.

When I checked our email in the early afternoon, I found one from our B&B mentor. I had sent her good wishes earlier and told her that we had opened on December 15th. She had responded that we needed to have positive thoughts and before we knew it, our first guest would arrive. It made me smile and decide I would do just that.

It was yet another rain-free day in Costa Rica. The big news of the day was an email from the bank that our paperwork was ready for a few signatures and the fee to enable us to process credit cards. Chuck returned the rented scaffolding to our contractor. He looked in good health, which was great news to hear. Also, since he still had leftover wood from our project in his wood shop, our contractor agreed to do our baseboards to complete our master bedroom and office. Chuck was thrilled. Overall, it sounded like a great day to me, given the fact nothing was stolen from our place the prior night. Chuck thought I was crazy to worry so much, but I was very thankful. I suppose I worried enough for both of us. Maybe that is why he figured he didn't have to worry so much about things. I planned to say my prayer again for God to watch after him and Jefe, and I was going to keep my positive thoughts for our first guests to arrive at our doorsteps with smiling faces.

Chuck sent me a few photos. Most were of the construction of the cabina, which included the footers and the start of the rebar. One was of a beautiful December sunset from our place. It was all so green in Costa Rica, compared to the dead of winter I was used to seeing in Tennessee. It was strange to be living in such different places so far apart, yet we were still closely connected.

I called Chuck and was shocked to hear him say he couldn't talk. We had our first guests! They had just driven up to the gate. Since I was paranoid about being ripped off, I was immediately worried if they were legitimate. It was a family with small kids, so he assured me that they were legitimate. I wished him good luck before hanging up the phone.

Mom and I were both really excited. When I had been envisioning our first guests, like our mentor had told us to do, I had been picturing a young couple. A family had never crossed my mind, but they had been chosen to visit us for a reason. If they were nice, I knew they would be blown away. I really hoped they were nice and enjoyed their time at our place. I knew Chuck had to be stressed out with them showing up out of the blue, on top of them being our first guests.

Chuck called me back later to say he had no food, and he wasn't sure the store would be open early enough the next morning. We decided he could run to a neighbor's house instead. Hopefully, they had food. It was hard to believe he did not have food in the house. I planned to say my prayers that all went well for Chuck the next morning. I certainly hoped we got off to a good start with our first guests. I was still in shock we had guests, and I was sure Chuck was too. They showed up at our place for a reason, so I had to believe it was destiny that brought them to us. I knew Chuck would do his best.

I had a hard time going to sleep. All I thought about was having our first guests. It was exciting. How many of them were there? How old? Where were they from? Why did they decide to stop at our place? Did they have plans already for their time? Did Chuck find enough food to feed them breakfast? I was stressed out for him. I hated I was missing out on all of it too, but I finally fell asleep.

The next morning, I awoke immediately wondering how things were going for Chuck and our guests in Costa Rica. I hoped everything was going all right. My workday was hectic, so I quickly forgot about what was happening there.

After work, I realized my cell phone was not in the office. When I grabbed it out of my purse, I saw I had missed three calls from Chuck that morning. It was disappointing. Hopefully, he had called to tell me things were going fine. He called back later that night. He was still waiting for our guests to return from their day out. They were a family from Silicon Valley in California, spending about a week and a half in Costa Rica. They had travelled around quite a bit already. They had stopped at a few hotels that were booked but tried us, since they liked our sign. It was well lit, and it was the first sign they came to that was not hand painted. When they were talking at breakfast that morning, Chuck discovered she was an architect too. I had said there was a reason why they picked us, and now I knew why.

Upon their arrival, Chuck told them we had just opened, and they were our first guests. It was obvious, since he was totally unprepared. It was a mad rush for him to get towels for the bathroom and the blankets for the bed. They knew they had driven up without a reservation, so they were very understanding. It made me smile. Still, he should have had the bed together, soap in the soap dispenser and towels in the bathroom. I thought he had everything staged when the bank came for their inspection three weeks earlier. I understood not having food on hand, since it spoiled, but I had hoped he would be more organized on the other items. Thankfully, he was able to grab some food at the corner store that morning. The couple ate Kosher, so it was good he had asked about any special food restrictions.

Our first guests spent their entire day at a few beaches. They took dinner to their rooms, so Chuck didn't have much opportunity to talk to them. When they checked out, they asked him for some of our business cards, which he took as a good sign. Overall, they really had not spent much time at our place to enjoy it, but it was a major hurdle. We had gotten over the hump of our first guests. I knew Chuck was better prepared for when our next guests arrived. I meant to ask him if he enjoyed it, but I was guessing it was probably too stressful to enjoy. I knew I felt it was stressful, and I was not even there. It was exciting but more stressful.

It was New Year's Eve, the last day of 2010. We had accomplished a lot during the past year. Chuck and I had each grown individually, in our own ways. Our relationship had grown stronger by living apart, as we had a deeper appreciation for each other. I had grown closer to my family here in Tennessee. Jefe had become a part of our family, and so had the many friends we made in Costa Rica. We had seen the construction of the B&B through completion and the house near completion. The B&B had officially opened, and Chuck had served our first guests. Progress was still needed on the B&B to get things going, but we were officially underway. We still had to work out the kinks. We had to figure out what needed to be done marketing-wise to get business going and move things in the right direction. These were all challenges for the upcoming year in 2011. Of course, the biggest hurdle was to get me to Costa Rica, so we could live together again.

Chuck had a good day. Some neighbors came over for dinner with their son, who was visiting from the U.S. There were a lot of fireworks going off in the neighborhood. Our crew told Chuck the Ticos stay up until early morning, like 4:00am, celebrating New Year's Eve. It was a big holiday tradition for them. Chuck's plan was to clean the dishes and go to bed by 10:00pm. The only upsetting news was that our contractor called from the hospital. Chuck thought he sounded very bad. All he could hear from the message was that his blood pressure was very high when he was checked into the local hospital. He told Chuck to call his wood guy on Monday about the woodwork he had promised to do for us. Chuck didn't make out more than that from the call. Unfortunately, our contractor never made it out of the hospital and passed away shortly into the New Year. He had put his heart into building our place. It was his perfection and love for wood along with Chuck's unique design ideas that made our place special. It was sad he never saw our entire project completed. However, we are reminded of him whenever we look around at our bamboo ceilings or at any of our woodwork, for he will be a part of Ocaso Cerro.

I was happy to move forward into 2011. I had high hopes for the year ahead. I was hoping for a healthy family, much financial success, and most of all, to find a way to get to Costa Rica and live happily together again. What was the road ahead going to be like for us? Only time would tell. However, we were going to do our best to control where the road was headed. Even though we were ringing in the New Year alone, I emailed Chuck to toast to Hope, Happiness and Pura Vida!

27 TIPS FOR DREAM CHASERS

IN COSTA RICA, WE ARE ON an adventure where every day we know there are new challenges. It is the sense of adventure and unknown that draws us to such a beautiful country. Life in Costa Rica is not about keeping up with the Jones's in a material world. Life in Costa Rica is simple. It is not simpler for us right now, living apart and starting up a new business, but I know it will be a simpler life for us one day when things settle down. In Costa Rica, we can eat healthier, have less stress and be happier. Ultimately, this will help us lead longer lives together and hopefully allow us to touch the lives of others, who visit us to make them happier people in the short time they spend with us at Ocaso Cerro. Happiness is a state of mind where you learn to live in the present moment. Costa Rica is unique in that it allows you to forget about the rest of the world and the future to live in the current moment of happiness. I believe part of this is the relaxing simplicity of nature, which is so prevalent in Costa Rica. It allows you to appreciate things that are bigger than yourself. I hope everyone who visits our B&B takes a little Costa Rica home with them, for it will enrich their lives and bring a smile to their faces. Who can't use more of that in this world?

At this point, we have opened the B&B. Therefore, after 5 years of taking notes on our journey, I have stopped writing with mixed emotions. I am saddened at the loss of a daily writing ritual, but I am relieved to spend my time on new goals. Although I have stopped writing, our journey has not ended. I still feel that one day, I will be found living a simpler life in Costa Rica with Chuck, the love of my life, because we are meant to be together. I just don't know what day that will be, but I hold out hope it will be one day soon. To learn how things continue to progress for us, please visit us in person as a guest at the B&B, or we'd love to hear from you on our website, www.ocasocerro.com.

For those who dare to pursue your dreams, here are some tips we learned along our journey. First, seek out the advice of others whose path you are following. This can be invaluable to help you keep from making the same mistakes as others. Second, don't panic when things go wrong. Hopefully, you won't have as many issues as we had, but it is highly likely you will meet obstacles along your dream path. Regardless of how bad things may seem at the moment, don't get caught up in the drama. Stay calm to reach the heart of the problem, and then take steps to find a solution that will work for you. Third, keep a positive attitude and a sense of humor without letting fear or excuses keep you from following your dreams. Times will get rough, but seeing the glass as half full of opportunities makes a huge difference in following your dream. Fourth, have a plan to follow, but be flexible. You may not get to follow the straight path you had in mind initially, so you have to be willing to make adjustments to reach your goal, even if the road to get there is a windy one. Finally, always have hope, but be realistic when it comes to making sacrifices. You will most likely have to make some sacrifices along your dream path, so be prepared before you start, knowing you will have to go backward before you can go forward again. Once you start working toward your dream, you may even surprise yourself at how far you are willing to sacrifice to reach your goal.

Thank you for taking time to read our story. I hope your life was enriched by it and by the lessons we learned along the way. Please remember happiness is a wonderful feeling, so add a little more to your life and the lives of others. Life is what we make it. It is unique to each of us, and nobody else can live it for us. How will you shape yours? Is your life on the right track, or is it time for a makeover? Whatever your path, I wish you "Pura Vida."

Insert chapter ten text here. Insert chapter ten text here. Insert chapter ten text here. Insert chapter ten text here. Insert chapter ten text here. Insert chapter ten text here. Insert chapter ten text here. Insert chapter ten text here. Insert chapter ten text here. Insert chapter ten text here. Insert chapter ten text here. Insert chapter ten text here.

EPILOGUE

BUSINESS AT THE B&B grew throughout the year in 2011 and was helped by the newspaper article published about our Ocaso Cerro dream in the St Petersburg Times (now renamed the Tampa Bay Times). Chuck loved running the business, and the result was lots of great guest reviews posted on-line. We also made a lot of friends from around the world, as our small B&B attracted guests from ten countries in its first year, and Jefe gained his own fan club. Many of our guests sent hugs and ear rubs to Jefe soon after their departure, and some still do today. It has even crossed my mind that he should write his own book of his many adventures. Although I didn't have the opportunity to meet many of the guests, Chuck relayed to me details about them from how they found our place to how they spent their day as he wanted to include me in the experience that I was missing. Along with managing the B&B, Chuck supervised and helped complete the construction of our house and the cabina, so it felt like everything was finally in place by the end of 2011. We believed that we had succeeded in our goal to get everything built and the business launched successfully. Although we had succeeded, I was still not in Costa Rica.

Despite seeing on the Internet since 2005 that telecommuting internationally was legal in Costa Rica, knowing many neighbors in Costa Rica who were telecommuting for their foreign employers and confirming the legality with some Costa Rican attorneys and tax accountants, my employer declined my request to telecommute there. Their research on the interpretations of the law concluded it was too risky for them. We waited almost seven months to hear that answer, a few weeks before Christmas 2011. It made for a long year of living apart from Chuck, with our lives hanging in the balance. The reality was that we needed my job to let me telecommute from Costa Rica to make our plans work financially. Eventually, we knew that we would earn enough money to pay off our construction debt and that the B&B would make enough money to support us, but time was not a luxury we had. We simply weren't willing to sacrifice living apart any longer.

I saw our house completed for the first time at Christmas, knowing that we would have to sell it along with the B&B. The thought of all the work we had done to get to that point was overwhelming. Chuck had only recently unpacked everything in our house to make it all perfect for us and was now going to have to pack it all up to move again. It was heartbreaking.

As you know by reading this book, we had solved a lot of problems to succeed on our Costa Rican adventure, but we couldn't find a solution to convince my corporate employer how international telecommuting worked in Costa Rica. It even crossed my mind to push the ARCR to try to change the Costa Rican laws to clarify them; but it just didn't seem right to try to change their laws to one that detailed everything like in the U.S. After all, it was a laid back culture there, and their current law seemed to work fine for practically everyone else except me. I didn't really want Costa Rica to become like the U.S. We finally realized that some things were just out of our control and came to the realization that maybe God just didn't mean for us to be together in Costa Rica, regardless of how badly we wanted it. We had done everything within our power, but I simply was not going to make it.

We jumped into a black hole when we started this journey, and we would do it all again. I am convinced it saved Chuck's life. He needed drastic measures to get him out of the stress of his architecture job years earlier. There is no price I wouldn't pay to still have Chuck around. We sacrificed years of living together, but our relationship has grown closer, despite living in separate countries. We have a stronger appreciation for each other than ever before. I realize more than ever what a priority family is. I had the opportunity to spend the final year with my grandmother in Tennessee before she died in early 2011, and I had the opportunity to grow closer to the rest of my family in Tennessee. There is no doubt that we learned many valuable lessons along our journey.

It is hard to think about starting over, but I know we can do it. As long as we can sell Ocaso Cerro, we will have the money to start fresh in the U.S. Despite how overwhelming, it is to start over, given we have to buy everything from big items like a house and a car to little items like brooms and vacuums. I am trying to look at the positive side on how exciting it will be to rebuild a new life. However, I am sad to leave our Costa Rican dream behind. I regret that I will not be able to live at our place for at least a year to eat all the Costa Rican pineapple I wanted, immerse myself in the Spanish language and culture, watch the hummingbirds feed on the plants and feeders we bought for them, visit with all of our neighbors to get to know them better, tour the countryside with Chuck on various trips we always wanted to do and enjoy the beauty of Costa Rica just sitting at our place like we had dreamed about for 6 years. I also grieve over the loss of what could have been our future. I think of all the future guests from around the world who would have visited us at the B&B that we will never tell us their story and teach us about their great part of the world. I had even dreamed we would retire someday to visit some of our guests at home in their cities, and maybe I would write a book about our experiences as we traveled around the world to tell others their story and the secrets of their great cities. Plus, we will not get to share in their Costa Rican experience as they are entranced by all Costa Rica and Ocaso Cerro has to offer. We will never know how we might have influenced them. Already some guests who stayed with us have fallen in love with Costa Rica and purchased property in our area. Chuck even helped design the home for one of them, and I hope that we will get to see it built one day.

Ocaso Cerro was built with love. Our realtors think it may not sell as a B&B but rather as a family compound or a corporate retreat. Regardless, my hope is it goes to a new owner who will love it as much as we do and continue to improve it. Although we will not get to live in Costa Rica, it will always be in our hearts, and I still hope that someday I will get to have the experience of living abroad. Regardless of the many stories that I hear from Chuck about living abroad from the ups on experiencing new things to the frustration of driving 3 hours to find a $12 box of Cascade, I believe the experience of living abroad will make me a better-rounded person.

Chuck loved running the B&B, so maybe we will have one here in the U.S. instead of Costa Rica. After all, our passion is to meet new people on vacation and make them happy. Although we still prefer Costa Rica, I suppose it is possible if the right place in the U.S. comes along, maybe we can make it work. Also, Chuck loves to cook, so maybe we will own a restaurant instead one day, or a B&B with a restaurant. I am still not sure why this is happening to us, but I like to think things happen for a reason. Maybe one day we will understand it better.

We are coming full circle back to where we started to begin a simple life. Maybe this is where we were supposed to end up at the end of our journey all along, but we just didn't know it. We are starting over in St Petersburg. I'm relocating my current telework job from Tennessee back to St Petersburg and can be reached at www.hopehappinesspuravida.com. Also, please visit the site to see photos that supplement the book and to follow my blog on topics related to living life with hope, happiness and Pura Vida. Chuck is going to begin a new career as a realtor at Coldwell Banker and can be reached at www.floridamoves.com/chuck.knight. I think his background in architecture and customer service will make him a great realtor. Plus, this new career will still allow him to meet lots of people and make them happy finding them or selling them a home, and I hope I can tag along to meet some of his clients as friends too.

The window of opportunity is wide open for us now. The most important part is after 21 years of marriage, during which we sacrificed over two years of living apart, we are finally together again, for our Costa Rica dream of a happier life was nothing without each other. We have learned many lessons for a happier life to begin fresh in Florida. And this time around, we have Jefe to add to our U.S. family. I hope he will like being a U.S. dog. Although many say he won the Tico lottery, in reality, Jefe will be losing his freedom to come to the U.S. It is a fact that weights on Chuck, but I know that they would be sad without each other. Whatever the future holds for Chuck and me, I know we will be happy together. I am holding Chuck's hand, and I am never going to let it go.

This brings me to the most valuable lesson of all the lessons I learned on our journey. Don't take for granted the ones who you love. Life is too short, so remember to take the time to let them know how much you appreciate them every day. Don't look back on your life and have regrets about not showing enough appreciation. Please take the time to get started, for there is no better day to start than today.

ABOUT THE AUTHOR

Debbie Knight grew up in Tennessee, north of Nashville. She graduated with a degree in Business Administration from Georgia State University with a major in Risk Management and Insurance. As an insurance nerd, you might not expect her to be an adventuresome person; however, she and her husband, Chuck, have been on quite a Costa Rican adventure since their first visit to Costa Rica in 2005. She is inspired to share their Costa Rican experiences and lessons learned with others as well as offer encouragement to help more people follow their dreams. To learn more about living a happier life, please visit her website at www.hopehappinesspuravida.com.

Made in the USA
Lexington, KY
17 October 2012